ROADSIDE GEOLOGY

of the NORTHERN ROCKIES

David D. Alt, Ph.D.
Donald W. Hyndman, Ph.D.

MOUNTAIN PRESS PUBLISHING COMPANY
287 West Front Street
MISSOULA, MONTANA 59801

Copyright, Mountain Press Publishing Company 1972

All rights reserved. No part of this book may be reproduced or trans-
mitted in any form or by any means, electronic or mechanical, including
photocopying, recording or by any information storage and retrieval
system, without permission in writing from the Publisher.

Library of Congress Catalog Card Number: 72-78039

ISBN Number: 0-87842-029-0

PREFACE

The geology of the northern Rocky Mountains is as varied and as spectacular as that of any region in the country. It is the foundation of the scenery because landscape, after all, is geology with trees growing on it.

Several generations of geologists have worked in the northern Rocky Mountains unraveling the complicated geology of the region. Unfortunately, most of the knowledge they have gained is in the technical literature and might as well be buried as far as the general public is concerned. We have written this book to help people who wish to know a little more about the rocky foundation of their world. We hope those who use it will find it improves their enjoyment of their surroundings.

The title of the book accurately describes its intent. We have dealt with the geology that can be appreciated from the roadside by the passing traveller, leaving out the kind of detail that would be charming only to a professional geologist. We have tried to answer the kinds of questions we thought might occur to an observant person interested in his environment but too busy to spend weeks in the library distilling answers from the technical literature. Along the way we have tried to guide people who are interested in collecting their own specimens of minerals, rocks, and fossils to a few of the choicer localities.

We have done our best to be resolutely non-technical and at the same time scientifically accurate in our descriptions. Our original intention was to avoid all technical terminology but a few of these words turned out to be unavoidable. We have tried to use those few in such a way that their meaning is self-explanatory. But this is not always easy to do, so we have added a short glossary.

We hope that users of this book will begin by reading the introductory section on the development of the northern Rocky Mountains, in which we attempt to paint the general picture by drawing with bold strokes on a large canvas. Each of the individual roadguides is intended to stand on its own with that section as a foundation. In cases where different roads cross similar rocks, we

iii

have provided cross-references so those who are interested can supplement their reading. The colored geologic maps in the front of the book should also be useful to people who want to grasp the larger picture. They show in a general way the kinds of rocks that outcrop in various parts of the region. The geologic time scale at the beginning of the roadguides will help to sort out the names of the geologic periods which are unfamiliar but essential to an understanding of the sequence of geologic events that formed the rocks and shaped the landscape.

Each roadguide consists of an outline of the main features of the geology of that stretch of highway — the most prominent rocks along the road and in adjacent ranges, and the processes that formed them. The roadguides are accompanied by maps outlining the names of the mountain ranges, the locations of the most abundant rocks, and specific localities where interesting rocks, minerals, and fossils may be seen or collected. Each roadguide also contains a cross-section to show diagrammatically the structural arrangement of the rocks below the surface. Most of the roadguides are written, paragraph by paragraph, in an east-west or south-north direction but we have made every effort to organize them so they can equally well be used by travellers going in the opposite direction.

We would like to take this opportunity to remind our readers that many of the places where they will want to collect specimens are on private property. Most landowners are quite generous about permitting collecting and they should be treated with every consideration. Collecting of any kind is, of course, forbidden in national parks and monuments. This should not pose a serious problem because similar rocks can invariably be found outside the park or monument in places where collecting is permitted.

We have garnered the information in this book in every way we could. Some was obtained by our own observations but much comes from our reading of the published geologic literature and many discussions with numerous professional colleagues. Space does not permit us to individually acknowledge everyone who has provided us with information but we thank them nonetheless. We especially appreciate the helpfulness of Jim Welch, Jim Talbot, Bob Curry, Bruce Johnson, the Geological Survey, and the U.S. Dept. of Agriculture all of whom generously gave us permission to use pictures in this book. We owe special thanks to Bill Melton for his help in finding collecting localities.

TABLE OF CONTENTS

ROADGUIDES TO U.S. HIGHWAYS

DEVELOPMENT OF THE NORTHERN ROCKY MOUNTAINS

Basement Rocks — The First Act

The oldest rocks in our region formed between 2.5 and 3 billion years ago and are nearly as old as any rocks anywhere in the world. Geologists call them the "basement rocks" because they lie beneath all the others.

Basement rocks are especially interesting because they make up the great bulk of the continental parts of the earth's crust. In most areas they are covered by younger rocks which conceal them the way a coat of paint covers a board. Here and there the younger rocks have been removed by erosion and the basement rocks lie exposed at the surface, giving us a glimpse into the interior of the continent. Large areas of basement rocks are exposed in several parts of southwestern Montana and northwestern Wyoming.

Basement rocks are usually beautiful. The outcrops are a colorful and complex mixture of red, pink, gray, and black rocks which actually look as though they had been through some interesting experiences during their long existence. Most of the rocks are coarsely crystalline so the individual mineral grains are large enough to be easily seen. Many contain unusual minerals which frequently make attractive specimens.

Most basement rocks began their long careers as mud and sand laid down on the bottom of the ocean. Then they were carried deep into the crust of the earth where they were cooked for millions of years at a red heat while being intensely squeezed under great pressure. So the original mudstones have now been metamorphosed into streaky-looking gneiss and schist composed of glassy grains of quartz, pink and milky-white grains of feldspar, and black grains of flaky mica or glossy hornblende. The difference between schist and gneiss

1

is not really very important: if the rock simply looks streaky, it is called gneiss; if it contains enough mica to make it actually flaky, it is called schist.

While the original sedimentary rocks were being cooked deep within the earth's crust, some of them got hot enough to melt, forming molten granite magma. This often squirted into fractures to form dikes which look like pink or white stripes on an outcrop. Sometimes large volumes of granite magma formed to create granite batholiths which outcrop over hundreds or thousands of square miles. Granite is composed of the same minerals found in schist and gneiss — quartz, feldspar, and mica — but in the granite they are randomly mixed together giving the rock a uniform instead of a streaky appearance. Frequently we see outcrops in which uniform-looking granite is mixed with streaky gneiss or schist, making a rock that looks a bit like a marble cake. These mixed rocks formed in places where the rocks were at just the right temperature to begin melting.

The kind of complicated assemblage of metamorphic and igneous rocks we see in the basement rocks is known to form in places where mountains are being created. The fact that we find such rocks with an age of 2.5 to 3 billion years, as established by analysis of their radioactive minerals, tells us that mountains must have formed in our region nearly 3 billion years ago. See map on page 4.

Precambrian Sedimentary Rocks — The Second Act

After the early mountains had formed, they were deeply eroded and finally reduced to a smooth, low-lying surface. This required removal of thousands of feet of rock by erosion before the basement rocks which formed deep within the crust were finally exposed at the surface. All this happened before there were any plants or animals living on the land, so the level landscape finally produced must have been barren and lifeless, frequented only by muddy streams restlessly shifting their courses.

Then, over a period of hundreds of millions of years, a thick blanket of sandstones and colorful mudstones was slowly laid down on top of the basement rocks that had once been exposed. Geologists have nicknamed these the "Belt" sedimentary rocks because they are *nicely exposed in the Belt Mountains of central Montana but they can be seen over tens of thousands of square miles of the northern Rocky Mountains in the United States and in the Canadian Rockies as well. See map on page 8.*

The term "Precambrian" refers to the age of these ancient sedimentary rocks. The oldest rocks containing animal fossils were laid down during the Cambrian Period, which began about 600 million years ago. Geologists use animal fossils to subdivide the rocks containing them into the various periods during which they formed. Rocks which formed before the Cambrian Period contain no animal fossils so can not be subdivided in this way. All sedimentary rocks older than about 600 million years are therefore lumped together and referred to collectively as "Precambrian" rocks.

Many Precambrian sedimentary rocks contain structures that are believed to be fossil seaweeds. Most geologists believe that the earth's atmosphere contained very little oxygen during most of Precambrian Time and was composed mostly of carbon dioxide. Seaweeds, like all green plants, use carbon dioxide in their life processes and give off oxygen. The fossil seaweeds we see in the Precambrian sedimentary rocks were probably among the first green plants to appear on the earth and may very well have been the plants that introduced the first oxygen into the atmosphere making it fit for animals to breathe. Their fossil remains are inconspicuous and unspectacular but should be viewed with an appropriate degree of respect and even gratitude!

Generations of geologists have looked hopefully for animal fossils in the Precambrian sedimentary rocks, so far without success. Apparently there are none. Surely there must have been some animals around, at least when the youngest of these rocks were deposited, but they must all have been soft-bodied creatures that left no fossil record of their existence.

Absence of animal fossils has made the Precambrian sedimentary rocks very difficult for geologists to work with because there is no way of being sure how the layers match from one outcrop to another. No one has yet figured out what their total thickness may be but the figure must surely amount to some tens of thousands of feet. We know from analysis of radioactive minerals that at least some of the Precambrian sedimentary rocks were deposited as long as 1500 million years ago.

Many of the red, yellow, and green Precambrian mudstones contain marvelously preserved sedimentary features such as mudcracks, ripple marks, and raindrop prints. These are usually so perfectly preserved and fresh-looking that it is difficult to believe they must be more than 600 million years old and may be well over a billion years old. They look as though they might have formed yesterday in a roadside mud puddle. Thousands of fascinating fireplaces, patios, and rock walls have been made of Precambrian mudstones. Their owners can look at surfaces that dried in the sun and were pockmarked by raindrops from a passing shower more than a billion years ago. Rain, wind, waves, and the sun were already working the face of the earth just as they do now.

Paleozoic and Mesozoic Sedimentary Rocks — The Third Act

Most of the Northern Rocky Mountain region was shallowly flooded by the sea at intervals during the Paleozoic Era, which lasted from 600 until 225 million years ago and again during the Mesozoic Era, which lasted from 225 until 60 million years ago. During these times more sedimentary rocks were laid down on top of the Precambrian sedimentary rocks, burying the basement rocks beneath still deeper.

Paleozoic sedimentary rocks total several thousand feet in thickness and are mostly limestones although there are also some sandstones and mudstones. Most of them contain fossils but these are usually hard to find. Paleozoic sedimentary rocks are not as colorful as the Precambrian ones and neither do they contain as many sedimentary features such as mudcracks and ripple marks.

Mesozoic sedimentary rocks are mostly brown sandstones but variously colored mudstones are common and there are even some limestones. These rocks also contain fossils but good ones are hard to find except in a few places. Dinosaurs roamed the earth during Mesozoic Time and their bones are found in some of the Mesozoic formations in Montana and Wyoming. Whole skeletons are very rare but fragments of dinosaur bones are quite common and have been found in many places. Toward the end of Mesozoic Time, during the Cretaceous Period, the sea flooded the eastern part of our region for the last time before finally draining away to the east as the Rocky

6

Mountains began to rise. Plant material accumulated in extensive swamps along the sea coast was finally buried to become thick beds of coal. The Mesozoic coals of the Rocky Mountains have not been much mined so far because they are so remote from large markets. But these coals contain very little sulfur so they can be burned with a minimum of atmospheric pollution. It seems ironic that the upsurge of environmental awareness will probably bring the scourge of large-scale strip mining to the Rocky Mountains.

Areas in which sedimentary rocks are found in our region are outlined on the map on page 8.

Formation of the Rocky Mountains — The Main Act

During most of the Precambrian, all of the Paleozoic, and most of the Mesozoic Eras the Northern Rocky Mountain region appears to have been essentially a flat plain partially flooded by shallow seas. Few, if any, mountains existed during all this time and geologically speaking the entire region seems to have been remarkably quiet. All the quietness came to an end during the Cretaceous Period, which began about 135 million years ago.

The crust of the earth floats on the dense interior of the earth the way a sheet of ice floats on water. Great masses of hot, semi-solid rock rise through the earth's interior toward the surface as they get hotter and then sink slowly back after they have lost some heat and cooled off a bit.

Apparently one of these masses of hot rock began to rise beneath western North America about 100 million years ago — lifting, stretching and heating the continental crust. When this happened the crust, which is about 25 miles thick, broke up into long, narrow blocks that run generally north-south. All of these blocks were lifted up but some were raised higher than others. The ones that rose the farthest became mountain ranges while the others became high, intermontane valleys. We frequently refer to the valley blocks as having been "let down;" we mean by this simply that they were let down relative to the adjacent mountain blocks.

Along the eastern edge of the uplifted region from Glacier Park south, the sedimentary rocks slid downhill to form the complicated structures of the Montana Sawtooth Range. One great mass of Precambrian sedimentary rock slid eastward as a single slab to form Glacier National Park.

Meanwhile, the heat building up in the crust was melting large volumes of rock to form molten magmas which rose upward. Some of these crystallized before they reached the surface to form igneous rocks such as granites which now outcrop over many thousands of square miles in our region (see the map of granite areas on page 4). Other bodies of molten magma actually reached the surface before they froze and were erupted from volcanoes to blanket large areas with volcanic rocks. Their distribution in this region is outlined on the map on page 12.

The result of all this activity is that most of the mountain ranges in the northern Rockies are uplifted fault-blocks which may contain almost any combination of Precambrian basement rock, Precambrian sedimentary rock, and Paleozoic or Mesozoic sedimentary rocks, depending upon which of these were originally present and which have been removed by erosion. A few of the mountain ranges are the remains of volcanoes and a few others are great masses of igneous granite called batholiths.

As the region was broken up into blocks which were raised to form mountains, the sedimentary rocks were folded. Layers of these rocks are flat when originally laid down but now they tilt at all angles. What had been a giant layer cake of sedimentary beds has now become a complicated jumble.

It would be a mistake to suppose that the Rocky Mountains formed during the Cretaceous Period. They began to form during that time, but the action has continued ever since then and still goes on today. Volcanoes have been active in the region during most of the past 100 million years and a new eruption would not be surprising to geologists. Frequent earthquakes in many parts of the region show that some of the fault-block mountains and valleys are still moving. No one can predict how many more million years will elapse before the interior of the earth takes its activity someplace else.

The Tertiary — An Aftermath of Deserts and Volcanoes

The interval between the end of the Cretaceous Period (also the end of the Mesozoic Era) about 60 million years ago and the beginning of the great ice ages about 3 million years ago is called by geologists the Tertiary Period. This was a time of continuing intense geologic activity in the Northern Rocky Mountains. The present-day pattern of fault-block ranges and valleys had already been established and continued movement of these crustal blocks was accompanied by widespread volcanic activity on a very large scale.

During about 40 million years, approximately the last two-thirds of Tertiary Time, the Northern Rocky Mountain region had a desert climate as dry as that of the modern southwestern states although probably not as hot. There was not enough rain to maintain a system of streams draining out of the region to the sea. Therefore, sediment washed out of the mountains during rains accumulated in the neighboring valleys simply because there were no streams to carry it farther. Consequently, most of the big fault-block valleys in the region accumulated several thousand feet of sand, mud, and gravel during these 40 million years. Their distribution is shown on page 16.

Tertiary valley-fill deposits can be seen wherever the highway crosses one of the big valleys. They are mostly light green to gray muds and brownish gravels not yet hardened into solid rock. Numerous fossils of animals that lived in the valleys during the Tertiary — including such things as camels, elephants, and various sorts of primitive horses — are found in these deposits. Scraps of bone and teeth can be collected in almost any roadcut in the Tertiary valley fill by someone willing to look for them very carefully with his nose close to the ground. Petrified wood, some of it very beautiful, can be found in the same way.

Active volcanoes were scattered here and there throughout the region during Tertiary Time, erupting rocks which still blanket large areas of the countryside. But the really big volcanic activity was eruption of flood basalts in eastern Washington at the western edge of our area and in southern Idaho at the southern edge.

Basalt is a dull black volcanic rock which pours out as a very fluid magma capable of spreading rapidly for long distances over the surface of the ground before it finally cools and solidifies. Early in

13

Tertiary Time, a long series of basalt eruptions began in eastern Washington burying large parts of Washington, Oregon, and western Idaho under the thick stack of lava flows which form the vast Columbia Plateau. Toward the end of Tertiary Time, and continuing until very recently, a similar series of basalt eruptions occurred in southern Idaho to form the Snake River Plain. These flood basalts are shown in the map on page 12.

Although basalt is a very common volcanic rock, basalt plateaus are not common. The two in our region are the only two in North America and among the very few known in the entire world.

The Pleistocene — Ice Ages and Volcanoes

The Tertiary Period ended about three million years ago with the onset of the first of the great Pleistocene ice ages of which there have been at least four — so far. Volcanic activity also continued through the Pleistocene. And our region ceased to be a desert.

The four great ice ages were not, as many people suppose, times of intense cold. Instead, they were wet. Glaciers formed because winter snowfalls were so heavy that they could not all melt during the summer. They gradually accumulated to form glaciers which covered most of the high mountain peaks in our region and filled some of the more northern valleys as well. The interglacial intervals between ice ages were times when the climate was probably more like the one we have now.

During the last three million years there has been enough rainfall in the Northern Rocky Mountain region to establish much more vegetation and to maintain a system of streams draining all the mountain valleys. They put an end to accumulation of valley-fill sediments. In fact, the streams have actually carried away much of the valley-fill sediment that had accumulated during the time of the Tertiary desert. Most of these valleys have lost about a thousand feet of such sediment so far and have another two or three thousand feet yet to go. The mountains that had been partially buried in their own debris are now being dug out again. Undoubtedly they look much higher today than they did three million years ago when the present streams first began to flow.

14

Most of the big valleys today have a deep stream valley cut into the Tertiary valley-fill sediments between high benches of the original valley fill left around the edges of the valley along the flanks of the mountains. These are the grassy "foothills" along the bases of the tree-covered mountains. The narrow canyons which the streams flow through as they pass from one broad fault-block valley to another were eroded in bedrock during the three million years of Pleistocene Time.

During the ice ages an immense ice cap covered most of Canada and extended down into the northern fringe of our area to the vicinity of Great Falls, Montana and Sandpoint, Idaho. One of the large valley glaciers flowed down out of British Columbia as far south as Pend Oreille Lake in northern Idaho where it dammed the drainage of the Clark Fork River to form an enormous lake called Glacial Lake Missoula. Its shorelines can still be seen on many mountainsides in western Montana. The lake drained suddenly when the ice dam broke, releasing an unbelievable flood which scoured the floors of several western Montana valleys, then spilled over much of eastern Washington to carve the barren scablands.

Volcanic eruptions continued on the Snake River Plain in southern Idaho all during the Pleistocene. Another large center of volcanic activity during this time was the Yellowstone Park area where a series of violent eruptions built up the high Yellowstone Plateau.

The Present — Geologic Activity Continues

The Northern Rocky Mountain region continues to be an area of intense geologic activity. Many of the mountain and valley blocks are still moving just as they have been ever since the Cretaceous.

Streams continue to erode their valleys and cut down into and carry away the valley-fill sediments that accumulated during the Tertiary Period when the region was a desert.

The glaciers are almost all gone now and the few that remain are so small and shrunken that no significant glacial erosion is now going

17

on. *Streams have taken up where the great ice age glaciers once filled the valleys and are now reshaping the landscape once again, slowly removing the marks left by the ice.*

No volcanoes have erupted during historic time but there have been a number of eruptions in the region during the 10,000 years that have passed since the last ice age ended. New eruptions would come as no surprise in Yellowstone Park or in the Snake River Plain.

Beds of sedimentary rock originally laid down as horizontal layers of mud and sand were crumpled into complex folds as the Rocky Mountains formed.

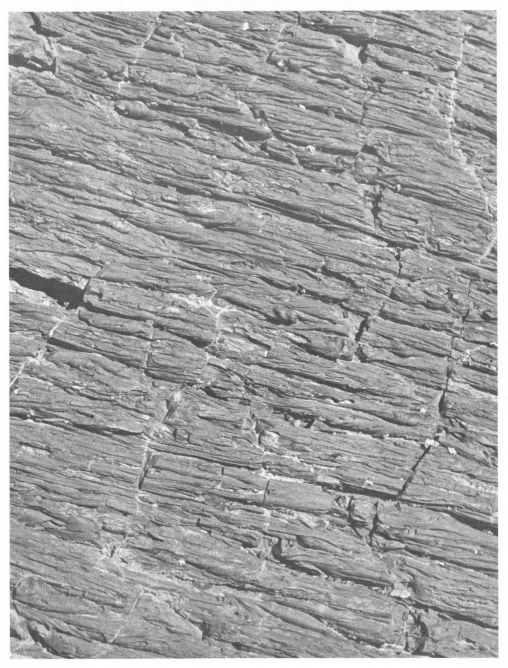

"Pahoehoe" surface on a basalt lava flow, direction of movement of molten magma is shown by the "grain" of the surface.

IDAHO FALLS — DILLON
146 miles

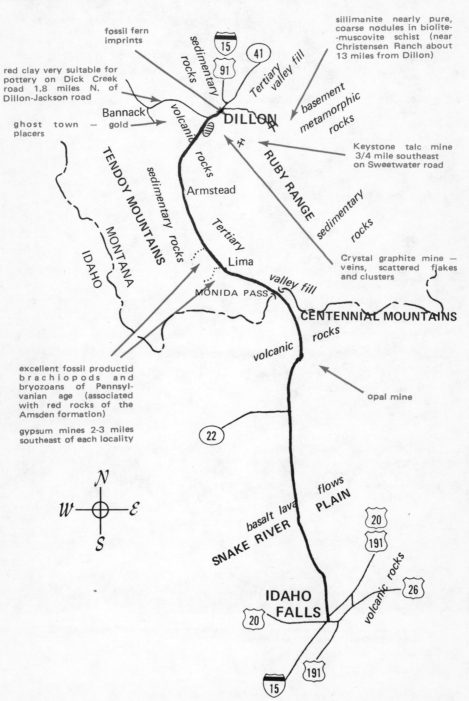

fossil fern imprints

sillimanite nearly pure, coarse nodules in biolite-muscovite schist (near Christensen Ranch about 13 miles from Dillon)

red clay very suitable for pottery on Dick Creek road 1.8 miles N. of Dillon-Jackson road

sedimentary rocks

Tertiary valley fill

basement metamorphic rocks

Bannack

volcanic rocks

DILLON

ghost town — placers

gold

RUBY RANGE

Keystone talc mine 3/4 mile southeast on Sweetwater road

TENDOY MOUNTAINS

Armstead

sedimentary rocks

MONTANA
IDAHO

Tertiary

Lima

sedimentary rocks

MONIDA PASS

valley fill

Crystal graphite mine — veins, scattered flakes and clusters

CENTENNIAL MOUNTAINS

rocks

volcanic

excellent fossil productid brachiopods and bryozoans of Pennsylvanian age (associated with red rocks of the Amsden formation)

gypsum mines 2-3 miles southeast of each locality

opal mine

22

N
W ⊕ E
S

flows

basalt lava

PLAIN

SNAKE RIVER

20
191

volcanic rocks

26

IDAHO FALLS

20

191

15

20

Interstate 15

IDAHO FALLS – DILLON

No other section of highway in our region takes the traveller through as wide a variety of geologic settings in as short a drive as Interstate 15 between Idaho Falls and Dillon.

Idaho Falls is near the eastern end of the Snake River Plain, a high volcanic plateau built up of a series of lava flows during the last several million years. The flows are all black basalt that welled up from long fractures in the earth's crust as incredible floods of molten magma. Some cover hundreds of squares miles to a depth of 100 feet or more.

The Snake River Plain is shaped somewhat like a giant crescent with its horns pointing north. Between Idaho Falls and Monida Pass, Interstate 15 heads straight up the eastern horn. Many fresh lava flows along the road show pressure ridges formed when a solid surface crust was carried along on still-molten lava flowing beneath. Most of them are 10 to 15 feet high and have fractures along their crests.

Fishermen are out of luck on the Snake River Plain because there are no streams. Lava flows are full of open spaces that quickly soak up any surface water, draining it away underground. The entire Snake River Plain is gently tilted down to the south so all this water seeping along below the surface moves slowly southward and finally gets into the Snake River through springs along the north wall of its canyon west of Pocatello. The gentle southward dip of the Snake River Plain is quite apparent along Interstate 15.

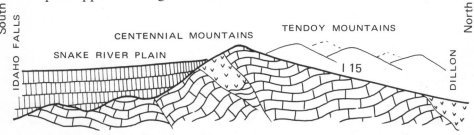

South-north cross section along the line of Interstate 15 between Idaho Falls and Dillon. Basalt lava flows of the Snake River Plain lap over a landscape eroded on folded Paleozoic and Mesozoic volcanic rocks.

The Centennial Range on the Idaho-Montana border is one of the very few mountain ranges in the Rocky Mountain region that trends east-west instead of north-south. Some geologists suggest that this is because the earth's crust beneath the Snake River Plain sank under the burden of thousands of feet of basalt lava flows, raising the Centennial Range in a kind of lever action. Outcrops in the Centennial Range are folded and faulted Paleozoic and Mesozoic sedimentary rocks capped in many places by light-colored volcanic ash deposits. The sedimentary rocks were deposited between 300 and 135 million years ago when this region was nearly flat plain shallowly submerged by the sea. Then, beginning about 70 million years ago, they were raised up and deformed into folds during formation of the Rocky Mountains. The volcanic ash was laid down within the last few million years after the range had already been carved by erosion into essentially its present shape.

Between Monida Pass, on the crest of the Centennial Range, and Armstead, 43 miles north, Interstate 15 follows the valley of the Red Rock River with the Tendoy Range dominating the skyline to the west. Low, rolling hills east of the highway are eroded into Tertiary valley-fill deposits laid down between about 40 and 3 million years ago when this area was a desert without streams to carry away debris eroded from the mountains.

The Tendoy Range contains Precambrian igneous and metamorphic basement rocks overlain by Paleozoic sedimentary rocks. Innumerable faults break the range into a jumble of blocks, making the geology rather complicated.

There really are red rocks along the Red Rock River. Most are outcrops of a red Paleozoic mudstone called the Amsden Formation. In the old days, many prospectors were fooled by this red formation because they mistook it for the kind of red rock (called "gossan") that forms on top of an ore body as it weathers into soil. This red sedimentary rock is especially conspicuous west of the highway a short distance south of Armstead.

For 22 miles south of Dillon, the highway passes through a low range of hills containing Paleozoic sedimentary rocks thickly blanketed by light-colored volcanic ash. These are in the southwestern edge of the Beaverhead Valley, a large fault-block let down as the surrounding mountain blocks came up during formation of the northern Rocky Mountains. Like other such valleys in our region, the Beaverhead

Valley is deeply floored by valley-fill deposits of mud, sand, and gravel laid down during Tertiary Time.

For more information on flood basalts of the Snake River Plain, see
         Interstate 15 W, 80 N: Idaho Falls — Twin Falls
         Interstate 80 N: Twin Falls — Boise
         U.S. 20: Idaho Falls — Arco
         U.S. 93A: Shoshone — Arco, Craters of the Moon

The black area at the lower right is the end of a basalt lava flow that poured over the Snake River Plain a few thousand years ago. Hills at the top of the picture are mountains at the north end of the lava plateau, partially buried by older lava flows. Viewed from the air.

DILLON – BUTTE – HELENA
131 miles

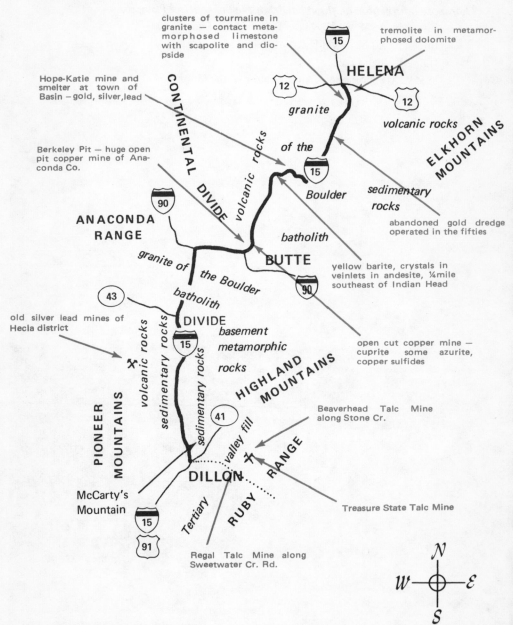

Interstate 15, U.S. 91
DILLON – HELENA

Dillon is in the Beaverhead Valley, a large block of the earth's crust let down along faults during formation of the northern Rocky Mountains. The valley is floored by valley-fill sediments formed during the Tertiary Period when this region had a desert climate.

Beaverhead Valley gets its name from Beaverhead Rock – an outcrop of Paleozoic sedimentary rock jutting prominently from the valley floor near Highway 41 between Dillon and Twin Bridges. It can not be seen from U.S. 91. Beaverhead Rock was the first landmark recognized by Lewis and Clark's Indian guide Sacajawea. From this point on, she was back in the country of her own people and would be familiar with the region ahead.

Beaverhead Valley is bounded to the southeast by the Ruby Range, a fault block composed almost entirely of Precambrian igneous and metamorphic basement rocks. A small patch of Paleozoic sedimentary rocks lies at the northern end. The Tobacco Root Range is on the far distant skyline to the northeast beyond the Ruby Range.

West of the Beaverhead Valley are the mountains of the Pioneer Range which parallel Interstate 15 to the west almost as far north as Butte. In its southern part, the Pioneer Range contains complexly folded Precambrian sedimentary rocks near the center and Paleozoic and Mesozoic sedimentary rocks near the flanks. The northern end of the range is composed largely of granites intruded as molten magmas about 70 to 75 million years ago.

McCarty's Mountain is on the east side of Interstate 15 several miles directly north of Dillon. Both McCarty's Mountain and the Highland Range farther north are composed mostly of granites intruded between 70 and 75 million years ago. The low area between them is Precambrian igneous and metamorphic basement rocks.

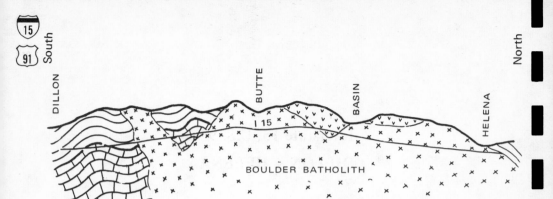

South-north cross section along the line of Interstate 15 between Dillon and Helena. Large masses of granite magma intruded older rocks to form the Boulder batholith. The volcanics formed when the molten granite magma erupted lavas to the surface.

From the area west of Butte on Interstate 90 all the way to within a few miles of Helena, Interstate 15 crosses granites belonging to the Boulder batholith and closely related volcanic rocks. The Boulder batholith has been very carefully studied by geologists because it has been the source of many valuable deposits of copper, silver, and gold along with several other metals. One of the interesting things they have found is that the batholith was not intruded as a single large mass of molten magma but instead as several smaller intrusions over a period of several million years between 75 and 70 million years ago. The granitic rocks intruded during these different stages actually look slightly different. If you stop at a number of widely spaced outcrops and examine the rocks very closely you may be able to detect subtle variations in color and texture.

Quite a few outcrops of volcanic rocks along U.S. 91 formed when the molten granite magmas being intruded to make the batholith erupted to the surface through volcanoes. Even though these volcanic rocks are closely related to the granites, they look quite different, being very fine-grained and typically fragmental.

Basin, one of the small towns between Butte and Helena, was once a very active mining community where mills and smelters treated the ores dug from the surrounding mines. Most of the mining was for silver and gold, now priced too low to make the ore bodies in this area commercially mineable. Apparently there are some radioactive minerals in the district because several of the old properties have become "health mines." A small fee is charged for the privilege of sitting in an old mine opening and basking in the radiation. Exactly how this can be healthful eludes the authors of this book.

About 12 miles north of Boulder a large old gold dredge is sinking into the bed of Prickly Pear Creek east of the highway. This dredge worked its way several miles up the creek during the 1950's, destroying the stream as it went, until the Montana Fish and Game Commission finally put a belated end to its activities. The spoil heaps of gravel it left behind are visible from the road.

The city of Helena was originally a placer mining community, with some of the principal workings along a stream called Last Chance Gulch, now the main business street of the community. Estimates of the amount of gold recovered from Last Chance Gulch before it was finally paved over run as high as 30 million dollars.

The hills immediately west and south of Helena are made of Precambrian and Paleozoic sedimentary rocks baked by the heat given off from the nearby Boulder batholith when it was still molten.

For more information on the Boulder batholith, see
Interstate 90: Bozeman — Butte

Vertical cracks (joints) and rounded pinnacle weathering in granite of the Boulder batholith.

HELENA – WOLF CREEK – GREAT FALLS
87 miles

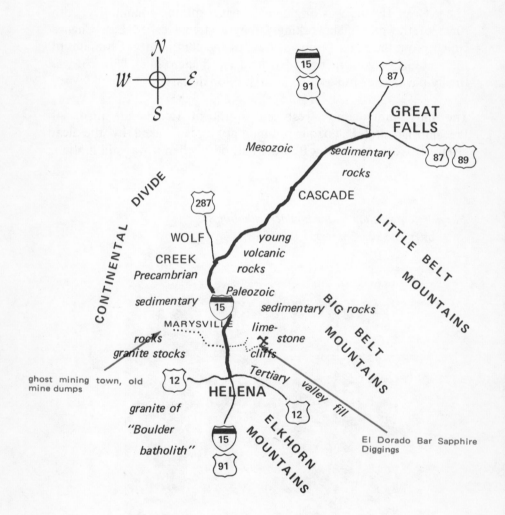

Interstate 15

HELENA – GREAT FALLS

For a few miles north of Helena, Interstate 15 crosses an extensive, nearly level surface called Prickly Pear Flat, the scene of feverish prospecting for gold a century ago. Many present-day Montanans have ancestors who went broke here trying to make their fortunes. A few small piles of gravel still stand as monuments to their efforts. The low, rounded granite hills rising above Prickly Pear flat west of the highway are called the Scratchgravel Hills. They are composed of granite related to the Boulder batholith which lies south of Helena.

Between 15 and 25 miles north of Helena there are occasional glimpses of the Gates of the Mountains east of the highway. Lewis and Clark first entered the Rocky Mountains here, through a narrow gorge cut by the Missouri River into large, white outcrops of Paleozoic limestone.

From about 25 miles north of Helena almost to Wolf Creek, the road passes through Prickly Pear Canyon which is eroded into red and green Precambrian mudstones. These rocks are full of beautifully preserved mudcracks, ripple marks, raindrop imprints, and little cubical impressions of salt crystals, all of which can be seen in many roadcuts. No one is sure how old these rocks may be but a billion years is fairly close.

Numerous small faults offset the layers of rock in Prickly Pear Canyon and occasional basalt dikes look like vertical black stripes in the roadcuts. The dikes are cracks that filled with molten basalt at the same time the volcanic rocks, which cover the surrounding hills, were being erupted – about 60 to 70 million years ago.

Two or 3 miles south of Wolf Creek the volcanic rocks which cap the hills in this area get down to the level of the road where they can be seen. A spectacular large roadcut on the east side of the highway 1 mile south of Wolf Creek is worth stopping to look at. Here a number of layers of dark-colored volcanic ash were broken by vertical fractures which filled with molten basalt magma to form dikes. Then the layers of ash slid on each other like a stack of buttered pancakes breaking the vertical dikes into short, upright segments. Near the bottom of the roadcut some thin, light-colored beds were rumpled into complicated folds by the sliding motion.

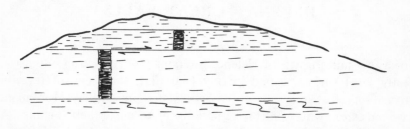

Diagram showing how vertical dikes of basalt are offset by horizontal faults in layers of volcanic material near Wolf Creek.

It is difficult at first to imagine how layers of rock can slide past each other like this because it would seem that there would be too much friction between them. Apparently this happens when the water trapped in the rocks is under sufficient pressure to float most of the load, thus greatly reducing the friction between the layers. The same sort of thing happened on a very much larger scale to form Glacier National Park and the Sawtooth Range between here and Glacier Park.

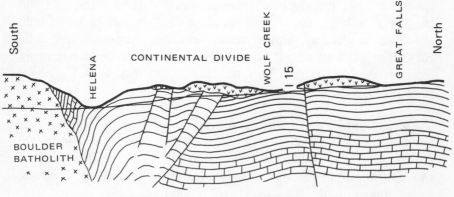

South-north cross section along the line of Interstate 15 between Helena and Great Falls. Gently folded sedimentary formations are intruded by granites of the Boulder batholith near Helena and locally overlain by dark-colored Mesozoic volcanic rocks.

Interstate 15 follows the valley of the Missouri River almost the entire distance between Wolf Creek and Great Falls. Between Wolf Creek and Cascade it crosses a thick section of volcanic rocks which were erupted over Cretaceous sandstones and mudstones roughly 70 million years ago. Most of these are greenish-black in color and many of the outcrops contain large, black crystals of augite which grew in the molten magmas before they were erupted to the surface. These volcanic rocks are part of an old volcano which had its center a few miles southeast of Interstate 15.

Between Cascade and Great Falls, the river flows on brown and yellow Cretaceous sandstones laid down between 70 and 90 million years ago before the volcanic rocks were erupted. Near Cascade the river has actually cut completely through the volcanics into the older rocks beneath but farther east, near Great Falls, there never were any volcanic rocks. In this area the Cretaceous sandstones were not folded during formation of the Rocky Mountains so their layers are still lying in nearly their original horizontal position.

Cascade Butte, immediately north of the town of Cascade, is an especially interesting type of intrusive igneous rock body which geologists call a laccolith. It formed when molten magma squirted between two layers of sedimentary rock to form a mushroom-shaped intrusion several miles across.

The area north of Interstate 15 and south of Montana 200 west of Great Falls contains one of the finest displays of laccoliths to be seen anywhere in the world — a swarm of them, each standing out as an isolated butte visible for miles. The best way to get a good view quickly is to take the secondary road between Cascade and Simms.

When the volcanic rocks exposed along Interstate 15 between Wolf Creek and Cascade were being erupted, tremendous pressures developed within the molten magma still beneath the surface. A system of vertical fractures opened in the earth's crust, radiating from the volcanic vent like spokes in a wagonwheel. Molten magma shot through these fractures for distances of as much as 20 miles from the vent and then spread horizontally between the layers of Cretaceous sandstone to form great blisters of magma several miles across and hundreds of feet thick. When the molten magma cooled, the fracture fillings became dikes and the blisters, laccoliths. Both have been exposed by erosion during the 60 million or so years that have elapsed since. Now the dikes look like great ruined walls running across the countryside in perfectly straight lines for several miles. They range in thickness from 15 to 100 feet and stand as much as 75 feet above the surrounding plains. The laccoliths make large buttes some of which still have their original, blister-shaped tops.

It is interesting to find one of the large dikes and follow it northward with the eye. Every one of the large ones stops at a laccolith. The dikes are clearly the conduits through which the molten magma was squirted to make the laccoliths. Geologists rarely have a chance to see the "plumbing" of igneous rocks so clearly displayed. Look closely at the sides of the lacoliths to see that they are broken by vertical shrinkage fractures that make them look like a log stockade fence. Similar fractures develop on a smaller scale in many lava flows.

One of the largest laccoliths, Square Butte, was a favorite of the great Montana artist C.M. Russell. It can be recognized in the background of several of his paintings.

Ripple marks pockmarked by splattering raindrops record a light shower that passed over a drying mudflat over a billion years ago.

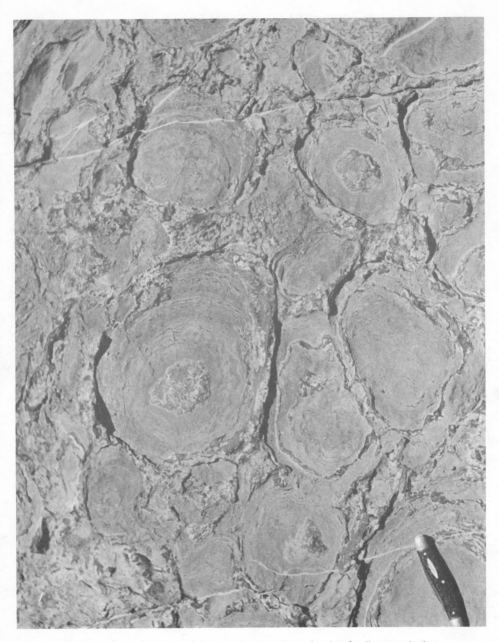

Upper surface of a layer of Precambrian limestone showing fossil seaweeds that grew in clumps about the size and shape of cabbage heads in a place where the water was stirred by waves.

IDAHO FALLS — POCATELLO — TWIN FALLS
159 miles

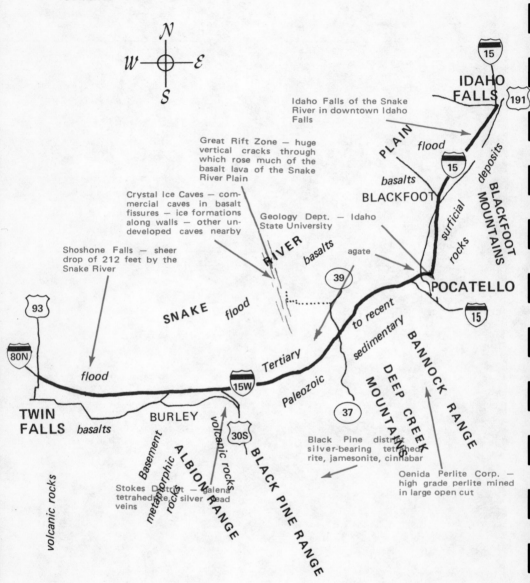

Idaho Falls of the Snake River in downtown Idaho Falls

Great Rift Zone — huge vertical cracks through which rose much of the basalt lava of the Snake River Plain

Crystal Ice Caves — commercial caves in basalt fissures — ice formations along walls — other undeveloped caves nearby

Geology Dept. — Idaho State University

Shoshone Falls — sheer drop of 212 feet by the Snake River

flood

basalts

PLAIN

BLACKFOOT

basalts

agate

POCATELLO

IDAHO FALLS

15

191

15

surficial rocks

deposits

BLACKFOOT MOUNTAINS

15

RIVER

SNAKE

flood

39

to recent

sedimentary

Tertiary

Paleozoic

BANNOCK RANGE

DEEP CREEK MOUNTAINS

flood

93

80N

15W

TWIN FALLS

basalts

BURLEY

37

30S

Basement metamorphic rocks

volcanic rocks

ALBION RANGE

BLACK PINE RANGE

Black Pine district — silver-bearing tetrahedrite, jamesonite, cinnabar

Oenida Perlite Corp. — high grade perlite mined in large open cut

Stokes District — galena tetrahedrite, silver-lead veins

volcanic rocks

34

Interstate 15W, 80N
IDAHO FALLS – TWIN FALLS

Between Idaho Falls and Twin Falls, Interstate 15W – 80N skirts the curving southern margin of the Snake River Plain, following the course of the Snake River.

The Snake River Plain is a high volcanic plateau built up of a thick stack of basalt lava flows all erupted within the last few million years. It covers a roughly crescent-shaped area of southern Idaho nearly 300 miles long in an east-west direction and as much as 60 miles wide north-south.

Molten lavas that built the Snake River Plain welled up in the earth's crust from great fissures that trended north-south and were many miles long. Immense floods of molten basalt magma poured out during each eruption, spreading out on both sides of the fissure to form enormous lava flows, some of which extend more than 100 miles and are more than 100 feet thick. It is commonplace to trace the boundaries of a single lava flow and find it covering several hundred square miles.

Eruptions of this kind do not form volcanic mountains because the molten basalt magma is very fluid and pours across the surface, building a flat plateau instead of piling up around the vent to form a volcano the way more viscous magmas do. This explains why there are so few volcanoes on the volcanic Snake River Plain.

Fresh basalt lava flows are intensely black and have a broken, rubbly surface which supports very little vegetation beyond a scattering of sagebrush. As time passes, the flow acquires a mantle of soil and begins to support more plants.

Most of the flows along the route of the Interstate highway are old enough to have developed a covering of soil and be somewhat carved up by erosion. But there are some recent flows in this part of the Snake River Plain and one of them, located a few miles north of Blackfoot, has a nice little roadside picnic area right on top of it.

This is almost as good a place to look at a fresh lava flow as Craters of the Moon National Monument, located on the northern edge of the Snake River Plain near Arco.

The walls of the Snake River Canyon, and its tributaries entering from the south, display very nice cross-sections of the black basalt lava flows that make up the Snake River Plain. All the rock ledges are horizontal, showing that the lava flows are still in their original position and have not been folded. Many of the ledges fracture along vertical shrinkage cracks in the basalt, causing the outcrop to look like a row of standing columns. Lava flows frequently do this, making it quite easy to recognize them from a distance.

All along the way the mountains bordering the southern edge of the Snake River Plain rise south of the highway. These are made mostly of Paleozoic sedimentary rocks laid down in shallow seas between 600 and 225 million years ago. They were folded, broken by faults, and intruded by molten granite magma early in the formation of the Rocky Mountains between 60 and 80 million years ago. In the area south of Burley the mountains are made of Precambrian igneous and metamorphic basement rocks which are very much older than the Paleozoic sedimentary rocks and formed the surface on which they were deposited.

After the sedimentary rocks had been folded and intruded by molten granite magma, they were eroded into mountains by streams until all of southern Idaho looked very much like the mountainous area south of the highway now does. Then the basalt eruptions flooded much of the older landscape under lava flows to make the Snake River Plain.

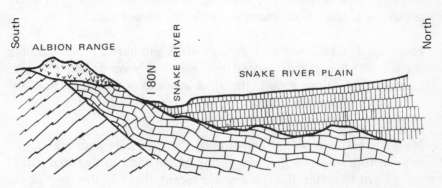

South-north cross section across the line of Interstate 80 N near Burley. Basalt lava flows of the Snake River Plain bury an older landscape eroded onto Paleozoic sedimentary rocks and volcanic rocks deposited on top of the Precambrian basement.

It is interesting that the Snake River flows right along the southern margin of the Snake River Plain almost exactly following the boundary between the basalt lava flows and the older mountains south of them. This is because the Snake River Plain is gently tilted southward so its southern margin is its lowest part. The lava flows north of the river are very porous and soak up water making it impossible for surface streams to cross them. This explains why the Snake River receives numerous tributaries from the mountains to the south but none from the volcanic plateau to the north.

The waterfalls at Idaho Falls are located right in town, just a few blocks from the downtown business district. They have been somewhat modified by dam construction but are still a wonderful place to see how very hard rock can be sculptured by running water.

Numerous cylindrical potholes have been cut into the hard basalt in places where a whirlpool catches rocks on the bottom and swirls them round and round, slowly drilling a hole. These are best seen in times of low water.

During the glacial periods an enormous lake, called Lake Bonneville by geologists who have studied it, existed in parts of Utah and southern Idaho. This enormous lake has almost completely disappeared in the dry climate that has prevailed since the last ice age ended leaving the Great Salt Lake of Utah as its most important remnant. At one time during its history, the waters of Lake Bonneville rose until they overflowed the rim of the basin through Red Rock Pass, south of Pocatello, and poured into the Snake River drainage. The material in the pass where the overflow occurred was mostly very soft and easily eroded so the outlet was cut down very rapidly releasing an enormous flood that poured down the Snake River Canyon with devastating effect. This occurred about 30,000 years ago but the effects of the flood are still plainly visible. In some places the canyon was scoured out and its walls scrubbed clean of loose rock debris. In other places large deposits of rounded basalt boulder gravel were laid down. These gravels are called the "Melon Gravel." Because the boulders suggest fields full of "fossil watermelons," some people have actually thought they were fossil watermelons. In many places where the interstate highway closely approaches the Snake River travellers can see the scoured appearance of the canyon or the deposits of incredibly large rounded boulders of basalt. During the flood, violently rushing waters must have filled the canyon brimful and even overflowed in places onto the surrounding plains. Deposits of boulders much too large to be moved by the modern stream were laid down high above the canyon floor. Estimates vary, but geologists who have closely studied the problem agree that the flood must have lasted a matter of a few days.

For more information on the Snake River Plain, see
    Interstate 80 N: Twin Falls — Boise
    U.S. 20: Idaho Falls — Arco
    U.S. 93 A: Shoshone — Arco, Craters of the Moon

Boulders of basalt rolled down the canyon of the Snake River by the catastrophic flood caused by sudden partial draining of Lake Bonneville about 30,000 years ago.

TWIN FALLS — BOISE
129 miles

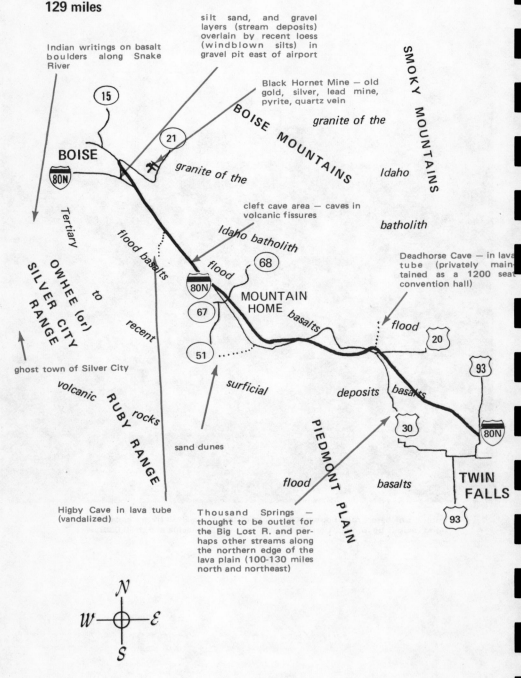

Indian writings on basalt boulders along Snake River

silt sand, and gravel layers (stream deposits) overlain by recent loess (windblown silts) in gravel pit east of airport

Black Hornet Mine — old gold, silver, lead mine, pyrite, quartz vein

granite of the

SMOKY MOUNTAINS

15

BOISE MOUNTAINS

21

BOISE

80N

granite of the

Idaho

batholith

cleft cave area — caves in volcanic fissures

Idaho batholith

68

Deadhorse Cave — in lava tube (privately maintained as a 1200 seat convention hall)

flood

80N

flood

Tertiary

flood basalts

67

MOUNTAIN HOME

basalts

flood

20

OWHEE (or) SILVER CITY RANGE

to

recent

51

93

ghost town of Silver City

surficial

deposits

basalts

80N

volcanic rocks RUBY RANGE

30

sand dunes

PIEDMONT PLAIN

flood

basalts

TWIN FALLS

Higby Cave in lava tube (vandalized)

Thousand Springs — thought to be outlet for the Big Lost R. and perhaps other streams along the northern edge of the lava plain (100-130 miles north and northeast)

93

N
W ⊕ *E*
S

Interstate 80 N

TWIN FALLS — BOISE

The Interstate highway between Twin Falls and Boise crosses the western part of the Snake River Plain, a high plateau built up of lava flows during the last several million years. All the lava on the Snake River Plain is basalt, which always has an intense black color. It is quite different in chemical composition from most other rocks commonly found on continents and is believed by geologists to have come from the interior of the earth. The continental crust is about 25 miles thick in most places and is composed mostly of lighter rocks, such as granite, floating on the considerably heavier rocks of the earth's interior. When for any reason the black, heavy rocks beneath the crust begin to melt, the first liquid to form is molten basalt magma which may then rise through fractures in the crust to be erupted on the surface of the continent. Exactly why this should have happened on such large scale beneath southern Idaho during the last few million years is something that geologists do not yet fully understand even though considerable work has been done on the problem.

Only about one-third of the earth's surface is continental and the rest is oceanic. There is no continental crust in the ocean basins; they are floored by basalt lava flows almost exactly similar to those in the Snake River Plain. So it is quite correct, and rather interesting, to think of the Snake River Plain as looking very much like the floor of the ocean would look if all the water were somehow to be drained away. Of course there is continental crust under the Snake River Plain but it is completely buried beneath the basalt lava flows.

Another area where large expanses of basalt lava flows resemble those on the Snake River Plain is in the maria (lunar seas) on the moon. These are the round, black spots that mark the surface of the full moon. Some of the astronauts landed on these areas and returned with specimens of basalt virtually indistinguishable from the rocks on the Snake River Plain.

Lava flows are full of open spaces. The rock itself contains holes formed by gas bubbles while it was still molten and the surfaces of many flows are broken and rubbly. Frequently a lava flow will cool on top to form a solid crust while the still-molten interior continues to run, leaving large caves within the flow. One result of all this is that surface water quickly sinks underground and moves within the flows beyond the reach of plant roots. This is why there are so few streams on the Snake River Plain and explains why the vegetation is so much sparser than rainfall amounts might lead us to expect.

A number of streams flow out onto the Snake River Plain from the mountains bordering it to the north, and sink into the flows. The largest of these is the Big Lost River which disappears underground near Arco. The entire Snake River Plain tilts gently southward so the underground water tends to seep slowly from north to south. This tilt probably explains why the Snake River follows the southern instead of the northern edge of the lava plateau.

Although the Snake River receives numerous tributaries from the mountains bordering the Snake River Plain to the south, it receives no tributaries entering from the Snake River Plain to the north. This can be seen by studying an ordinary road map. However, this does not mean that the Snake River doesn't receive water from the Snake River Plain. Instead of coming in through tributary streams, the water from the north enters the river from numerous springs along the north wall of the canyon. The Snake River Plain can be compared to a big, water-soaked sponge slightly tilted to the south and leaking from its downhill side.

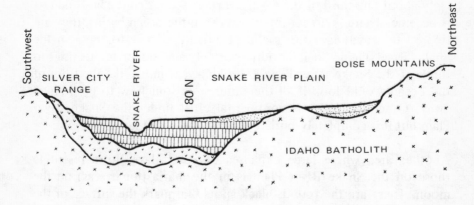

Southwest-northeast cross section across the line of Interstate 80 N between Mountain Home and Boise. Basalt lava flows of the Snake River Plain bury an older landscape eroded on granites and volcanic rocks. Sediments eroded from the Boise Mountains cover the northern part of the Snake River Plain.

Thousand Springs, located about 15 miles west of Twin Falls, is one of the largest springs in the country. Tradition has it that the water issuing from Thousand Springs is actually the Big Lost River which sinks into the ground over 100 miles to the northeast. In fact, this is probably no more than partly true. Many streams soak into the ground along the north edge of the Snake River Plain and then completely lose their individual identities as their water seeps slowly southward underground. Thousand Springs is almost certainly a mixture of water from many sources. It would be most incorrect to imagine that the Big Lost River actually flows as an underground stream beneath the Snake River Plain.

Mountains north of the Snake River Plain near Boise are mostly granite intruded as a molten magma between 60 and 90 million years ago while the Rocky Mountains were beginning to form. The granite magma rose into older Paleozoic sedimentary rocks, mostly limestones, deposited between 600 and 225 million years ago and folded while the granite was being intruded. Erosion then carved the sedimentary rocks and the granite into mountains. Finally the basalt lava flows were erupted, burying the mountains under the Snake River Plain.

The contact between the mountains and the lava flows along the northern margin of the lava plateau looks almost like the shore of a lake. It is easy to imagine the molten lava pouring against the sides of the mountains, burying them a bit deeper with each successive flow.

For more information on the Snake River Plain, see
Interstate 80 N: Twin Falls — Boise
U.S. 20: Idaho Falls — Arco
U.S. 93 A: Shoshone — Arco, Craters of the Moon

BILLINGS – BIG TIMBER
80 miles

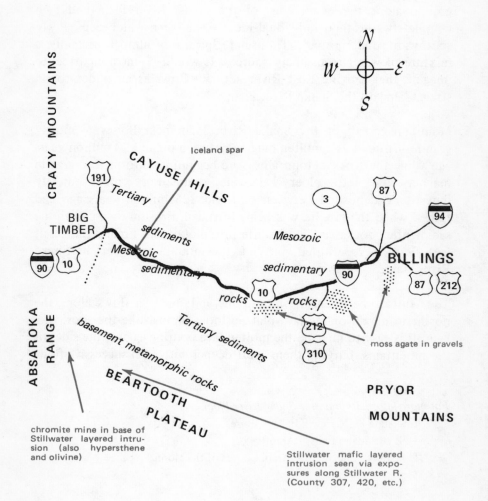

N
W ⊕ E
S

CRAZY MOUNTAINS

CAYUSE HILLS

Iceland spar

191

Tertiary

BIG TIMBER

sediments

Mesozoic

90 10

sedimentary

Mesozoic

3

87

94

sedimentary

BILLINGS

90

rocks

10

rocks

87 212

Tertiary sediments

212

310

moss agate in gravels

ABSAROKA RANGE

basement metamorphic rocks

BEARTOOTH

PLATEAU

PRYOR

MOUNTAINS

chromite mine in base of
Stillwater layered intru-
sion (also hypersthene
and olivine)

Stillwater mafic layered
intrusion seen via expo-
sures along Stillwater R.
(County 307, 420, etc.)

Interstate 90
BILLINGS – BIG TIMBER

Between Billings and Big Timber, Interstate 90 follows the valley of the Yellowstone River past outcrops of Cretaceous and early Tertiary sandstones and mudstones laid down between 50 and 90 million years ago. The Rocky Mountains were beginning to form to the west in those days and volcanoes were active. Large quantities of volcanic ash blew in on the wind and even more was washed in by streams so these sedimentary rocks are composed largely of volcanic materials. Some of the beds consist entirely of wind-blown ash; others are a hodge-podge of angular volcanic chunks washed in by flooding, muddy streams; most are just muddy brown sandstones.

These rocks are far enough east to have escaped most of the geologic excitement during formation of the Rocky Mountains. This can be seen from the highway by observing that in most places the sedimentary layers are still in their original, nearly horizontal position.

The total thickness of sedimentary rocks below the surface here is very great, amounting to many thousands of feet. These are the kinds of rocks in which oil is found and for many years oil companies have been looking for deposits in this part of Montana. They have found a few oil fields but not nearly as many as they expected to when they started, and many companies have now given up and left the area. Nevertheless, these are the kinds of rocks that should contain oil and a few companies still persist in the search.

All the way from Billings to Big Timber, the Beartooth Plateau looms as a bold, snowcapped mountain front south of the highway. The rocks there are mostly Precambrian igneous and metamorphic basement rocks lifted up as a block during formation of the Rocky Mountains.

Rock Creek Canyon, a magnificent example of a glaciated valley, cuts the eastern end of the Beartooth Plateau. The flat upper surface of the plateau, carved by erosion more than 500 million years ago, was covered by Paleozoic sedimentary rocks until they were eroded away after the block was uplifted.

Of course, basement rocks similar to the ones in the Beartooth Plateau exist thousands of feet below the surface in the area crossed by the highway but here they are still thickly covered by Paleozoic and Mesozoic sedimentary rocks. These same sediments once covered the basement rocks in the Beartooth Plateau but have been almost completely stripped away by erosion. The high peaks thrusting above the general surface of the plateau are the only remaining remnants of the former sedimentary cover.

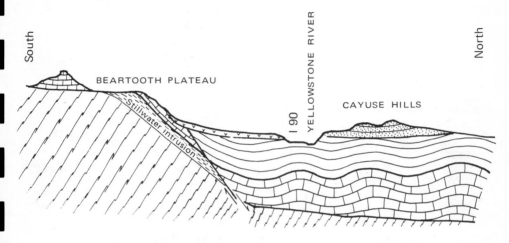

South-north cross section across the line of Interstate 90 near Big Timber. Layered igneous rocks of the Stillwater intrusion form the northern edge of the high Beartooth Plateau block of Precambrian basement rocks.

Except for the few high peaks formed by remnants of the old sedimentary cover, the Beartooth Plateau has a remarkably even skyline and an extensive, flat upper surface. This is a smooth erosion surface originally cut on the Precambrian basement rocks more than 550 million years ago when they had been reduced by erosion to a flat plain. Thousands of feet of Paleozoic sedimentary rock were deposited on top of this flat plain burying it. After the Beartooth block was uplifted during formation of the northern Rocky Mountains, the soft Paleozoic sedimentary rocks were stripped away by erosion, leaving the hard surface of the Precambrian rocks beneath essentially untouched. So the upper surface of the Beartooth Plateau is an old erosion surface buried for hundreds of millions of years and now exhumed.

For more information on the Beartooth Plateau, see
U.S. 212: Laurel — Cooke City, Beartooth Plateau

BIG TIMBER — BOZEMAN
62 miles

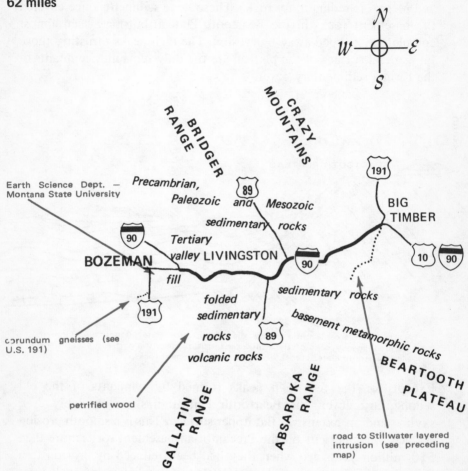

N
W — E
S

BRIDGER RANGE

CRAZY MOUNTAINS

191

BIG TIMBER

Earth Science Dept. — Montana State University

Precambrian, Paleozoic and Mesozoic sedimentary rocks

89

90

BOZEMAN

Tertiary valley LIVINGSTON

90

10 90

fill

sedimentary rocks

191

basement metamorphic rocks

corundum gneisses (see U.S. 191)

folded sedimentary rocks

89

volcanic rocks

BEARTOOTH PLATEAU

GALLATIN RANGE

ABSAROKA RANGE

petrified wood

road to Stillwater layered intrusion (see preceding map)

Interstate 90

BIG TIMBER — BOZEMAN

The Beartooth Plateau is the high, flat-topped mountain front south of Interstate 90 between Big Timber and Livingston. It is a large block of the earth's crust that was lifted many thousands of feet vertically upward during formation of the Rocky Mountains. Paleozoic and some Mesozoic sedimentary rocks originally capped it but these have been almost entirely stripped off by erosion so that now mostly Precambrian igneous and metamorphic basement rocks remain.

Small glaciers still surviving on the top of the Beartooth Plateau do not compare with the ice cap that covered it during the last ice age. The ice poured over the side of the plateau in large glaciers that pushed far out onto the surrounding plains. County road 298, south of Big Timber, follows the course of Boulder Creek, once filled by one of these streams of ice and now a magnificent example of a glaciated stream valley. A chromite mine about 30 miles south along the road is in a very famous body of rock called the Stillwater Complex. Geologists have long been fascinated by the fact that it contains layered igneous rock (rocks that look as though mineral grains settled through the molten magma just as sand settles through water to form sedimentary layers of sandstone).

Between Big Timber and Livingston, Interstate 90 crosses nearly horizontal beds of mudstone and sandstone laid down between 50 and 90 million years ago when this area was along the shores of a shallow sea and the northern Rocky Mountains were first beginning to rise in the country to the west.

Volcanoes were active nearby during those days and streams washed large quantities of volcanic debris into these sedimentary deposits. Some of this material was very coarse and formed beds of volcanic gravel which frequently contain quantities of petrified wood. Apparently trees were washed in by the same floods that brought the gravel. Considerable quantities of petrified wood have been found in some outcrops of volcanic gravel about halfway between Big Timber and Livingston.

Between Big Timber and Livingston, the highway passes the southern end of the Crazy Mountains which fill the skyline to the north. These are old volcanoes active about 50 million years ago and now so carved by erosion that they have lost their original volcanic shapes.

One of the interesting things about the southern end of the Crazy Mountains is a swarm of igneous dikes that radiate outward from the volcanic center like the spokes in a wagonwheel. Apparently pressure generated near the center of the volcano opened in the surrounding rocks a radial set of fractures that were squirted full of molten magma. The magma cooled to form igneous dikes which, being resistant to erosion, now stand above the surface like walls radiating from the volcanic center. These are spectacular when seen from the air but a bit difficult to spot from the road. Look very carefully for long, narrow ridges that look like segments of ruined stone walls running down the mountain slopes toward the road.

Between Livingston and Bozeman, Interstate 90 passes outcrops of rocks folded during formation of the Rocky Mountains. Most of those farther east missed the action and are still lying nearly as flat as they were when originally deposited.

Bozeman Pass is in the saddle between the Bridger Range to the north and the Gallatin Range to the south. Both of these ranges contain Precambrian rocks in their cores and are covered by complexly folded Mesozoic and Paleozoic sedimentary rocks. Big

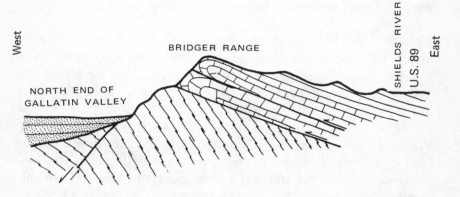

West-east cross section of the Bridger Range north of Bozeman showing how slices of sedimentary rock are pushed over one another on the eastern flank of the range.

folds are visible in the Mesozoic sedimentary rocks near the highway east of Bozeman Pass and in the Paleozoic rocks, mostly limestones, on the west side of the pass. Even where the complete folds are not visible, their existence can be recognized by the fact that the rocks along the highway are standing at steep angles instead of lying flat.

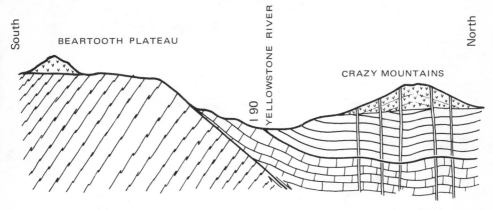

South-north cross section across the line of Interstate 90 between Livingston and Big Timber. Young volcanic rocks form occasional high peaks atop the Beartooth Plateau, a high block of Precambrian basement rock. Vertical dikes, fractures filled with igneous rocks, were the channels through which the volcanic lavas of the Crazy Mountains rose to the surface.

BOZEMAN – BUTTE
82 miles

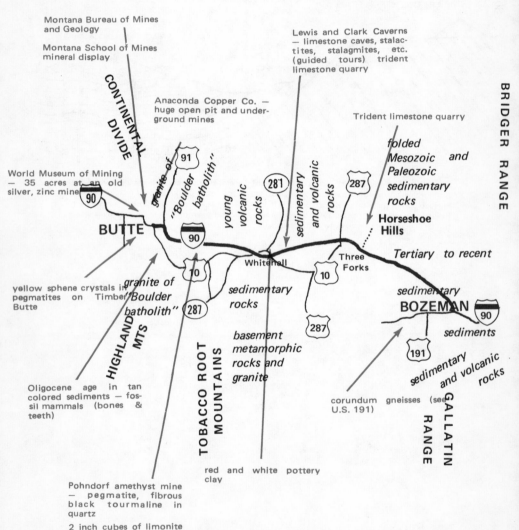

Montana Bureau of Mines and Geology

Montana School of Mines mineral display

Lewis and Clark Caverns — limestone caves, stalactites, stalagmites, etc. (guided tours) trident limestone quarry

Anaconda Copper Co. — huge open pit and underground mines

Trident limestone quarry

CONTINENTAL DIVIDE

BRIDGER RANGE

granite of "Boulder batholith"

91

World Museum of Mining — 35 acres at an old silver, zinc mine

90

folded Mesozoic and Paleozoic sedimentary rocks

281

287

Horseshoe Hills

young volcanic rocks

sedimentary and volcanic rocks

BUTTE

90

Tertiary to recent

Whitehall

Three Forks

10

yellow sphene crystals in pegmatites on Timber Butte

granite of "Boulder batholith"

10

287

sedimentary rocks

287

sedimentary

BOZEMAN

90

sediments

191

Oligocene age in tan colored sediments — fossil mammals (bones & teeth)

HIGHLAND MTS

TOBACCO ROOT MOUNTAINS

basement metamorphic rocks and granite

sedimentary and volcanic rocks

corundum gneisses (see U.S. 191)

GALLATIN RANGE

Pohndorf amethyst mine — pegmatite, fibrous black tourmaline in quartz

2 inch cubes of limonite after pyrite at picnic area

red and white pottery clay

Interstate 90

BOZEMAN — BUTTE

Interstate 90 crosses the broad, flat floors of the Madison and Jefferson Valleys for most of the distance between Bozeman and Butte. Except for the stretch between Three Forks and Cardwell and the route over Homestake Pass east of Butte, the materials exposed in roadcuts are almost entirely Tertiary valley-fill deposits.

Bozeman is in the Gallatin Valley, bounded on its eastern margin by the Bridger Range running northward from town and the Gallatin Range extending to the south. The Bridger Range is composed largely of folded Paleozoic sedimentary rocks but also contains Precambrian sedimentary rocks as well as some Precambrian igneous and metamorphic basement rocks. Its rough, jagged outline shows that it was heavily glaciated during the last ice age.

Low hills on the north side of the Gallatin Valley are folded sedimentary rocks of all ages from Precambrian through Mesozoic. Some of the folding can be seen by looking north from the highway at the arid hills a few miles east of Three Forks.

The low hills on the south side of the valley are the Precambrian igneous and metamorphic rocks crossed by U.S. 287 in the vicinity of Norris.

A very large and high mountain range on the southwest side of the Madison Valley can be seen on the distant skyline from as far away as Bozeman. This is the Tobacco Root Range, composed largely of Precambrian igneous and metamorphic basement rocks intruded about 70 million years ago by a large body of molten granite magma that now forms the core of the range.

The north side of the mountains is flanked by folded sedimentary rocks of all ages. Like the other high mountains in this region, the Tobacco Roots were heavily glaciated during the last ice age.

Lewis and Clark Caverns State Park is located south of Interstate 90 in Jefferson Canyon on old U.S. 10, about 10 miles east of the Cardwell Interchange. The caverns are briefly discussed at the end of the Roadguide to U.S. 287 (West Yellowstone-Townsend) and are well worth a visit.

Indiana University has operated a geologic field station in the northern part of the Tobacco Root Range for many years. Hundreds of active professional geologists received their first exposure to study of rocks outdoors in summer courses taught in these rugged mountains. The station is located on the South Boulder River about 17 miles south of Cardwell.

Between Three Forks and Cardwell, Interstate 90 crosses a tract of hills in which Precambrian, Paleozoic, and Mesozoic sedimentary rocks are complexly folded and faulted. These hills are fairly barren making it possible to see some of the folds in the rocks north of the highway. This area lies between the Madison Valley to the east and the Jefferson Valley to the west.

Northwest of the Cardwell Interchange are the workings of the Sunlight Mine easily visible from the road on the east side of a large hill. This large gold mine managed to stay in production until recent years when it was finally closed down by the fixed price of gold. An ore body formed where molten granite magma intruded Paleozoic limestones. The property is not abandoned so the dumps, which contain spectacular specimens of sulfide minerals, are not accessible to collectors.

Bull Mountain, the ridge extending northward from the Sunlight Mine, forms the eastern margin of the Jefferson Valley. It is composed mostly of Cretaceous volcanic rocks erupted between 70 and 75 million years ago.

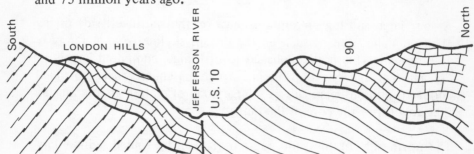

South-north cross section across the line of Interstate 90 between Three Forks and Whitehall. No Precambrian sedimentary rocks exist south of a large east-west fault approximately along the line of the Jefferson River.

54

Travellers crossing the Jefferson Valley on Interstate 90 pass the northern end of the Tobacco Root Range. West of Whitehall they can look southwest down the Jefferson Valley to see the peaks of the Ruby and Pioneer Ranges in the distance.

The mountain front west of the Jefferson Valley is the continental divide, underlain in this area by granites intruded about 70 to 75 million years ago during the Cretaceous Period. These are part of the Boulder batholith which occupies thousands of square miles of the mountainous country between Butte and Helena. It is curious that this imposing range does not seem to have a name.

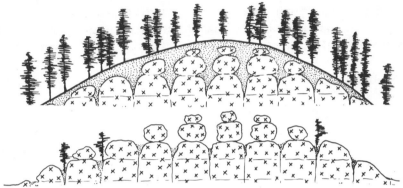

Schematic diagram showing two-stage development of bouldery terrain on Boulder batholith. During the first stage granite weathers to soil along fractures while ground is protected from erosion by forest cover. During the second stage the forest cover is removed because the climate is arid and the soil developed during the first stage is washed away by erosion.

The outcrops of the Boulder batholith granite passed by Interstate 90 as it crosses the continental divide over Homestake Pass are dramatically picturesque. Spires, pinnacles, ridges and boulders of pink granite thrust up through the soil and clumps of trees grow between them and from cracks in the rock. Apparently this landscape began its development as the granite weathered into soil along fractures. Then the climate became very dry — probably during one of the interglacial periods of the past million years — and the vegetation died as the area became a desert. Soil that had formed along cracks in the rock was left unprotected and was splashed away by the rain, leaving the solid unweathered rock behind to form boulders we now see.

Butte calls itself the "richest hill on earth," boasting that more mineral wealth has been recovered here than from any other mining camp in the world. Such claims are difficult to judge, but this one may not be far from the truth.

Mining began in Butte during the 1860's and attempts to recover gold and silver were not very successful because there isn't much gold and silver here. Early miners ignored the copper ore for 20 years before it finally occurred to some of them that they should be mining it. That was the real beginning of mining at Butte.

Until 1956 when the Berkeley Pit was started all the mines at Butte were underground. Now most of the underground mines are closed, probably permanently. Old headframes that dot the skyline in Butte are mostly abandoned.

One mine is kept going largely for the benefit of visitors who wish to tour an underground mine. It makes a very worthwhile trip, as does a visit to the World Museum of Mining on the west side of town.

It is impossible to give directions to a place where a visitor can get a good view of the Berkeley Pit because the streets and traffic patterns in that area are constantly changing as mining operations expand. Nevertheless, it is usually possible to find a place where the pit can be closely approached by walking a short distance. Usually, but not always, there is a visitors' overlook somewhere on the south side of the pit.

The thing to look for when you do get a good view of the side of the Berkeley Pit is the thick band of brownish rock near the surface, sharply underlain by greenish rock below. Processes of weathering have removed the copper from the rocks near the surface leaving them brown. The copper they once contained has been carried downward by seeping rainwater and redeposited in the greenish rocks below. These contain a double dose of copper − that which they originally possessed plus that washed out of the brownish rocks above them. This is the best ore.

The brown rock near the surface contains no copper and is stripped off and dumped. The greenish rock below is then mined and sent to the mill near the mine where the copper ores are separated from the waste rock. Finally, the separated copper minerals are shipped to the smelter in Anaconda, 22 miles west of Butte.

The gray rocks deep in the pit below the greenish zone contain their original complement of copper but have not been enriched by weathering and redeposition. These are the leaner ores. Much of this material is stacked in huge piles visible north of the pit where it is treated with acid to dissolve out the copper. Copper-bearing solutions that trickle from the bottoms of the piles are run across beds of old steel cans collected from garbage pits to recover the copper.

Rich copper veins that were the basis of underground mining at Butte for many years are now exposed in the walls of the Berkeley Pit. These are not easy to spot; look closely for faint greenish stains running vertically down the sides of the pit. The veins were thoroughly mined out in the underground workings so there isn't much left to see today.

Like most large copper mines, the Berkeley Pit operates on very low-grade ores. Copper content runs considerably less than 1% on the average so it is very difficult to see any copper minerals in most specimens of the ore. The smaller trucks carry a load of over 100 tons, so each truckload of ore contains several hundred pounds of copper.

No one but the Anaconda Company knows how much copper is left at Butte but indications are that a great deal still remains. We can probably expect to see this pit become much larger, finally swallowing up most of the older part of Butte.

For more information on Lewis and Clark Caverns, see
    U.S. 287: West Yellowstone — Townsend

For more information on the Boulder batholith, see
    Interstate 15: Butte — Helena

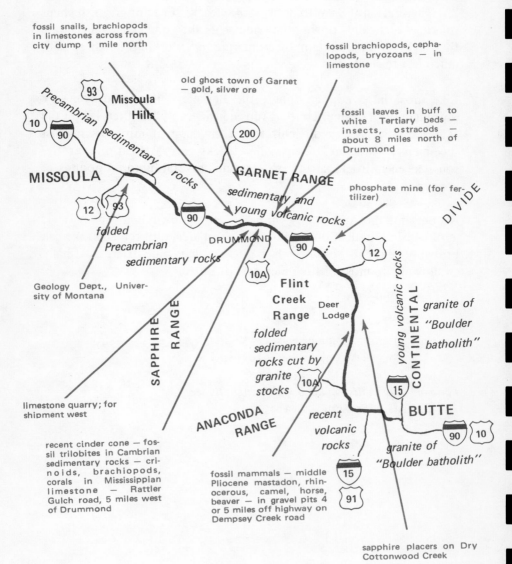

BUTTE — GARRISON JCT. — MISSOULA
118 miles

N
W ⊕ E
S

fossil snails, brachiopods
in limestones across from
city dump 1 mile north

old ghost town of Garnet
— gold, silver ore

fossil brachiopods, cepha-
lopods, bryozoans — in
limestone

93

Missoula
Hills

Precambrian

10

90

200

fossil leaves in buff to
white Tertiary beds —
insects, ostracods —
about 8 miles north of
Drummond

MISSOULA

sedimentary

GARNET RANGE

rocks

*sedimentary and
young volcanic rocks*

phosphate mine (for fer-
tilizer)

DIVIDE

12 93

90

DRUMMOND

*folded
Precambrian
sedimentary rocks*

90

12

10A

young volcanic rocks

Geology Dept., Univer-
sity of Montana

Flint
Creek
Range

Deer
Lodge

*granite of
"Boulder
batholith"*

SAPPHIRE RANGE

*folded
sedimentary
rocks cut by
granite
stocks*

10A

CONTINENTAL

15

limestone quarry; for
shipment west

ANACONDA
RANGE

*recent
volcanic
rocks*

BUTTE

90 10

recent cinder cone — fos-
sil trilobites in Cambrian
sedimentary rocks — cri-
noids, brachiopods,
corals in Mississippian
limestone — Rattler
Gulch road, 5 miles west
of Drummond

*granite of
"Boulder batholith"*

fossil mammals — middle
Pliocene mastadon, rhin-
ocerous, camel, horse,
beaver — in gravel pits 4
or 5 miles off highway on
Dempsey Creek road

15

91

sapphire placers on Dry
Cottonwood Creek

58

Interstate 90 – U.S. 10

BUTTE – MISSOULA

For a few miles west of Butte, the highway cuts across the southern part of the Boulder batholith which outcrops very picturesquely as low, rolling hills dotted with little trees growing among big boulders of pink granite. These hills are liberally sprinkled with small spoil heaps, mostly left by prospectors active during the early period of frantic exploration around Butte.

Between Butte and Garrison Junction, the highway runs the full length of the Deer Lodge Valley, a big, downdropped fault block floored by thick deposits of Tertiary valley-fill sediments. Several well known vertebrate fossil localities in this valley include one in the precincts of the state penitentiary that requires rather special qualifications for admission. Collecting has also been good in several gravel pits southeast of Deer Lodge on the Dempsey Creek Road which turns east from the highway about 6 miles south of town.

Bordering the Deer Lodge Valley to the east are the granites of the Boulder batholith which form the mountains of the continental divide. In places the granite is covered by patches of volcanic rock believed to have been erupted onto the surface from the same body of molten magma that cooled at depth to form the granite.

Along the west side of the Deer Lodge Valley are the peaks of the Flint Creek Range, made of a complexly folded assortment of Precambrian, Paleozoic, and Mesozoic sedimentary rocks intruded in the middle of the range by several large bodies of granite.

The mill south of the highway at Garrison Junction formerly made fertilizer from phosphate rock mined from the Paleozoic Phosphoria Formation in the hills a few miles north of town. However, there was considerable trouble over excessive emissions of fluorides from the smokestack and the mill is now burning limestone to make lime.

Between Garrison Junction and Drummond, the northern end of the

Flint Creek Range is south of the highway. North of the road is the east end of the Garnet Range, composed mostly of folded Precambrian and Paleozoic sedimentary rocks intruded by several small bodies of granite and capped in places by volcanics. The rocks exposed in roadcuts along the highway are Cretaceous sandstones, mudstones, and limestones deposited between 60 and 80 million years ago.

Gold Creek, located south of the highway about 7 miles west of Garrison, is believed to be the site of the first discovery of gold in Montana in 1858. The strike was a small one. Although they aren't visible from the highway, piles of gravel left by the early placer miners still mark the area.

Drummond is at the north end of the Flint Creek Valley, another downdropped fault-block floored by deposits of Tertiary valley-fill sediments. The small hills surrounding the town are folded Cretaceous sedimentary rocks deposited between 60 and 130 million years ago. Folding can be seen by following with the eye the prominent ledge of limestone in the hills north of town. This same ledge of limestone is full of little fossil snails which appear to be a kind that would have lived in fresh water. Apparently at least some of these rocks were deposited on land instead of in a shallow sea.

For about 7 miles west of Drummond the road continues across folded Mesozoic sedimentary rocks in various shades of red, yellow, and brown which outcrop as smooth slopes on both sides of the valley. Father back from the river, the hills both north and south of the road are Paleozoic sedimentary rocks. The arrangement of these rocks is interesting and can best be understood by looking at the cross-section below.

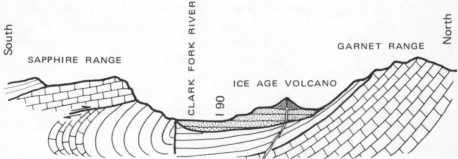

South-north cross section across Interstate 90 and the Clark Fork River Valley about 5 miles west of Drummond. South of the river, Paleozoic sedimentary rocks have slid northward over Mesozoic sedimentary rocks. North of the river, a large fold in the sedimentary rocks has a small volcano erupted on top of it.

The road between Garrison Junction and Missoula follows the line of a major fault – the same one that Interstate 90 continues to follow almost to Spokane. As usual, the fault itself cannot be seen because it is concealed by river gravels and soil but many of the rocks along this valley have been severely contorted as the mountains north of the highway moved west. A striking example is near Bearmouth Canyon where conspicuous cliffs of white limestone form bluffs rising from both sides of the river. Look very carefully at the cliffs above the south side of the river and, if the light is good, you will see large, intricate folds in the rock. Another effect of the movements on this fault is the conspicuous fracturing of many of the rocks exposed in roadcuts.

Bearmouth Canyon, which enters the Clark Fork River from the Garnet Range to the north about 15 miles west of Drummond, was the site of large-scale placer gold mining during the late years of the last century and the early years of this one. Miles of creek gravels were worked over by hand and by dredges, leaving a sea of spoil heaps where once there was an attractive creek. Some of these piles of gravel can be glimpsed from the highway. Bedrock ores were mined high in the mountains where several ghost towns still remain. One of these, the town of Garnet, can be reached from old U.S. 10 by taking the road up Bearmouth Canyon. Interesting mineral specimens, including specimens of garnet, are found on the old mine dumps around the ghost town. Garnet is now being preserved as a historic monument and is well worth a visit in its own right.

About 25 miles west of Missoula the road crosses the last Paleozoic sedimentary rocks, all the rocks west of there are sandstones and mudstones deposited more than 600 million years ago during Precambrian time.

Milltown Dam, about 6 miles east of Missoula on the Clark Fork River, was built as a power generating facility. During the last 40 years the reservoir behind the dam has almost completely filled with sediment brought in by the river so that now very little water storage capacity remains and extensive grassy marshes have grown up over much of the former area of the reservoir. This can easily be seen south of Interstate 90 just west of its junction with Montana 200 at Bonner.

For more information on the Butte mines, see
Interstate 90: Bozeman – Butte (preceding section)

MISSOULA — LOOKOUT PASS
105 miles

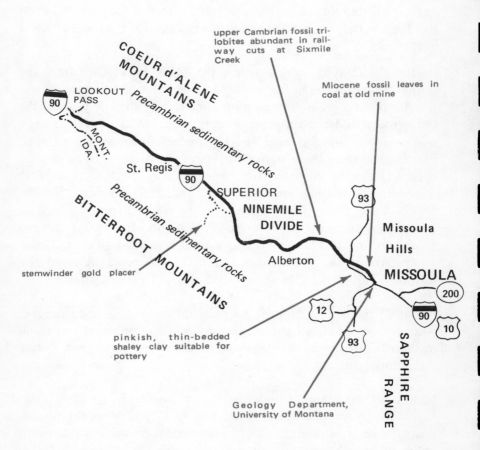

Interstate 90

MISSOULA – LOOKOUT PASS

For about 15 miles west of Missoula the highway goes through the western end of the broad Missoula Valley, a large fault-block let down as the adjacent mountain blocks rose during formation of the Rockies. Large roadcuts of gravel along the highway north of Missoula are excellent exposures of the valley-fill deposited during Tertiary Time when for 40 million or so years the climate was too dry to maintain a stream drainage. Fossil leaves and bone have been found in these gravels along with some beautiful petrified wood but there isn't much material and the collecting is rewarding only to the most patient.

The bare, grassy mountains at the east side of Missoula are made of hard Precambrian sandstone. About 35 shorelines recording different depths of Glacial Lake Missoula appear as faintly grooved horizontal lines on their slopes.

Missoula County Airport is laid out on a flat terrace of fine silts deposited in the bottom of Glacial Lake Missoula during the last ice age when the valley was inundated under as much as 1400 feet of water.

A much better exposure of Glacial Lake Missoula silts is right on the interstate highway, about 20 miles west of Missoula, immediately west of the Ninemile Exit where the road goes down a long slope toward the Clark Fork River. Large roadcuts through a thick deposit of horizontally-bedded light gray silts are on both sides of the highway.

Glacial lakes deposit a peculiar kind of sediment consisting of alternating layers of light-gray silt released from the melting ice during spring and summer, and black organic material which settles slowly to the bottom of the lake during winter. Each such pair of beds (usually less than an inch thick) records one year in the life of the lake and is called a varve. Varves in this roadcut have been very carefully studied and have shown that Glacial Lake Missoula was filled with water at least 36 times. The longest period of filling was for 58 years and the shortest for 9 years. A total of 967 varves have been counted in this exposure.

The Missoula Valley ends about 18 miles west of town and the highway follows the narrow canyon of the Clark Fork River from there to St. Regis. From St. Regis to Lookout Pass it follows the even narrower canyon of the St. Regis River. These valleys cut diagonally between the northern part of the Bitterroot Range to the south and the Coeur d'Alene Range to the north. All these mountains are composed almost entirely of Precambrian sedimentary rocks deposited between 500 and 1500 million years ago.

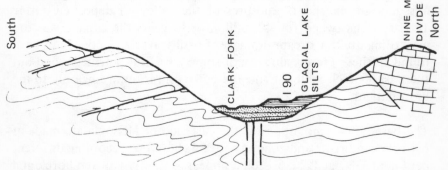

South-north cross section across the line of Interstate 90 about 20 miles west of Missoula. Several large slices of Precambrian sedimentary rocks pushed over the tops of each other make complicated geologic structures south of the highway. Light gray Glacial Lake Missoula silts cover parts of the valley floor.

Red and green mudstones form conspicuous outcrops between the Tarkio and Ninemile Exits a short distance west of Missoula. These are thought to be among the younger Precambrian sedimentary rocks in the region. They are full of beautifully preserved sedimentary structures including mudcracks, ripple marks, raindrop impressions, and cubical imprints of salt crystals. These features make it possible to deduce that the rocks were once layers of mud cracked in the sun and wetted by passing showers on mudflats that existed here between 1000 and 500 million years ago. Almost any of the conspicuous outcrops along the road for several miles on either side of Alberton are good places to look for sedimentary structures.

Farther west, all the way to Lookout Pass, the rocks contain ripple marks, which form underwater, but are mostly lacking the kinds of sedimentary structures that form when mud dries in the sun. Apparently these sediments were laid down under deeper water.

Several enormous white boulders scattered through the town of Alberton and easily visible just north of the highway are the remains of a prehistoric rock fall. They came from the light-colored ledges visible high on the mountain slope north of town. These are especially interesting because they are Paleozoic limestone (Cambrian age), the only such outcrops anywhere within 30 miles of Alberton. It seems likely that these rocks once covered the whole region and have since been removed by erosion except in this one area.

Most of the road between Missoula and Lookout Pass is along the line of a major fault which appears to be responsible for the directly northwestward course of the Clark Fork Canyon. As is usually the case with large faults, this one is not exposed in outcrops because the rocks along it have been crushed and broken, so are easily eroded away. In order to recognize the existence of such a fault it is usually necessary to do considerable geologic work over a sizeable area to show that the rocks on opposite sides of the fault do not match.

Red and green mudstones around Alberton are very close to the fault and have been complexly folded. Many of the layers are actually turned upside down so that the mudcracks and ripple marks appear to be on the under surfaces of the beds instead of on top where they belong. It is surprisingly difficult, however, to tell the difference between a mudcrack or ripple mark on the upper surface of a rock layer and the cast of the same feature on the under surface of the layer above.

The huge fault which Interstate 90 follows between Missoula and Lookout Pass is the same one that controlled emplacement of the large ore bodies in the Coeur d'Alene Mining District of northern Idaho. All of the major ore bodies appear to be in Idaho but a few small ones have been found in Montana, especially near Superior, once the site of several productive mines. Attractive mineral specimens are found in the old mine dumps around town.

For more information on Glacial Lake Missoula, see
   Montana 28: Plains — Elmo
   Montana 200: Ravalli Jct. — Sandpoint
   County 382: Perma — Hot Springs
   U.S. 195: Lewiston — Spokane

LOOKOUT PASS — SPOKANE
105 miles

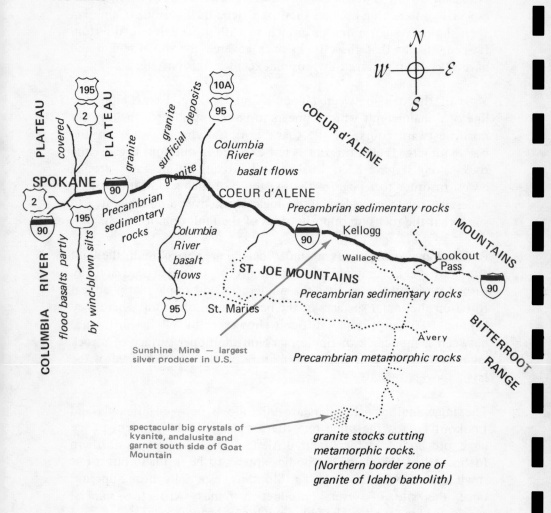

PLATEAU

covered

PLATEAU

granite

195

2

granite

surficial deposits

10A

95

Columbia River basalt flows

N

W — E

S

COEUR d'ALENE

SPOKANE

granite

90

COEUR d'ALENE

Precambrian sedimentary rocks

MOUNTAINS

2

195

90

Precambrian sedimentary rocks

Kellogg

90

Wallace

Lookout Pass

90

Columbia River basalt flows

ST. JOE MOUNTAINS

Precambrian sedimentary rocks

95

St. Maries

Avery

BITTERROOT RANGE

COLUMBIA RIVER

flood basalts partly

by wind-blown silts

Precambrian metamorphic rocks

Sunshine Mine — largest silver producer in U.S.

spectacular big crystals of kyanite, andalusite and garnet south side of Goat Mountain

granite stocks cutting metamorphic rocks. (Northern border zone of granite of Idaho batholith)

Interstate 90

LOOKOUT PASS – SPOKANE

Between Lookout Pass on the Montana-Idaho line and Spokane, the traveller goes through the Coeur d'Alene Mining District which has been producing lead, zinc, silver, and gold continuously since the 1880's. The towns in this area are authentically colorful places with long histories extending back to the wild times of the last century. Anyone who fears that the exuberant spirit of the old western mining camp is a thing of the past should try Wallace on a Saturday night.

White settlement in this area (near Coeur d'Alene Lake) began in the 1840's with a Jesuit mission which was moved to its present site at Cataldo in 1853. Tradition has it that the priests and Captain John Mullan, who laid out this road, knew of the presence of gold in the region as early as 1854 but said nothing. But such a secret could not keep and word did get out in the early 1860's, touching off a series of gold rushes in northern Idaho. These continued sporadically through the 1880's. Things gradually calmed down and the district settled into the serious business of large-scale mining. A railroad was built and the first concentrating mill began operation in 1890. The Coeur d'Alene district was one of the focal points of the labor struggles that shook the nation during the 1890's. The miners organized into unions and the operators responded by trying to bring in non-union labor from outside the district. Several properties were dynamited, a number of people were shot, and the National Guard was called in to restore order during a seesaw struggle that went on for years before the miners finally succeeded in establishing powerful unions.

All the ore bodies between Mullan and Coeur d'Alene were emplaced along the same great fault zone that appears to continue into Montana along the line of Interstate 90 – it can be followed for a total distance of at least 300 miles. The time of ore emplacement is in considerable dispute with some geologists claiming that this took place during Precambrian Time, about 1200 million years ago, while others insist that it took place during formation of the Rocky Mountains, only about 70 million years ago.

Most of the mines are lead-zinc producers which also recover small amounts of silver, gold and cadmium as by-products. Four of the 10 largest lead mines, 2 of the 10 largest zinc mines, and 4 of the 5 largest silver mines in the country are in this district. About 90% of the total national production of silver comes from this area.

Dumps around the larger mines are not good places to collect mineral specimens because the ores are thoroughly milled. Good specimens are occasionally found on some of the smaller dumps and around old prospect pits.

The hills surrounding Kellogg and Smelterville have been thoroughly defoliated by poisonous gasses emitted from the smelter stack providing an excellent example of what uncontrolled sulfur dioxide emissions can do to the landscape. The river is choked with silt eroded from the hills stripped of their protective cloak of vegetation. Greater efforts are now being made to control the emissions by converting the sulfur dioxide, which used to go up the smokestack, into sulfuric acid. A part of this production is used to treat phosphate rock from the Paleozoic Phosphoria Formation, making phosphoric acid used mainly in the fertilizer industry. The fact that the trees in most of the entire district, even away from the smelter, are scrubby is the aftermath of a great forest fire that burned much of northern Idaho during the late summer of 1910.

An interesting geological relationship is exposed along the north side of Coeur d'Alene Lake a few miles east of town. Black basalt lava flows of the Columbia Plateau can be seen on top of Precambrian sedimentary rocks in several roadcuts. The lava flows were erupted between about 40 and 15 million years ago over an older erosional landscape which they buried almost completely except for a few hills that now stick up above the flows like islands in a lake. Coeur d'Alene Lake is at the eastern margin of the Columbia Plateau where the black basalts lap over the much older light-colored Precambrian rocks.

During the last ice age a large glacier came south out of British Columbia as far as the northern edge of Coeur d'Alene Lake. There it

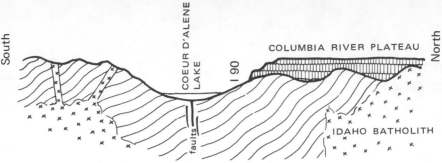

South-north cross section across Interstate 90 at Coeur d'Alene Lake showing how basalt lava flows of the Columbia River Plateau lap over an older landscape eroded into Precambrian sedimentary rocks intruded by granite.

finally came into an area where the climate was warm enough to melt the ice front as fast as it advanced and the glacier ended at the point where this balance was struck. Glaciers carry tremendous amounts of rock and soil which they deposit at the edge of the ice to form a heap of debris called a moraine. At the north edge of Coeur d'Alene Lake a moraine dumped by this glacier formed the lake by damming the drainage of the St. Joe River which flows into the area from the south. Unlike most glacially created lakes, this one does not occupy a basin scoured by the glacier. Coeur d'Alene Lake is entirely south of the area where the glacier once existed.

Between Coeur d'Alene and Spokane, Interstate 90 crosses a very flat area called Rathdrum Prairie which held a lake on at least two occasions. About 20 million years ago, during Miocene time, basalt lava flows of the Columbia Plateau dammed up the drainage creating a large lake which seems to have lasted for millions of years. Sediments accumulated in this lake are exposed in a number of places around Spokane. They contain abundant plant fossils which include such things as Magnolia leaves suggesting that the climate at that time may have been considerably milder than it now is. Much later, during the last ice age which ended only about 10,000 years ago, the drainage in this area was dammed a second time by the same glacier that left the moraine which impounds Coeur d'Alene Lake. Once again lake sediments accumulated and their flat surface is the floor of the prairie we see today.

For more information on the Columbia River Plateau, see
    U.S. 95: Lewiston — Coeur d'Alene
    U.S. 195: Lewiston — Spokane

The following roadguides on the Snake River Plain give additional information on more recent basalt lava flows
    Interstate 80 N: Twin Falls — Boise
    U.S. 20: Idaho Falls — Arco
    U.S. 93A: Shoshone — Arco, Craters of the Moon

69

BROWNING — GLACIER PARK — KALISPELL
103 miles

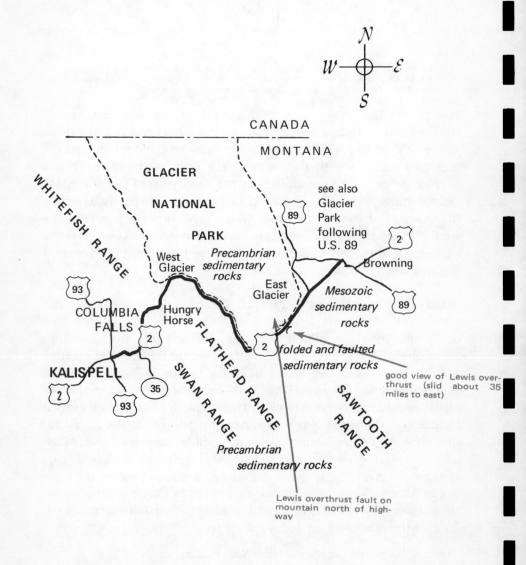

N
W ⊕ E
S

CANADA
MONTANA

GLACIER

NATIONAL

PARK

see also
Glacier
Park
following
U.S. 89

89

2

West
Glacier

*Precambrian
sedimentary
rocks*

Browning

East
Glacier

*Mesozoic
sedimentary
rocks*

89

WHITEFISH RANGE

93

COLUMBIA
FALLS

Hungry
Horse

FLATHEAD RANGE

2

2

*folded and faulted
sedimentary rocks*

good view of Lewis over-
thrust (slid about 35
miles to east)

KALISPELL

2

35

SWAN RANGE

SAWTOOTH
RANGE

93

*Precambrian
sedimentary rocks*

Lewis overthrust fault on
mountain north of high-
way

U.S. 2

BROWNING – KALISPELL

From Browning to the top of Marias Pass, U.S. 2 passes through roadcuts in Cretaceous sandstones and black mudstones laid down in a shallow sea between 60 and 80 million years ago. These rocks are very tightly folded and torn by movements which created the Sawtooth Range and the mountains in Glacier Park about 50 million years ago. This can best be seen in some of the railroad cuts north of the highway.

South of the highway between Browning and Marias Pass is the Sawtooth Range, made of huge slabs of Precambrian limestone and mudstone that have slid eastward and stacked on top of each other. All the slabs tilt westward and lap over each other.

North of the same stretch of highway are the mountains in Glacier Park, carved by erosion from a single large slab of Precambrian sedimentary rocks that slid eastward over the Cretaceous sedimentary rocks on the Lewis Overthrust Fault. The fault can easily be identified from the road as the point on the mountainside where gently rolling, tree-covered topography abruptly gives way to steep, rocky cliffs above.

An obelisk in the center of U.S. 2 at the top of Marias Pass was erected there to honor the memory of Theodore Roosevelt. This is a good place to get a view of the Lewis Overthrust Fault north of the highway. It shows up as a nearly straight line slanting gently upward to the east across the face of the high mountains that form the southern edge of Glacier National Park. At first glance, it looks almost as though it might be a railroad grade high on the mountain slope north of the pass.

The thin, buff-colored zone above the Lewis Overthrust is the Precambrian Altyn Limestone, well over one billion years old. Immediately beneath it are Cretaceous sandstones and mudstones only 60 to 80 million years old. This is a truly spectacular geologic situation — rocks more than one billion years old have been pushed up and slid over the top of rocks only 60-80 million years old. Older rocks should be underneath younger ones instead of on top.

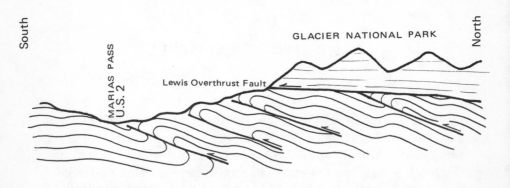

North-south cross section showing how a large slab of Precambrian sedimentary rock slid over Mesozoic sedimentary rocks along the Lewis Overthrust Fault to form the mountains of Glacier National Park.

Cretaceous rocks disappear beneath the Precambrian a short distance west of Marias Pass and do not appear again at the surface anyplace farther west. No one knows how far they may extend beneath the surface. All the rocks exposed along the road west of Marias Pass are Precambrian mudstones and limestones similar to those in Glacier Park.

The mountains south of Highway 2 west of Marias Pass are not slabs of Precambrian rock that have slid eastward. Instead, they are fault blocks lifted up during formation of the Rocky Mountains. From Marias Pass to Hungry Horse, the highway skirts the northern end of the Flathead Range, which is one fault block; from Hungry Horse to Columbia Falls, it skirts the northern end of the Swan Range, which is another.

Between Hungry Horse and Columbia Falls, the highway passes through Bad Rock Canyon which gets its name from a fight among the Indians that occurred many years ago. The walls of the canyon are in red and green Precambrian mudstones full of nice ripple marks and mudcracks.

A large aluminum smelter is operated by the Anaconda Company at Columbia Falls. Power generated at Hungry Horse Dam is used to process aluminum ores brought in from the Caribbean region.

Fluorides emitted from the smokestacks have poisoned trees along the road near the mouth of Bad Rock Canyon and on the slopes of Teakettle Mountain north of Bad Rock Canyon.

Between Columbia Falls and Kalispell, U.S. 2 crosses the broad Flathead Valley which is near the southern end of a long fault-block valley that extends far into northern British Columbia. Geologists call it the Rocky Mountain Trench. The Salish Ranges visible in the distance west of the Flathead Valley are Precambrian sedimentary rocks resembling those of Glacier Park.

An enormous glacier filled the Rocky Mountain Trench during the last ice age, flowing southward out of British Columbia as far as the area a few miles south of Flathead Lake. Glacial debris dropped as the ice melted at the end of the last age, about 10,000 years ago, deeply covers the floor of the Flathead Valley. This material is the basis of the soil that supports the valley's richly productive agriculture.

For more information on the geology of Glacier National Park, see
> Glacier National Park (after roadguide for U.S. 89: Great Falls – Browning)
> U.S. 89: Browning – Chief Mountain

For more information on continental ice age glaciers, see
> U.S. 93: Missoula – Kalispell
> U.S. 93: Kalispell – Eureka

KALISPELL – BONNERS FERRY
136 miles

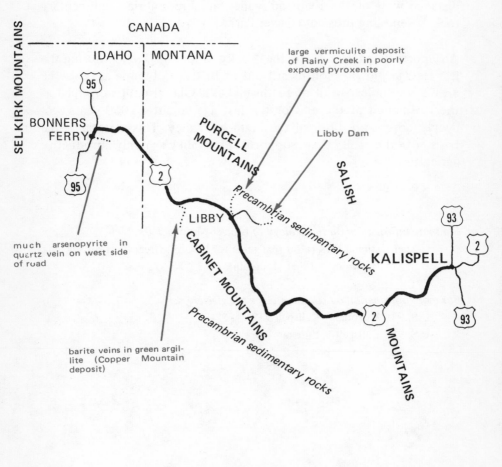

CANADA

IDAHO MONTANA

SELKIRK MOUNTAINS

95

BONNERS FERRY

95

2

large vermiculite deposit of Rainy Creek in poorly exposed pyroxenite

Libby Dam

PURCELL MOUNTAINS

SALISH

Precambrian sedimentary rocks

much arsenopyrite in quartz vein on west side of road

LIBBY

CABINET MOUNTAINS

Precambrian sedimentary rocks

KALISPELL

93

2

2

93

MOUNTAINS

barite veins in green argillite (Copper Mountain deposit)

U.S. 2

KALISPELL – BONNERS FERRY

Kalispell, at the eastern end of this highway, is in the Flathead Valley which was occupied by a very large glacier during the last ice age and is now completely floored by debris dumped from the ice when it melted about 10,000 years ago. Bonners Ferry, at the western end of the highway, is in the Purcell Trench, another large fault-block valley also filled with ice during the last ice age and also blanketed by glacial debris when the ice melted.

The highway between Kalispell and Bonners Ferry passes through heavily forested country in which very little of the bedrock geology can easily be seen from the road.

Except near Bonners Ferry, all the bedrock exposed along the highway and in the mountains visible from the highway is Precambrian mudstone and sandstone deposited between 600 and 1500 million years ago, then folded during the past 70 million or so years while the Rocky Mountains were forming. These rocks have not been as severely deformed as those in most of the other parts of our region so the folds are relatively flat and gentle.

The rather low mountains on the west side of the Flathead Valley near Kalispell are called the Salish Ranges. Farther west, the higher mountains north of U.S. 2 between Libby and Bonners Ferry are the Purcell Range, whereas those south of the same stretch of highway are the Cabinet Range. All these ranges contain the same Precambrian sedimentary rocks and are basically quite similar in their geology.

A very large mass of molten granite magma moved up into the earth's crust, in what is now the northern panhandle of Idaho, about 60 to 80 million years ago to form the Kaniksu batholith. After the batholith had cooled a long narrow segment of it was let down on faults to form the Purcell Trench in which Bonners Ferry is located.

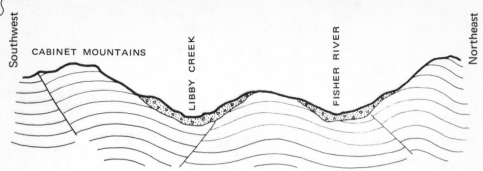

Southwest-northeast cross section across the line of U.S. 2 near Libby. Glacial debris in the valleys covers gently-folded beds of Precambrian sedimentary rock.

High granite mountains on the west side of the Purcell Trench are the Selkirk Range. The westernmost ends of the Purcell and Cabinet Ranges where they end east of the Purcell Trench are also granite.

Numerous exposures of glacial lake silts are conspicuous in roadcuts along the valley of Libby Creek. They are recognizable as soft-looking outcrops of very light-gray silt showing faint horizontal layers. A little bit of digging in one of these roadcuts will shortly turn up glacial lake varves, alternating layers of dark and light-colored silt that record the winters and summers of the years during the ice age when the glacial lake existed. Light layers were deposited during the summer when glacial ice was melting and releasing finely ground rock flour into the lake. Dark layers were deposited during the winter as the remains of small organisms that had flourished during the previous summer sifted slowly to the bottom.

The number of years the lake existed can be determined by counting the pairs of light and dark layers in its deposits. And something can be learned about the climate during those years by studying the thicknesses of the layers. For example, an unusually thick white layer records a long, warm summer that melted a lot of ice releasing a great deal of pulverized rock into the lake. A thin white streak within a dark winter layer tells us of a midwinter thaw.

Sediments like these are deposited only in glacial lakes so we can be sure that one formerly flooded this valley. Unfortunately, no geologic research has been done on this particular lake so we don't know much about it. It seems likely that it must have formed when a glacier dammed the drainage of Libby Creek somewhere near Troy.

For more information on continental glaciers and glacial deposits, see
   U.S. 93: Missoula – Kalispell
   U.S. 93: Kalispell – Eureka

Boulders dumped from melting ice litter a glacially scraped bedrock surface.

OPPORTUNITY JCT. (Anaconda) — DRUMMOND
63 miles

N
W E
S

oyster, snail, marine fossils 1 mile east of New Chicago

boulders on valley floor brought in by mud flow

GARNET

DRUMMOND

RANGE

Douglas Creek Phosphate Mine

SAPPHIRE

RANGE

Precambrian sedimentary rocks

FLINT

CREEK

RANGE

folded sedimentary

rocks cut by granite stocks

Philipsburg

Hilltop Manganese Mine — manganese oxide minerals, garnet, epidote

Amazonstone as large pale green masses in pegmatite at base of falls on Lost Creek

ANACONDA

folded sedimentary rocks cut by granite batholiths

young volcanic rocks

ANACONDA

RANGE

old ghost town of Granite and Granite Bi-Metallic Mine (silver)

Anaconda copper smelter

Browns limestone quarry

U.S. 10A

OPPORTUNITY JUNCTION (ANACONDA) – DRUMMOND

U.S. 10A follows a route that is both beautiful and geologically interesting. Travellers with a few extra minutes to spend may prefer it to Interstate 90 which is a faster road but not as interesting.

Between Opportunity Junction and Anaconda, the highway crosses the south end of the Deer Lodge Valley, past the enormous Anaconda smelter with its giant smokestack visible for miles. This smelter has processed the ores mined at Butte for many years and is one of the world's major producers of copper. A number of other metals are recovered as by-products. Barren hillsides surrounding the smelter testify to the poisonous effects of sulfur dioxide fumes on plant life. Waste piles of shiny black material south of the road are iron-rich smelter slag.

North of Anaconda, on the west side of the Deer Lodge Valley, is the Flint Creek Range, composed mostly of large masses of intrusive granite surrounded by Precambrian, Paleozoic, and Mesozoic sedimentary rocks. The mountains northeast of Anaconda, on the east side of the Deer Lodge Valley, are the granites of the Boulder batholith along the continental divide. And the big mountains southwest of Anaconda belong to the Anaconda Range, composed mostly of strongly folded Precambrian and Paleozoic sedimentary rocks intruded by granites and related igneous rocks.

Between Anaconda and Georgetown Lake, the road follows a valley that was occupied by a large glacier during the last ice age. Glaciers form when large amounts of snow accumulate in high mountain valleys and begin to flow slowly downhill as a stream of ice. The downhill end of the glacier is always at a place where the rate of ice advance is exactly equalled by the rate of melting. At this point the soil and rock the glacier had been carrying is deposited as a ridge of material called a moraine which remains after the ice melts to mark the place where it once stood. Between Anaconda and Georgetown

Lake, the road crosses several glacial moraines distinctively recognizable in roadcuts as small ridges of bouldery material. Each one marks a place where the ice stood for a few years as it melted back in stages at the end of the last ice age.

Most of the bedrock outcrops in the valley between Anaconda and Georgetown Lake are Paleozoic limestones ranging in age from Cambrian (about 550 million years old) to Mississippian (about 325 million years old).

About a mile northwest of Georgetown Lake, just below the crest of the hill, are some very large roadcuts on the north side of the highway that are well worth stopping to examine more closely. Huge slabs of red, yellow, and green Precambrian mudstones contain spectacular displays of ripple marks, mudcracks, raindrop imprints, and other sedimentary features – a natural outdoor museum. Watch for the big, flat surfaces sloping down toward the north side of the highway. See photograph, page 89.

Philipsburg, near the south end of the Flint Creek Valley, is a fine old mining town with a long and colorful history. Great quantities of gold and silver were mined here in the early days, and more recently, manganese. Total value of ores mined at Philipsburg probably approaches the 100 million dollar mark. Numerous old mine dumps in the area contain attractive mineral specimens.

Granite ghost town is about 5 miles east of Philipsburg, high in the Flint Creek mountains. It is accessible from Philipsburg during the summer months over well-graded roads poorly marked by small Forest Service signs and easily passable by cars with healthy cooling systems. Granite was a gold and silver mining community with a population of about 5000. They abandoned the town almost in a single day when one of the financial panics early in this century closed the mines.

Douglas Creek Phosphate Mine is in the northern portion of the Flint Creek Range and can be reached by a marked road that turns east from U.S. 10A near Hall. Phosphate rock mined here from the Paleozoic Phosphoria Formation, was shipped to Trail, British Columbia to be processed into fertilizer.

Ravages made by an old effort to mine gold hydraulically, now mercifully overgrown by trees, scar a low ridge east of the highway between Philipsburg and Hall.

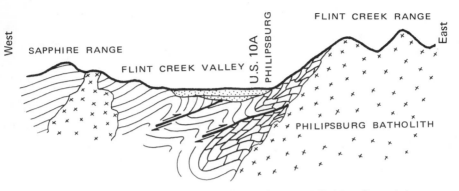

West-east cross section across the line of U.S. 10A near Philipsburg. Precambrian and Paleozoic sedimentary rocks in the Flint Creek range are intensely deformed near the Philipsburg batholith where they contain numerous valuable ore bodies.

Near the little community of Maxville, about halfway between Philipsburg and Drummond, the valley floor is strewn for a distance of several miles with thousands of large granite boulders. Apparently they were carried there by a large mudflow and flood that occurred several thousand years ago. A natural glacial moraine dam impounded a lake several miles up the valley of Boulder Creek in the Flint Creek Mountains east of Maxville. The dam broke and the water from the lake rushed down Boulder Creek carrying the large blocks of granite out onto the valley floor where we see them now.

Flint Creek Valley, between Philipsburg and Drummond, is another large fault-block valley floored by deep deposits of sand and gravel. The Flint Creek Range on the east side of the valley is mostly granite pushed up through Precambrian and Paleozoic sedimentary rocks, which outcrop along the highway. West of the Flint Creek Valley is the lower‘ Sapphire Range, named for the placer deposits of gem-quality sapphires in the gravels of the West Fork of Rock Creek about 12 miles west of Philipsburg. These can be reached by taking Montana 38 (Skalkaho Highway) west from Porters Corner or Philipsburg. Rocks in the Sapphire Range are folded Precambrian sedimentary rocks intruded by numerous small bodies of granite.

WHITE SULPHUR SPRINGS — HELENA
74 miles

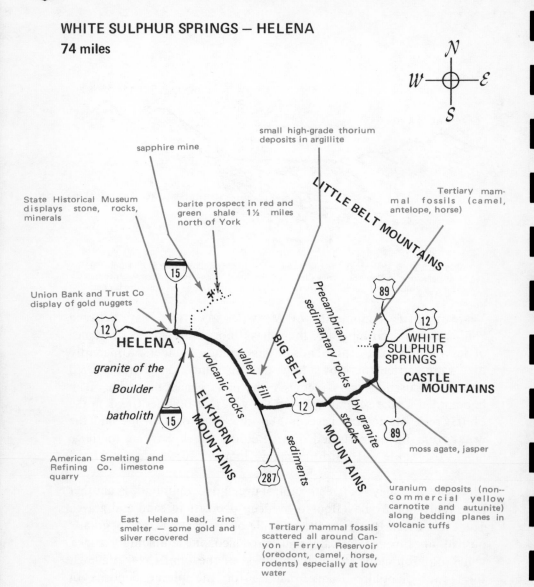

sapphire mine

small high-grade thorium deposits in argillite

State Historical Museum displays stone, rocks, minerals

barite prospect in red and green shale 1½ miles north of York

LITTLE BELT MOUNTAINS

Tertiary mammal fossils (camel, antelope, horse)

Union Bank and Trust Co display of gold nuggets

Precambrian sedimentary rocks

89

12

WHITE SULPHUR SPRINGS

HELENA

granite of the

Boulder

batholith

volcanic rocks

valley fill

BIG BELT

CASTLE MOUNTAINS

ELKHORN MOUNTAINS

12

by granite stocks

89

MOUNTAINS

moss agate, jasper

American Smelting and Refining Co. limestone quarry

sediments

287

uranium deposits (non-commercial yellow carnotite and autunite) along bedding planes in volcanic tuffs

East Helena lead, zinc smelter — some gold and silver recovered

Tertiary mammal fossils scattered all around Canyon Ferry Reservoir (oreodont, camel, horse, rodents) especially at low water

U.S. 12

WHITE SULPHUR SPRINGS – HELENA

From White Sulphur Springs to the junction of U.S. 89 and U.S. 12, eleven miles to the south, the road follows the Smith River Valley along the west side of the Castle Mountains, a granite intrusion punched up through Paleozoic and Mesozoic sedimentary rocks. Visible to the southeast is the north end of the Crazy Mountains. These are mostly Mesozoic sedimentary rocks that contain large numbers of igneous intrusions. The western skyline is dominated by the Big Belt Mountains which U.S. 12 passes through by way of Deep Creek Canyon.

The Big Belt Mountains are a large block raised up while the Rocky Mountains were being formed during the last 70 million or so years. It is composed mostly of intensely folded and faulted Precambrian, along with lesser amounts of Paleozoic, sedimentary rocks. Several bodies of granite in the central part of the range were intruded as molten magmas during the time these rocks were being folded and uplifted. However, the only kind of rocks actually visible along U.S. 12 are Precambrian mudstones (slates) and sandstones.

Between Townsend and Helena, U.S. 12-287 follows the valley of the Missouri River going past Canyon Ferry Reservoir for part of the distance. The Big Belt Mountains fill the view east of this stretch of highway and the low, rounded Spokane Hills are between the highway and the north end of Canyon Ferry Reservoir. The Spokane Hills are red and green Precambrian mudstones similar to those seen along Interstate 15 between Helena and Wolf Creek.

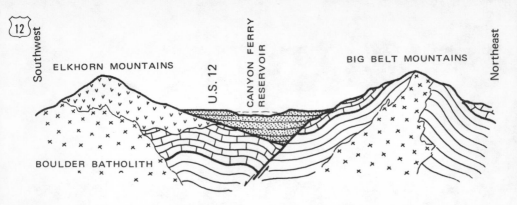

Southwest-northeast cross section across the line of U.S. 12 between Helena and Townsend. Volcanic rocks erupted from the molten magmas of the Boulder batholith make the superstructure of the Elkhorn Mountains. Small masses of granite intrude Precambrian and Paleozoic sedimentary rocks in the Big Belt Mountains.

West and south of U.S. 12-287 between Townsend and Helena are the Elkhorn Mountains, thickly capped by volcanic rocks erupted about 75 million years ago from the same body of molten magma that formed the Boulder batholith granites west of Helena. Some large gold mines were active in these mountains during the last century near the ghost town of Elkhorn on the southwestern flank of the range.

Helena is built on Precambrian and Paleozoic sedimentary rocks on the eastern edge of the Boulder batholith, an enormous mass of granitic rock intruded into the area between Helena and Butte about 75 million years ago. Sedimentary rocks around Helena were strongly heated when this mass of hot granite magma was emplaced nearby. This thoroughly recrystallized them so that the limestones, for example, have been turned into marble. Rocks recrystallized by heat become coarse-grained in the same way that fine snow on a sidewalk slowly turns into granular ice.

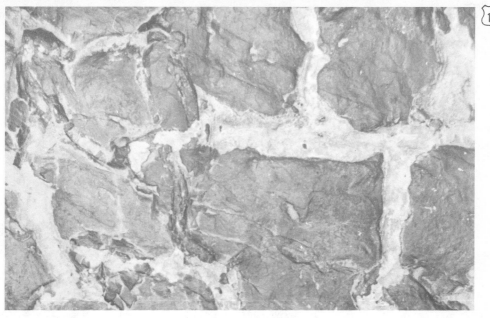

Mudcracks in Precambrian sedimentary rocks — about a billion years old.

Raindrop imprints in suncracked mud on the side of a modern mudpuddle. Identical features are preserved in Precambrian sedimentary rocks laid down more than one billion years ago.

HELENA – GARRISON JCT.
45 miles

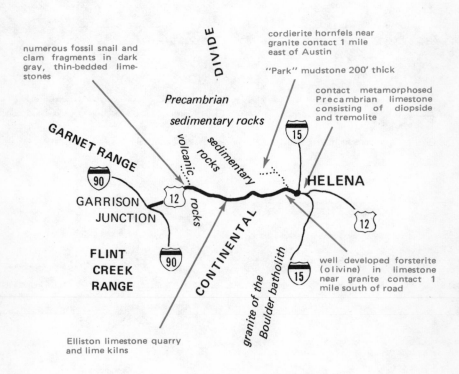

numerous fossil snail and clam fragments in dark gray, thin-bedded limestones

cordierite hornfels near granite contact 1 mile east of Austin

"Park" mudstone 200' thick

contact metamorphosed Precambrian limestone consisting of diopside and tremolite

Precambrian sedimentary rocks

volcanic rocks

sedimentary rocks

DIVIDE

GARNET RANGE

(90)

(12)

GARRISON JUNCTION

(90)

FLINT CREEK RANGE

(15)

HELENA

(12)

CONTINENTAL

granite of the Boulder batholith

well developed forsterite (olivine) in limestone near granite contact 1 mile south of road

(15)

Elliston limestone quarry and lime kilns

U.S. 12

HELENA – GARRISON JUNCTION

Helena is located just east of the northern part of an enormous body of granite called the Boulder batholith, intruded as a molten magma between 70 and 75 million years ago while the northern Rocky Mountains were first being formed. The town is built on Precambrian limestones and mudstones that were cooked by the heat from the nearby granite.

A very interesting small roadcut in Precambrian limestone (marble) is on the south side of U.S. 12 a short distance west of Helena, exactly 1.8 miles west of the ruins of the old Broadwater Hotel. This roadcut contains as spectacular a display of Precambrian fossil seaweeds as can be seen anywhere in our region. Most of them appear as small, vertical lines which squiggle their way through an inch or so of the rock. Many geologists nickname these "molar tooth structures" because they suggest (with a little imagination) big fossil molar teeth. They are actually leaf-like seaweeds that were buried in soft mud and then crumpled as the mud compacted. These are almost certainly among the oldest fossils known anywhere in the world. No one knows exactly how old they are but a billion years is probably too young.

Between a point several miles west of Helena and the area on the west side of Rogers Pass, U.S. 12 crosses granites of the Boulder batholith. Many roadcuts are in rather deeply weathered rock offering an opportunity to observe the way solid granite weathers to loose, sandy soil when exposed at the ground surface.

On the west slope of MacDonald Pass the road leaves the granite, crossing onto volcanic rocks. Most of these are reddish- or greenish-brown rocks that outcrop in large, rather plain-looking exposures without much layering.

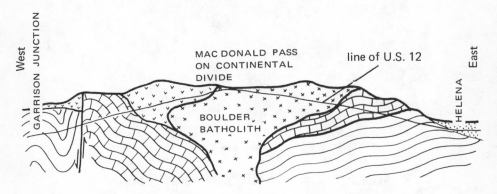

West-east cross section along the line of U.S. 12 between Garrison Junction and Helena. Molten granite magma rose through the older sedimentary rocks and was the source of the lavas erupted to form the volcanic rocks. During the last stages of intrusion the granite magma rose into its own volcanic roof now exposed west of MacDonald Pass.

Geologists believe the volcanics were erupted from the same large body of molten granite magma that solidified below the surface to form the Boulder batholith. They blanketed an older landscape eroded into folded sedimentary rocks. As the volcanics were being erupted, the still-molten granite magma beneath continued to move upward until it finally intruded its cover of volcanic rocks. While this was happening, 70 million years ago, this area must have been very much the way Yellowstone Park is today — a high plateau of volcanic rocks with still-molten granite magma beneath. Now most of the volcanics have been stripped off the granite by erosion but patches remain to tell the story. Older sedimentary rocks west of the granite that had been covered by the volcanics are being exposed by erosion for a second time.

Between MacDonald Pass and Garrison Junction the highway passes outcrops of volcanic rocks lying on top of the older sedimentary rocks. The two can easily be distinguished because the sedimentary rocks are conspicuously layered whereas the volcanics are not.

For more information on the Boulder batholith, see
    Interstate 90: Bozeman — Butte
    Interstate 15: Butte — Helena

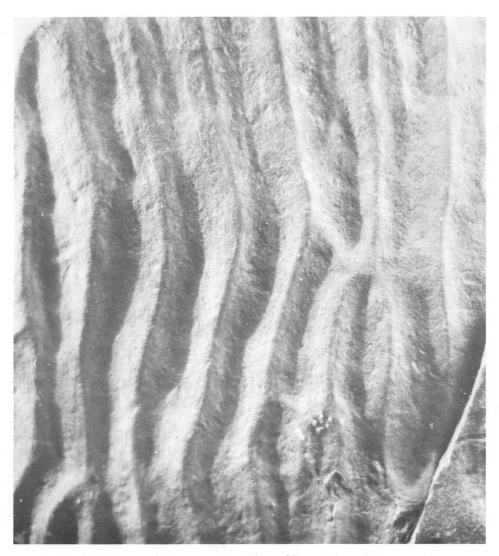

Ripple marks beautifully preserved on surfaces of Precambrian sedimentary rocks tell of mud stirred in the bottom of shallow pools of water ruffled by the wind more than a billion years ago. Approximately natural size.

MISSOULA – LOLO PASS – KOOSKIA
145 miles

ancient fossils

Precambrian algal beds 7 miles east of Lolo Hot Springs

Smoky quartz crystal mine on Granite Creek reached to west and southwest about 6 miles from Lolo Hot Springs

miarolitic cavities (angular) gas holes) in granite are lined by well-formed crystals of quartz and feldspar

Precambrian sedimentary rocks

MISSOULA

MONT.

IDAHO

granite

transparent, green crystals of beryl have been found in pegmatite dikes in old landslide

schists and gneisses (strongly metamorphosed)

granite of the Idaho batholith

CLEARWATER

barite vein on west bank of Pattee Creek, north of Mt. Mitten

basalts of the Columbia

MOUNTAINS

schists

KOOSKIA

and

LOWELL

granite of the Idaho batholith

BITTERROOT MOUNTAINS

River Plateau

CLEARWATER MOUNTAINS

gneisses

spectacular metamorphic rocks and granite along highway in this vicinity

U.S. 12

MISSOULA — KOOSKIA

U.S. 12 between Missoula and Kooskia parallels the route taken by Lewis and Clark as they nearly starved while crossing the Bitterroot and Clearwater Mountains. They followed the ridge north of the present highway which follows the valleys of Lolo Creek and the Lochsa and Clearwater Rivers through beautiful country almost as wild as it was when the first white men saw it. The rocks are unusually interesting too and add considerably to the pleasure of the drive.

The easternmost end of the trip, between Missoula and Lolo Hot Springs, takes the traveller through tightly folded Precambrian sandstones, mudstones, and limestones in which the layers can be seen tilting at all angles.

Lolo Creek closely follows the line of a large fault which runs generally parallel to the road a short distance to the south. The high peaks of the Bitterroot Mountains south of the highway are metamorphic rocks formed when Precambrian sedimentary rocks were deeply buried in the crust and thoroughly cooked during Mesozoic time — 70 to 100 million years ago.

Between Lolo Hot Springs and the top of Lolo Pass, the road crosses one end of the Lolo batholith, a very large body of granite extending many miles into Idaho. Molten granite magma rose into the crust about 50 or so million years ago. Although the time is a bit uncertain, the Lolo batholith appears to be one of the youngest large bodies of granite in the region. Light-colored volcanic rocks which outcrop in a few places were formed when part of the magma was erupted through a volcanic neck in the hills north of the highway.

Lolo Hot Springs really are hot. Lewis and Clark had a bath here and enthusiastically described the springs in their journals. The water emerges along the contact between the granite and its surrounding

Precambrian sedimentary rocks. Probably fractures permit rain water to circulate deep enough to get well heated by the still-hot batholith before it returns to the surface at the springs.

Granite of the Lolo batholith cooled at a shallow depth and is full of very small gas holes lined with crystals. The granite is also cut by very coarse-grained veins (called pegmatites) which contain much larger gas holes lined with beautiful crystals of feldspar and smoky quartz. Mineral collectors had a wonderful time when the new roadcuts for U.S. 12 were blasted. The easy pickings are cleaned up now but any new excavation in the Lolo batholith is a likely place to look for gem quality smoky quartz.

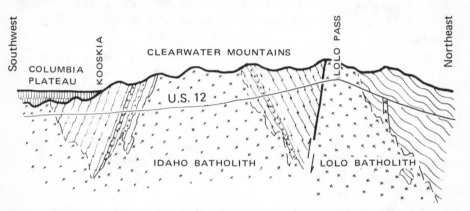

Southwest-northeast cross section along the line of U.S. 12 between Lolo and Kooskia. Large masses of granite intrude very complexly folded gneisses and schists. Basalt lava flows of the eastern edge of the Columbia River Plateau lap over the older rocks near Kooskia.

Between the top of Lolo Pass and Kooskia, U.S. 12 goes through dozens of beautiful roadcuts in igneous and metamorphic rocks. Although these rocks are similar to those elsewhere in the Precambrian basement, they are much younger, having formed between 70 and 100 million years ago during part of Mesozoic time.

Travellers who stop to look at roadcuts will find a variety of streaky-looking gneisses and flaky mica schists injected by varying amounts of granite magma. Some roadcuts contain no granite at all, others a few scattered dikes showing where molten magma was squirted into fractures, still others are blasted entirely in uniform pink granite. Many roadcuts contain streaky-looking metamorphic rocks and uniform-looking granite mixed together looking something like a marble cake. These are believed to form where the metamorphic rocks were so strongly heated that they began to melt.

U.S. 12 is one of the few highways that cross part of the enormous Idaho batholith, a body of granite intruded as a molten magma sometime between 70 and 90 million years ago, early in the history of the northern Rockies. Much of the route between Lolo Pass and Kooskia approximately follows the northern edge of the batholith so there are long stretches of road built through very uniform-looking pink and gray granite. The mixed granite and metamorphic rocks that also outcrop along this road formed in the border zone of the batholith.

Most of central Idaho is underlain by granites of the Idaho batholith. They extend south as far as Boise, west almost to the Idaho-Washington line, and east into the Bitterroot Mountains along the Idaho-Montana line. Approximately 14,000 square miles are underlain by this one enormous batholith, so a huge volume of rock within the earth's crust must have melted to form all that magma.

For more information on the Idaho batholith, see
    Idaho 15: Boise — New Meadows

Light-colored dikes of granite crossing banded gneiss. In roadcut along U.S. 12 a few miles west of Lolo Pass.

KOOSKIA – LEWISTON
71 miles

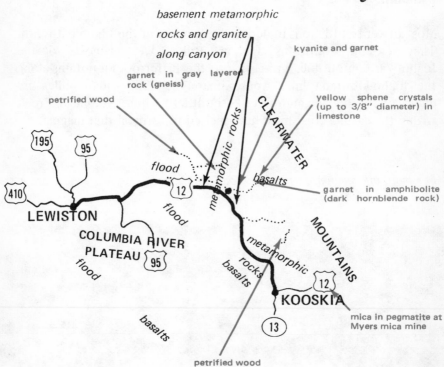

basement metamorphic
rocks and granite
along canyon

kyanite and garnet

garnet in gray layered
rock (gneiss)

yellow sphene crystals
(up to 3/8" diameter) in
limestone

petrified wood

flood

195   95

410

flood

LEWISTON

COLUMBIA RIVER
PLATEAU   95

flood

basalts

metamorphic rocks

CLEARWATER

basalts

garnet in amphibolite
(dark hornblende rock)

MOUNTAINS

metamorphic

rocks

basalts

KOOSKIA   12

13

mica in pegmatite at
Myers mica mine

petrified wood

U.S. 12

KOOSKIA – LEWISTON

In the vicinity of Kooskia U.S. 12 crosses the boundary between two major geologic provinces. The Clearwater Mountains to the east are underlain by granites and strongly metamorphosed sedimentary rocks, whereas the Columbia Plateau to the west is underlain by basalt lava flows.

The granites and metamorphic rocks of the Clearwater Mountains formed during Mesozoic Time between 70 and 100 million years ago and were then uplifted and exposed by erosion. Rivers developed and carved their valleys creating a landscape that probably looked about like the one we see today.

About 40 million years ago, a series of volcanic eruptions began in what is now eastern Washington. Dozens of enormous flows of black basaltic lava poured out, first filling the stream valleys, then covering the mountains until the entire landscape of eastern Washington and Oregon and western Idaho was buried beneath the thousands of feet of basalt that make up the Columbia Plateau.

About 15 million years ago the eruptions finally ceased and a new set of streams appeared and began to carve new valleys into the lava plateau. In the vicinity of Kooskia, on the edge of the basalt plateau, these new streams have cut completely through the lava flows into the light-colored granites and metamorphic rocks beneath. These had once been exposed, then buried, and are now being exposed a second time. Old stream valleys filled with basalt lava are now cut across by new streams and can be seen in the walls of the modern canyons.

Between Kooskia and Orofino the road keeps crossing from light-colored granites and metamorphic rocks to coal-black basalt and then back again to the light-colored rocks.

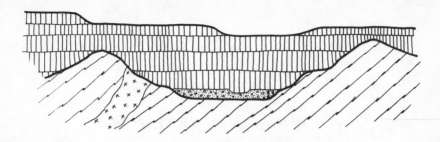

Cross section showing how basalt filling an old stream valley is exposed in the walls of a modern canyon. Vertical cracks called columnar joints form by shrinkage of lava as it cools and solidifies.

The western end of the route, between Orofino and Lewiston, passes entirely through basalt flows of the Columbia Plateau. The Clearwater River hasn't cut deeply enough here to expose the underlying igneous and metamorphic rocks.

It is interesting to try to pick out the individual flows which outcrop as nearly horizontal layers in the hillsides. Some of the roadcuts are good places to stop to look at individual basalt columns which form when the lava flow shrinks as it solidifies and cools. Most of the columns are five- or six-sided and they range in size from some about as big around as a fence post to others the diameter of a large tree. Early settlers sometimes used basalt columns as ready-made building blocks and some old cabins made of them still stand.

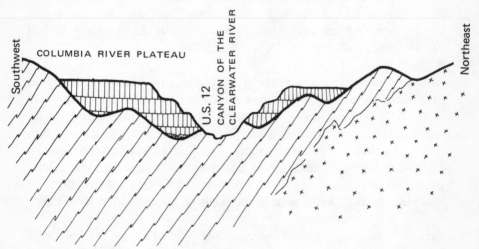

Southwest-northeast cross section across the line of U.S. 12 between Kooskia and Lewiston. The Clearwater River has eroded its canyon down through basalt lava flows, cutting into the older rocks buried beneath them.

Travellers continuing west across Washington, cross the Columbia Plateau all the way to its western margin at the Cascade Mountains.

For more information on the Columbia River basalt flows, see
U.S. 95: Lewiston – Coeur d'Alene
U.S. 195: Lewiston – Spokane

Mixed igneous and metamorphic rock formed when gneiss buried miles deep in the crust of the earth got hot enough that it began to melt to form granite magma. Streaky-looking rocks are gneiss, more uniform-looking, light-colored rock is granite. Outcrops like this are common in the Precambrian basement rocks.

CODY, Wyo. — EAST ENTRANCE YELLOWSTONE PARK
53 miles

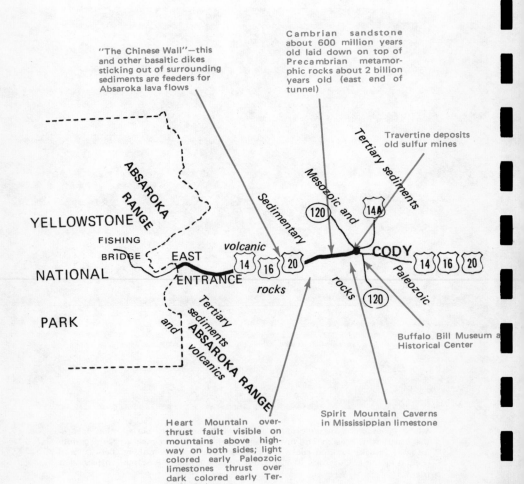

"The Chinese Wall"—this and other basaltic dikes sticking out of surrounding sediments are feeders for Absaroka lava flows

Cambrian sandstone about 600 million years old laid down on top of Precambrian metamorphic rocks about 2 billion years old (east end of tunnel)

Travertine deposits old sulfur mines

Heart Mountain overthrust fault visible on mountains above highway on both sides; light colored early Paleozoic limestones thrust over dark colored early Tertiary shale

Spirit Mountain Caverns in Mississippian limestone

Buffalo Bill Museum and Historical Center

U.S. 14-16-20

CODY – YELLOWSTONE PARK

U.S. 14-16-20 follows the valley of the Shoshoni River all the way from Cody to Yellowstone Park. The river gravels contain agate and petrified wood carried down from the Absaroka Mountains west of Cody.

Cody is built on an old flat floodplain of the Shoshoni River that was left high and dry when the stream eroded its valley down to its present lower level.

Bedrock exposed along the road and in the hills immediately west of Cody is mostly Paleozoic sedimentary rocks, although there are also a few outcrops of Mesozoic sedimentary rock.

About 3 miles west of Cody the highway passes porous, white travertine deposits laid down by large hot springs formerly active in this area. These were mined for sulfur many years ago and specimens can still be collected around the old workings.

About 6 miles west of Cody, the canyon of the Shoshoni River abruptly narrows at a place where a fault has brought the igneous and metamorphic rocks of the Precambrian basement to the surface. These hard rocks are much less easily eroded than the softer sedimentary rocks upstream and downstream, so the river has not been able to cut as wide a valley through them. Buffalo Bill Dam was built here to take advantage of this narrow place in the valley with very strong foundation rocks on both sides.

The Precambrian rocks contain a thick, horizontal sill of black basalt that conspicuously outcrops right along the road. Molten basalt magma was squirted into a fracture in the granite to form the sill.

Immediately west of the western end of Buffalo Bill Reservoir, the Shoshoni River has eroded its valley down through a big slab of Paleozoic sedimentary rocks that were pushed up and over the top of the much younger Mesozoic rocks on which the river is flowing. We normally expect to see younger rocks lying on top of the older ones but here they are backwards with the older ones on top.

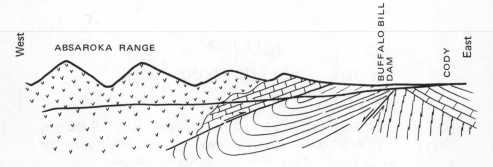

West-east cross-section along the line of U.S. 14, 16, 20 between Cody and the East Entrance of Yellowstone National Park. A large fault brings the tip of a block of Precambrian basement rock to the surface at Buffalo Bill Dam. Absaroka volcanic rocks blanket an erosion surface carved into older sedimentary rocks.

From the west end of Buffalo Bill Reservoir to Yellowstone Park, most of the outcrops along the road and in the hills above are dark-colored volcanic rocks of the Absaroka Range. These were erupted during early Tertiary Time (about 50-60 million years ago) from a number of volcanoes that eventually coalesced to form a volcanic plateau extending in a broad north-south band through part of western Wyoming and southwestern Montana. Since then, stream erosion has carved the plateau into mountains.

These Absaroka volcanics contain lava flows interlayered with beds of volcanic ash and volcanic material washed in by streams. They are discussed further in the following section on Yellowstone Park.

For more information on Yellowstone National Park, see the following pages.

Layers of light-colored volcanic ash and welded ash exposed along the Loop Road south of Mammoth in Yellowstone National Park.

101

YELLOWSTONE NATIONAL PARK

Yellowstone National Park is on a high plateau made up of three parts. Precambrian igneous and metamorphic basement rocks formed more than two billion years ago and then vertically uplifted along faults during formation of the northern Rocky Mountains are the oldest rocks in the park. The next oldest part, the Absaroka volcanics, were formed by eruption of large volumes of dark-colored volcanic rocks about 50 to 60 million years ago. The youngest part was created by eruption of the light-colored Yellowstone volcanic rocks during the last two million years. Portions of the surface of this composite plateau have been carved to different degrees by stream and glacial erosion.

Precambrian basement rocks in Yellowstone Park are actually the westernmost end of the Beartooth Plateau. Before they were uplifted, these rocks were thickly covered by Paleozoic and Mesozoic sedimentary rocks now almost completely stripped away by erosion. But the western end has been covered again, this time by volcanic rocks, so now the basement rocks outcrop only in two small areas of the northern part of the park. Look for them about five miles east of Tower Junction along the road between Tower Junction and Cooke City. Basement rocks are mostly gneisses, streaky-looking pink and black rocks containing glassy grains of quartz, pink and white crystals of feldspar, and black flakes of mica or needles of hornblende.

Between 50 and 60 million years ago, large volumes of molten magma erupted along the western edge of the Beartooth Plateau to form the Absaroka volcanic range. The magmas were of a kind intermediate between black basalt, such as we find on the Snake River Plain, and light-colored rhyolite, such as we find in much of Yellowstone Park.

102

Intermediate volcanic rocks formed from these magmas come in various colors ranging from dark red through many shades of brown to black. Visitors to the park can recognize the Absaroka volcanic rocks by their dark colors.

Sometimes intermediate magmas pour quietly out of a volcano to form lava flows but more often they are coughed out in bits and globs by escaping steam to form volcanic fragments. Larger fragments settle around the volcanic vent to build a volcano while smaller ones drift off downwind to settle eventually as beds of volcanic ash. Often fragments of all sizes are eroded and then redeposited elsewhere by streams. A volcanic range like the Absarokas is a complex pile of lava flows interlayered with all sorts of volcanic fragmental rocks.

The Absaroka Range is old enough to be deeply carved by streams which have cut nice cross-sections through the volcanic pile. Lava flows outcrop in the valley walls as solid looking ledges which usually break into vertical columns along shrinkage fractures making them easy to recognize. Volcanic fragmental rocks look like a hodge-podge of various-sized pieces stirred together.

Forests grew while the Absaroka volcanics were erupted and a great deal of wood was buried in the volcanic deposits. The rocks themselves were full of gas holes when they were first laid down. Eventually, with passage of millions of years, the buried trees were petrified and the holes in the rocks filled in with agate. So the Absaroka volcanic rocks are now the source of tremendous quantities of petrified wood and agate which streams have spread over a large part of Wyoming and southern Montana. Look for them east and north of Yellowstone Park in the gravels along the Shoshoni and Yellowstone Rivers.

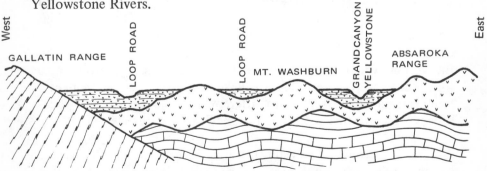

West-east cross section across the northern part of Yellowstone National Park. The Absaroka volcanic rocks were erupted over an erosion surface developed on older rocks and were themselves eroded before the much younger Yellowstone volcanic rocks were erupted.

Today the Absaroka volcanic rocks outcrop in a broad north-south band that passes through the eastern third of Yellowstone Park. Some of the best exposures are east of the park in the canyon of the Shoshoni River along the road between the east gate and Cody. They also outcrop along the road between Fishing Bridge and the east entrance as well as along the roads between Fishing Bridge and Tower Junction and between Tower Junction and Silver Gate.

Long after the Absaroka volcanic activity had ceased, new volcanoes became active a few miles to the west. These volcanoes, which have been erupting during the last two million years, were the source of the light-colored rocks that make up most of the present-day Yellowstone Plateau. Molten magmas that formed these rocks would eventually have crystallized to make granite had they not been erupted from volcanoes before they had a chance to cool slowly. Visitors to the park can recognize the Yellowstone volcanics rocks by their light colors, various shades of light gray, yellow, and pink. The only exception is obsidian (volcanic glass) which is black. Light-colored Yellowstone volcanics are exposed along all park roads except those between Fishing Bridge and the east entrance, and between Tower Junction and Silver Gate.

Molten magmas that cool to form light-colored volcanic rocks are extremely thick and viscous; they have a consistency resembling that of window putty. Magmas this thick can not possibly pour across the surface to form lava flows. Instead, they are blown out of the volcanic vent as shreds of molten lava that cool as they settle to the ground. Such eruptions are frequently violent; many volcanoes have actually exploded.

Some eruptions blow large quantities of magma high into the air where it cools and settles to the ground as volcanic ash which eventually sets up to form ash deposits called tuff. Other eruptions blow shreds of magma out of the volcano so rapidly and in such quantities that they do not cool in the air but settle still molten to the ground where they immediately weld themselves together to form a hard welded tuff. Black volcanic glass, obsidian, is frequently found in welded tuffs. It is no different from the light-colored rocks except that it is glass instead of a mass of minute crystals.

As large quantities of volcanic material are erupted, the top of the volcano frequently sinks into the space left underground by the escaping magma. This creates an enormous circular basin several

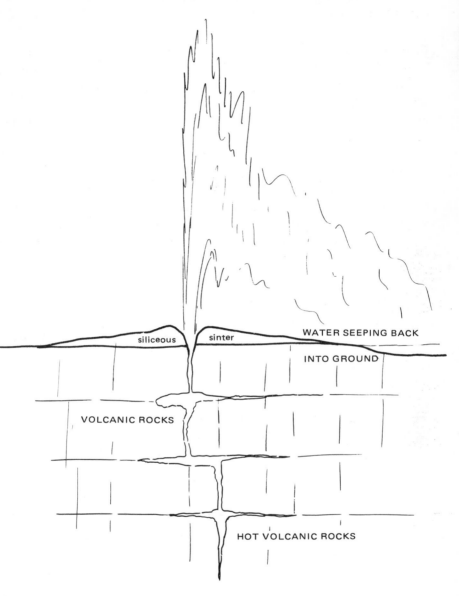

siliceous   sinter   WATER SEEPING BACK
INTO GROUND

VOLCANIC ROCKS

HOT VOLCANIC ROCKS

Schematic diagram showing the underground "percolator" plumbing of a typical geyser. Surface water penetrates to hot rocks at shallow depth along fractures, boils, and returns to the surface through the geyser.

miles across called a caldera which may then be partially filled by later volcanic rocks. Several calderas on the Yellowstone Plateau are not easily seen or identified because they are partially filled.

Many geologists believe that molten magma still exists a few thousand feet below the surface of the Yellowstone Plateau so future eruptions are a distinct possibility. If this magma is not erupted, it will eventually crystallize to form a granite batholith that will someday be exposed at the surface after the volcanic rocks covering it have been eroded away.

Geysers and hot springs are part of the cooling-off process. Surface water soaking downward into the hot rocks a few hundred feet below the surface is heated and returns to the surface as hot water or steam which may be mixed with a small amount of steam given off directly from the molten magma at depth.

Water circulating through hot rocks below the surface dissolves mineral matter from them and then deposits it around the mouth of a spring or geyser. This is the origin of the crusty white material around the hot spring areas in the park.

Geysers are a special type of hot spring which operate on exactly the same principle as a percolator coffee pot. What is needed in both cases is a long, vertical tube filled with water being heated at the bottom. Eventually the water at the bottom of the tube reaches the boiling temperature and would boil if it were not prevented from doing so by the weight of water in the tube above. So, instead of boiling, the water becomes superheated. But even if the water in the base of the tube can't boil, it can expand; finally, it expands enough to push some water out of the top of the tube. This relieves the pressure on the superheated water beneath which immediately flashes into steam, blowing the whole column of water out of the tube and causing the geyser to erupt, or the coffee pot to perk.

Just before a geyser erupts, water flows quietly out of the vent. When this happens, pressure below is reduced and the superheated water at the bottom of the tube flashes into steam causing the actual eruption.

After a geyser has erupted, it must refill with water which must then be heated before another eruption can happen. Geysers with a good

106

source of water and heat tend to erupt regularly and often. Those short of either water or heat erupt irregularly and at long intervals.

Of course geysers don't operate out of underground channels as straight and smooth as the column in a percolator coffee pot. The underground plumbing of geysers is complicated, irregular, and changing as time goes on. This accounts for the unpredictability of most geysers.

For more information on volcanic rocks related to those in Yellowstone National park, see
>U.S. 89: Mammoth Hot Springs – Livingston
>U.S. 191-20: Idaho Falls – West Yellowstone

For more information of the Beartooth Plateau, see
>U.S. 212: Laruel – Cooke City (Beartooth Highway)

For more information on individual roads in Yellowstone Park, see the following pages.

Steam and other volcanic gasses slurping to the surface through mud create small mud "volcanoes" in Yellowstone Park. This one is about a foot high.

107

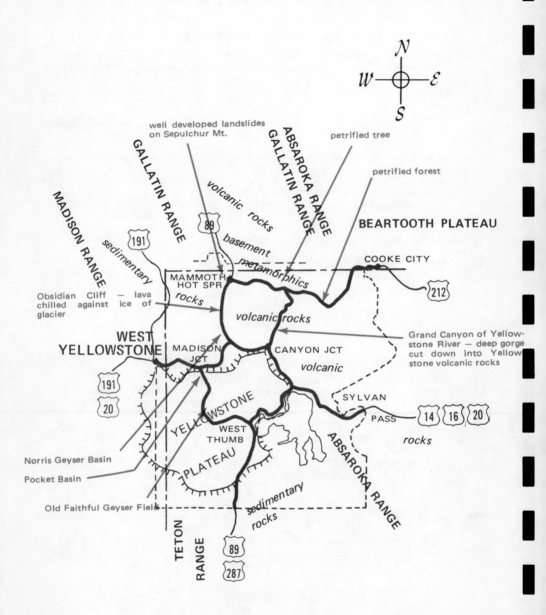

YELLOWSTONE PARK ROADS

Entrance Roads — East, South and West

Dark-colored volcanic rocks of the Absaroka Range erupted about 50 million years ago outcrop along the road between East Entrance and Sylvan Pass. West of Sylvan Pass, to the shore of Yellowstone Lake, these are mostly covered by light-colored volcanic ash belonging to the much younger Yellowstone volcanics erupted sometime within the last two million years. Glacial gravels conceal the bedrock all along the shores of Yellowstone Lake.

All the rocks exposed along the roads between South Entrance and West Thumb and between West Entrance and Madison Junction are light-colored Yellowstone volcanics erupted within the last 2 million years. Dense forest along both roads makes the geology difficult to see.

Silver Gate — Tower Junction

From Silver Gate to Tower Junction, the road follows the valley of Soda Butte Creek to its junction with the Lamar River which it follows the rest of the distance to Tower Junction.

Rocks underlying the valley of Soda Butte Creek are mostly Paleozoic limestones laid down in the waters of a shallow sea roughly 300 million years ago, then folded and broken by faults early in the formation of the Rocky Mountains — perhaps 70 million years ago. About 50 million years ago these old sedimentary rocks were deeply buried beneath dark-colored volcanics of the Absaroka Range. Now Soda Butte Creek has cut down through the volcanic cover, back into the Paleozoic limestones beneath. They are being exposed at the surface after having been buried for 50 million years.

109

The dark-colored volcanic rocks are composed of beds of fine-grained volcanic ash interlayered with lava flows and beds of coarse fragments moved in by streams and mud flows. Forests growing while these volcanic rocks were being erupted 50 million years ago, were buried and petrified. A fossil forest exhibit beside the road about 11 miles east of Tower Junction is directly across the valley of the Lamar River from a famous fossil forest locality. Here no fewer than 27 successive fossil forests are buried, one on top of the other, in layers of volcanic material.

Soda Butte is beside the road in the valley of Soda Butte Creek about 2 miles northeast of where it joins the Lamar River. It was built up by a hot spring that dissolved limestone from the Paleozoic sedimentary rocks beneath the surface, then redeposited it as a travertine cone around the mouth of the spring.

Lamar Canyon, about 7 miles east of Tower Junction, is a narrow gorge cut through very hard Precambrian igneous and metamorphic basement rocks. Most of them are streaky-looking gneisses made of glassy grains of quartz, pink and white feldspar, and black flakes of mica or needles of hornblende. Analysis of their radioactive minerals shows them to be 2.7 billion years old. Buffalo Plateau, north of the Lamar River between Lamar Canyon and Tower Junction, is underlain by Precambrian basement rock similar to that in the canyon beside the road. It is actually the westernmost extension of the Beartooth Plateau, a large block of basement rock lifted high along faults during formation of the northern Rockies then stripped by erosion of its cover of Paleozoic sedimentary rock.

Sizeable glaciers filled the valleys of Soda Butte Creek and the Lamar River during the last ice age. Thick glacial deposits dumped when the ice melted now cover much of the floors of these valleys. In numerous places these deposits are littered with large boulders transported by the ice but much too big to be moved by any process of erosion now operating. Small ponds mark spots where large chunks of ice were buried in the glacial deposits then later melted to form sinkhole ponds.

Canyon Junction — Tower Junction

Between Canyon Junction and Tower Junction, lower lying parts of the road cross light-colored, young volcanic rocks of the Yellowstone

110

Plateau. The Grand Canyon of the Yellowstone River is visible from the road for a short distance north of Canyon Junction, providing a good view down into the light-colored volcanic rocks altered by passage of hot water through them. These rocks are briefly discussed in the Lake Junction to Canyon Junction section.

Rocks exposed along the higher parts of the road, where it goes across Dunraven Pass on the flank of Mt. Washburn, are the much older, darker-colored rocks belonging to the Absaroka Range. Like islands in a lake, these rise above the younger rocks that fill in the lower areas.

Most of these dark Absaroka volcanics along the road are a hodge-podge of fragments all mixed together and solidified into rock. Probably, these are material moved by streams and mud flows down the slopes of volcanoes that erupted about 50 million years ago. After these volcanoes had ceased erupting, they were deeply carved by erosion, then partly buried under the much younger, light-colored volcanic rocks of the Yellowstone Plateau erupted within the last two million years.

The view from the top of Dunraven Pass is magnificent. Peaks of the north end of the Absaroka Range are visible to the east, and beyond them to the northeast the high Beartooth Plateau never completely free of snow. Several of the high mountain ranges in southwestern Montana form the ragged skyline to the north.

Between Dunraven Pass and Tower Junction, the road passes mostly dark-colored volcanic rocks of the Absaroka Range but crosses onto the light-colored Yellowstone volcanics in several places, finally getting onto them continuously several miles south of Tower Junction.

The wall of the Yellowstone Canyon across from Tower Falls is a wonderfully interesting geologic cross-section. Look across the canyon from the road just north of Tower Falls. The lowest rocks exposed are light-colored volcanic ash deposits of the Yellowstone Plateau. These are capped by a black basalt lava flow low in the canyon and hard to see, with well-developed vertical shrinkage cracks that give the outcrop the appearance of a row of vertical black columns standing in the cliff. About 100 feet of layered stream gravels are on top of the first basalt flow and these are capped by a second, higher, very prominent lava flow. Apparently molten basalt

111

flowed down the valley of the stream filling it with lava. The upper lava flow is covered by glacial lake deposits that are in turn covered by glacial gravels. Since the canyon is cut through glacial gravels, it must be younger than they are, perhaps no more than a few thousand years old.

Immediately north of Tower Falls a high, black cliff of basalt rises above the west side of the road. Well-developed vertical shrinkage fractures cause the basalt to break into neat columns about the size of telephone poles. This large lava flow appears to fill an old stream valley since cut across by the Yellowstone River. There are a number of such lava-filled stream valleys in this part of the park; several of them can be glimpsed from the highway.

Tower Junction — Mammoth Hot Springs

Along most of the distance between Tower Junction and Mammoth Hot Springs, the road crosses young volcanic rocks of the Yellowstone Plateau, all erupted within the last 2 million years. Most of these are light-colored ash deposits but some are black basalt lava flows. Except between about 3 and 8 miles west of Tower Junction, there are very few outcrops of the older dark-colored Absaroka lava flows. Large glaciers covered the area during the last ice age so deposits of glacial debris, including many large boulders, cover much of the bedrock.

In the distance a few miles north of the road are hills of the Buffalo Plateau, geologically the westernmost end of the Beartooth Plateau, a block of Precambrian igneous and metamorphic basement rock lifted up along faults during formation of the Rocky Mountains, then covered in places by younger volcanic rocks. No outcrops of these old rocks are along the road between Tower Junction and Mammoth Hot Springs but specimens can be found in some of the glacial boulders. Most of the Precambrian rocks are streaky pink and black gneisses containing large grains of glassy quartz, pink and white feldspar, and black flakes of mica and needles of hornblende.

Between Geode Creek, about 6 miles west of Tower Junction, and Oxbow Creek about 8 miles west, the road passes through an old stream channel that was eroded by glacial meltwater flowing along the edge of the ice. Now that the ice has melted, there is no longer a stream in this segment of valley.

About 10 miles west of Tower Junction, the road crosses outcrops of white Paleozoic limestone sticking above the much younger light-colored volcanic ash deposits on either side. This is probably the top of what was once a high limestone hill now almost completely buried under volcanic ash.

Wraith Falls and Undine Falls are close to each other — about 14 miles west of Tower Junction. Undine Falls spills over a lip of hard, black basalt lava that filled an old stream channel and was then buried under the light-colored volcanic ash of the Yellowstone Plateau. The stream cut a gorge down through the soft volcanic ash and now has a much more difficult time eroding through the harder basalt beneath.

Mammoth Hot Springs has built a series of travertine terraces made of limestone dissolved out of rocks beneath the surface by circulating hot water and then redeposited around the mouths of the springs. Quite a number of such terraces have been built in the area as the springs issued first from one place and then from another. All the older ones are now abandoned and covered by vegetation but they are still recognizable as big flat stairstepped places on the hillsides. Travertine terraces around the present spring opening are one of the largest such deposits in the country.

Many hot springs in Yellowstone Park deposit mineral matter around their mouths, but most of them lay down a crust of white siliceous sinter, a form of quartz. Mammoth Hot Springs is one of the few that deposits travertine, a form of the mineral calcite — the same mineral that makes up limestone and marble. This difference results from the fact that most of the other springs in the park issue from volcanic rocks rich in quartz while Mammoth Hot Springs comes out of limestone.

Rimmed pools form in the travertine terraces because water carrying dissolved limestone must give off carbon dioxide gas in order to deposit the limestone as travertine. Deposition is controlled by the fact that carbon dioxide gas can only be lost through the water surface. As water flows over the lip of a rimmed pool, the surface is stretched, producing more area from which gas can escape. Travertine is deposited right where the carbon dioxide is lost, so the rims of the pools are constantly built higher.

Circulating hot water dissolves limestone beneath the surface and then redeposits it around the mouth of Mammoth Hot Springs to form travertine terraces.

Lake Junction — Canyon Junction

All the bedrock crossed by the short stretch of road between Lake Junction and Canyon Junction belongs to the light-colored Yellowstone volcanics erupted within the last 2 million years. This part of the park is heavily blanketed by deposits laid down by glaciers which existed during the last ice age and finally melted only about 10,000 years ago. Such good bedrock exposures are few except in the Grand Canyon of the Yellowstone River where the stream has cut down through the glacial deposits.

Hayden Valley was occupied by a glacier during the last ice age and is now completely floored by glacial gravels. It was named for Dr. F. V. Hayden, a prominent geologist of the last century, who led the first scientific expeditions into the Yellowstone Park region and prepared reports to Congress that were instrumental in getting the park established in 1871. Hayden's reports were lavishly illustrated by beautiful photographs taken by the pioneer photographer W. H. Jackson and paintings done by the landscape artist Thomas Moran. Had it not been for the work of these men, Yellowstone Park might never have been set aside for public use. Various landmarks have been named to honor their memory.

Large ledges of beautiful, shiny-black obsidian outcrop below the road where it passes Hayden Valley. Look for them by scrambling a short distance below the road but collecting is forbidden. Obsidian is

114

volcanic glass commonly found in small quantities in light-colored volcanic rocks. Large masses of it, such as those found here and there in Yellowstone Park, are unusual. Perhaps they may have formed where an eruption occurred beneath a glacier. The melting ice would have cooled the volcanic rock very quickly causing it to solidify into glass instead of crystallizing into the light-colored rocks normally formed.

The Grand Canyon of the Yellowstone River is geologically fascinating as well as scenically magnificent. A deep gorge cut by the Yellowstone River through the light-colored volcanic rocks exposes a beautiful cross-section that fills in the blank spaces in the picture presented by the geyser and hot spring areas of the park.

Nearly all the hot spring and geyser basins are crusty with white deposits of mineral matter laid down by the thermal waters. This material is leached out of the rocks at depth, then deposited on the surface by the circulating waters. In the Grand Canyon of the Yellowstone we see what the circulating water does to the rocks below the surface. Volcanic rocks in the canyon walls have been worked over by circulating hot water that leached out some minerals and deposited others.

Look carefully at the canyon walls to see a criss-crossing pattern of light-yellow lines in the darker-yellow rock. These are traces of fractures through which the water moved. Rock in the light-colored lines has had mineral matter dissolved from it and is distinctly softer and easier to scrape than the darker-colored, less-affected rock. Mineral matter removed from the light-colored lines was undoubtedly deposited somewhere as crusty white material around a hot spring.

By looking very carefully, you may also find very small, brassy-yellow crystals of iron pyrite (fools gold) in the rocks of the canyon walls. This was deposited in the rock at the same time other minerals were dissolved away. Pyrite is worthless but many other minerals that may be deposited are valuable. Many large ore bodies of valuable minerals are in rocks altered in exactly the same way as those in the canyon walls. Unfortunately, such rocks are rather easily eroded so they are rarely well exposed at the ground surface. Geologists must usually study them in the walls of mines and hardly ever have a chance to see them freshly exposed in broad daylight.

Hot springs and geysers active today in Yellowstone Park show that hot waters are operating on the rocks at depth, dissolving some minerals and depositing others. It is perfectly possible that valuable ore bodies may be forming somewhere within the plateau. Similar rocks exposed by stream valleys frequently contain deposits of silver, gold, lead, copper, and other minerals. Many of the bonanza gold and silver deposits of the Rocky Mountain region are in rocks exactly like those cross-sectioned in the Grand Canyon of the Yellowstone.

Madison Junction — Mammoth Hot Springs

All the rocks exposed along the road between Madison Junction and Mammoth Hot Springs are light-colored volcanics erupted within the last 2 million years and still cooling off, as is shown by the numerous hot springs and geysers.

Terrace Spring, west of the road about a mile north of Madison Junction, differs from most other springs in this part of the park in that it deposits travertine instead of siliceous sinter around its mouth. Travertine, a form of the mineral calcite, is chemically identical to limestone and usually forms where water has circulated through limestones before coming to the surface. Since this part of the park is deeply underlain by volcanic rocks and no limestone is known to exist nearby, the travertine poses an interesting problem. Perhaps the water has circulated a greater distance than such waters normally do or there may be some buried limestone hidden not far beneath the surface.

For several miles between Madison Junction and Norris Geyser Basin, the road follows the canyon the Gibbon River has cut through volcanic ash deposits. The geology in this area is interesting but almost impossible to appreciate from the road. Very briefly, a large caldera formed in this part of the park when an area of the surface several miles across subsided into space left underground by eruption of large quantities of molten magma.

Later, lava and ash flows largely refilled the caldera basin so it no longer appears as a surface depression. Some of the rocks exposed along the Gibbon River formed before the caldera subsided and others are the ones that filled it in afterward. However, all are light-colored volcanic rocks and it is quite impossible to tell one from another without making detailed observations.

116

Gibbon Meadows and geyser basin is about 10 miles north of Madison Junction. Paintpot Hill, a high hill south of Gibbon Meadows, is an interesting feature called a rhyolite dome. Rhyolite is a technical term used to refer to light-colored volcanic rocks like those in Yellowstone Park. Molten rhyolite magmas are extremely stiff and viscous so it is quite impossible for them to flow liquidly across the ground surface to make a lava flow. Normally these magmas are sprayed violently from the volcanic vent by escaping steam, to make clouds of volcanic ash. If the ash is still very hot when it hits the ground, the particles fuse together to make a deposit of welded ash; if it is cool, it simply makes ash beds. Most of the light-colored volcanic rocks in Yellowstone Park are ash beds of one kind or another. Occasionally, rhyolite magmas manage to reach the surface without being blown to shreds by escaping steam. They push slowly up almost like rising bread dough to make dome-shaped extrusions such as Paintpot Hill and several others in the park. In Japan, a hill similar to this and about the same size rose slowly out of the ground during a period of several months in 1943.

Norris Geyser Basin, about 14 miles north of Madison Junction, is one of the most interesting in the park because of the wide variety of different kinds of water it produces. Some are strongly acid. During the summer of 1967, the United States Geological Survey drilled a hole there that penetrated to a depth of 812 feet where the water temperature was slightly more than twice that of water boiling at the surface.

Obsidian Cliff, 9 miles north of Norris Junction, is one of the most spectacular outcrops of volcanic glass in the country. Obsidian forms when molten magma is cooled very quickly so no crystals have time to grow. Small globs of obsidian are quite common in young, light-colored volcanic rocks but massive outcrops of it are rare. Obsidian Cliff probably formed when molten magma was erupted against glacial ice that was able to chill large quantities of magma quickly enough to prevent growth of crystals.

Look closely at the shiny black rock in Obsidian Cliff to see the swirling flow banding that records the last movements within the molten magma before it was suddenly chilled. Look also for small, spherical cavities about the size of peas, lined with smooth, brownish rock. Geologists have a name for these (lithophysae) but no good explanation for how they form. The ones at Obsidian Cliff are small; other outcrops along this road contain larger ones, some almost as

117

big as tennis balls.

Just south of Mammoth Hot Springs, the road passes out of the main area of light-colored volcanics onto the older sedimentary rocks that were here before the volcanoes erupted. The high cliff overlooking Mammoth Hot Springs is a block of these rocks uplifted along a fault. Their conspicuous layering makes it easy to identify them as sedimentary rocks even from a distance.

West Thumb – Madison Junction

All the rocks exposed between West Thumb and Madison Junction are light-colored volcanic rocks of the Yellowstone Plateau erupted within the last 2 million years. Numerous hot spring and geyser basins along the road are evidence that these rocks are still hot and still cooling off.

Rainwater soaks into the ground and circulates deeply along fracture systems within the young volcanic rocks. It returns to the surface hot and loaded with mineral matter dissolved from the rocks below. This mineral matter, which in this part of the park is mostly quartz, is deposited around the spring vents forming the white crust called siliceous sinter, a form of quartz.

Different springs differ considerably in temperature and in the chemistry of their waters. Presumably the hottest ones are discharging water that has ciruclated deepest beneath the surface. In a few cases, the water is believed to be coming from depths as great as 10,000 feet.

The most obvious difference in water chemistry involves its content of sulfur. Some springs discharge water containing very little sulfur; others bring up water heavily laden with hydrogen sulfide, which smells like rotten eggs. Still others emit water containing sulfur dioxide which has a pungent, acrid smell. A few springs vent enough sulfur into the atmosphere to kill nearby trees. Spring waters heavily laden with sulfur support growths of sulfur bacteria looking almost like bits of old, dirty gray rags in the water. Other kinds of springs support different sorts of bacteria and algae which produce various brightly colored coatings on the rocks in the water.

The United States Geological Survey has been doing a lot of research into the hot springs and geysers of Yellowstone Park during recent years and has drilled a number of small-diameter bore holes deep into several geyser basins to study directly what is going on beneath the surface. One of these, near Pocket Basin, went to a depth of 514 feet where the temperature was found to be 196°C (405° Fahrenheit), nearly twice the temperature of water boiling at the surface. They drilled a number of other holes which also revealed high temperatures a short distance below the surface. Extreme care was taken while these holes were drilled to be sure that the hot springs and geysers would not be damaged in any way.

Most of the larger hot spring basins occupy low places bounded by the edges of volcanic ash flows. In a few cases, the edge of the volcanic ash flow appears to have been against a glacier so the hot spring basin now is where the ice formerly stood. This appears to be true of the west sides of both Upper and Midway Geyser Basins. A few of the smaller basins occupy craters blasted out by single large steam explosions. This is true of Pocket Basin and also of a small basin adjacent to Twin Buttes west of Midway Basin. Twin Buttes are deposits of glacial debris laid down against the edge of the ice and then cemented into solid rock by mineral matter brought up by the hot springs.

Mud volcanoes are places where hot spring water or steam is slurping to the surface through thick, gooey mud. The mud probably formed as hot spring water chemically attacked the rock. Light-colored volcanic rocks are full of the mineral feldspar which turns into clay when it is subjected to prolonged attack by hot water.

Old Faithful Geyser has been erupting regularly every hour or so ever since records have been kept. Obviously, it must have an excellent supply of water to refill the "plumbing" after each eruption. Probably the water comes directly from the nearby river. Heat from the rocks at depth raises the temperature of the water in the bottom of the geyser tube to a point well above the boiling temperature. Just before the geyser erupts, a small amount of water splashes out of the vent, thus relieving the pressure on the water beneath and permitting it to flash into steam. Watch for this signal that the geyser is about to start.

West Thumb — Lake Junction

From West Thumb to Lake Junction the road follows the north side of Yellowstone Lake across light-colored volcanic rocks of the Yellowstone Plateau, all erupted within the last 2 million years. This is one of the parts of the park that were heavily covered by deposits dumped from ice age glaciers as they melted about 10,000 years ago. So there are not many good bedrock exposures.

Yellowstone Lake probably fills a basin between the Yellowstone Plateau on the west and the Absaroka volcanic range on the east. The lake has an irregular outline unlike the nearly circular form normally expected in caldera basins. Undoubtedly glaciers that covered much of the Yellowstone Plateau during the last ice age modified the form of the basin by gouging in some places and dumping morainal heaps of debris in others.

Watch the shoreline of the lake; it has many of the features of ocean shorelines developed in miniature so they can easily be seen. Large offshore bars parallel the main shoreline in many places. They form where waves break and build a beach in shallow water before they reach the shore.

Clearly, Yellowstone Lake was once fuller than it is now. An abandoned shoreline marked by a sharp break in slope parallels the present shoreline several feet above it. Probably the lake level has been dropping as the Yellowstone River cuts the outlet lower.

Cross-section of a basalt lava flow exposed in the wall of the Yellowstone River canyon near Tower Falls, Yellowstone National Park. Outcrops of lava flows frequently form vertical columns because of the pattern of vertical shrinkage fractures that form in the rock as it cools.

Light-colored volcanic rocks exposed in the walls of the Grand Canyon of the Yellowstone have been chemically attacked by hot water circulating through them along fractures. The nearly-flat surface of the Yellowstone Plateau, visible on the skyline, was created by deposition of volcanic ash.

121

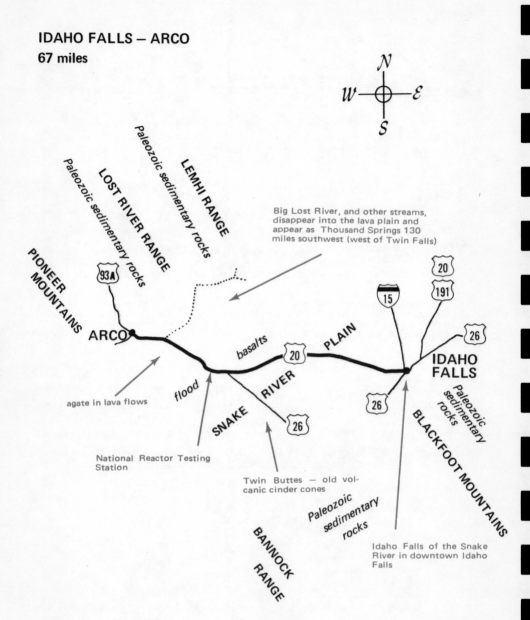

IDAHO FALLS – ARCO
67 miles

Big Lost River, and other streams, disappear into the lava plain and appear as Thousand Springs 130 miles southwest (west of Twin Falls)

PIONEER MOUNTAINS

LOST RIVER RANGE
Paleozoic sedimentary rocks

Paleozoic sedimentary rocks

LEMHI RANGE
Paleozoic sedimentary rocks

93A

ARCO

20

15

20

191

26

IDAHO FALLS

basalts

PLAIN

20

26

26

SNAKE RIVER

flood

agate in lava flows

National Reactor Testing Station

Twin Buttes — old volcanic cinder cones

BANNOCK RANGE

Paleozoic sedimentary rocks

BLACKFOOT MOUNTAINS

Paleozoic sedimentary rocks

Idaho Falls of the Snake River in downtown Idaho Falls

U.S. 20

IDAHO FALLS — ARCO

Both Idaho Falls and Arco are on the Snake River Plain, a high plateau built up of basalt lava flows erupted during the past several million years. U.S. 20 crosses lava flows all the way between these two cities. All of them are young, geologically speaking, and some are very young indeed.

It is interesting to try to recognize individual lava flows and guess at their relative ages. Those having a very rough, intensely black surface with little or no soil on it are the youngest. They support little vegetation beyond a scattering of sagebrush and bunchgrass. As time passes, a cover of soil slowly develops and blankets the flow, enabling it to support more and more vegetation. Part of the soil develops in place as the basalt weathers and breaks down, but most is blown in by the wind from elsewhere. Wind-blown dust settles first in the low places and behind obstructions to the wind, forming patches of soil that slowly spread as the vegetation growing on them catches more dust. All stages of this process can be seen between Idaho Falls and Arco.

Fresher lava flows show a great deal of interesting surface detail. When basalt lava is first erupted, it pours across the ground surface making a puddle of white-hot liquid. The surface quickly cools, freezing solid to form a crust over the still-molten and flowing lava beneath. Where the crust is very thin, it may be wrinkled into a smooth, ropy-looking surface (sometimes called pahoehoe) somewhat resembling the kind of surface we see in the skin that forms on hot milk.

If the solid crust is thick, it may be pushed up into a series of large pressure ridges. These are usually between 10 and 30 feet high and look like long, narrow ridges with large, open cracks along their crests. Occasionally places can be seen where still-molten lava squeezed out through these cracks like black toothpaste.

Frequently the liquid lava runs out from under the solid crust leaving caves beneath. While the flow is still young it is possible to enter the larger ones and walk around in them. As time passes and the flow begins to weather, the roofs of these caves collapse creating open sinkholes on the surface.

Basalt lavas do not always build volcanoes because the flows, which are erupted from long fissures, are very fluid and tend to spread widely over the surface instead of piling up around the vent. This is why the volcanic Snake River Plain is very flat and contains very few volcanoes.

The few volcanoes that do exist are made of light-colored volcanic rocks similar to those in Yellowstone Park. A good example is Great Southern Butte about 10 miles south of U.S. 20 and visible for very long distances.

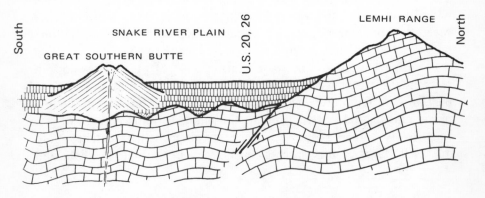

South-north cross section across the line of U.S. 20, 26 between Arco and Idaho Falls. Great Southern Butte, a volcano made of light-colored rocks, is partly buried beneath the black basalt lava flows of the Snake River Plain.

One of the most noticeable things about the Snake River Plain is the almost complete absence of streams. Of course, this is partly because these lava flows are so young that streams have had very little time to develop. But the most important reason is that there are so many open lava caverns, fractures, and other kinds of porous spaces beneath the surface that rainwater quickly soaks into the lava flows and never has a chance to flow across the surface as streams. As time goes on, these open spaces will gradually fill up with soil, making the

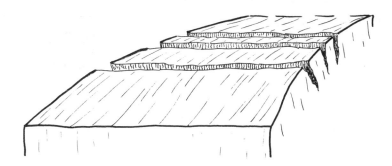

Vertical cracks form in the crests of wrinkles (pressure ridges) that develop as the solidified crust of a lava flow is carried along on still-flowing molten magma beneath. Sometimes little bulges of magma squeeze up through the cracks which may be anywhere from several inches to a few feet wide at the surface.

lava flows less absorbent. Then rainwater will finally flow over the surface forming streams that will carve valleys into the plateau converting it into a region of high, eroded mountains.

For more information on flood basalts of the Snake River Plain, see
    Interstate 80 N: Twin Falls – Boise
    U.S. 20: Idaho Falls – Arco
    U.S. 93 A: Shoshone – Arco; Craters of the Moon

Two small volcanoes (Twin Buttes) interrupting the level surface of the Snake River Plain between Arco and Idaho Falls.

125

JACKSON – IDAHO FALLS
100 miles

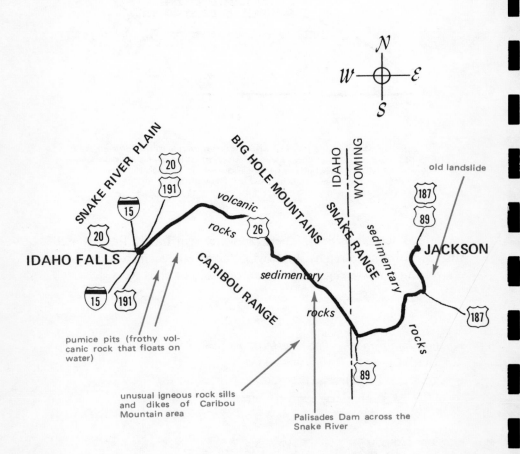

U.S. 26 – 89

JACKSON – IDAHO FALLS

Early fur traders and explorers in the northern Rocky Mountains called the big fault-block valleys "holes"; Jackson Hole in Wyoming and the Big Hole in Montana are two that still retain their old names.

Between Jackson and Hoback Junction, U.S. 89 passes through the southern end of Jackson Hole and into the northern end of the Grand Canyon of the Snake River. Rocks along this stretch of the highway include Paleozoic and Mesozoic limestones and mudstones as well as some younger gravel conglomerates deposited in Jackson Hole after it had already become a valley. Idaho's Snake Range makes the skyline west of the highway. The Grand Canyon of the Snake River cuts through the southeastern end of this range between Hoback Junction and Alpine, providing an excellent cross-sectional view of the rocks.

Rocks in the Snake Range are sedimentary layers of Paleozoic and Mesozoic limestones and mudstones, folded and then slid past each other in slices on a series of large faults. Mesozoic rocks predominate toward the east end of the Grand Canyon of the Snake River and Paleozoic rocks toward the west end. Folded beds tilted at various angles are visible from the highway, along with several large faults. Spotting faults is often difficult for a non-geologist. Look for places where two different kinds of rock or topography meet along a line that cuts across the sedimentary layers.

At Alpine, on the Wyoming-Idaho border, the Snake River leaves its eroded canyon and heads northwest through the Grand (Swan) Valley, a long, narrow fault-block let down within the last few million years, one of the youngest such valleys in the entire region. Grand (Swan) Valley has remarkably straight walls defined by faults along which the valley was let down. They are too young to have been much carved by erosion.

Southwest-northeast cross section across the line of U.S. 26 showing the Snake River and Caribou Ranges separated by the Swan Valley, a downdropped fault-block. Both ranges contain slices of Paleozoic and Mesozoic sedimentary rocks that slid past each other on faults before the Swan Valley formed.

The Caribou Range southwest of the Grand (Swan) Valley is made of Paleozoic and Mesozoic sedimentary rocks similar to those in the Snake Range except that they are not so complexly deformed. Caribou Mountain, located about 10 miles southwest of Palisades Reservoir, contains a number of large bodies of igneous rock intruded into Paleozoic limestone about 50 to 60 million years ago. There was at one time a mining district around Caribou Mountain but this activity ceased years ago; nothing remains now but two ghost towns.

U.S. 26 enters the eastern end of the Snake River Plain a few miles north of the community of Swan Valley and continues on it all the way to Idaho Falls. The Snake River Plain is a volcanic plateau built up of black basalt lava flows erupted as great floods of molten magma during the past several million years. As each successive flow built the plateau higher, the mountains surrounding it were buried deeper beneath the basalt. Some of the flows flooded into the north end of the Grand (Swan) Valley so the northwest end of the Caribou Range juts out into the Snake River Plain like a peninsula into a lake.

Before the black basalt lava flows were erupted, large outpourings of light-colored volcanic ash blanketed some of the mountains.

Scattered low hills of this material are visible from the highway near the margins of the Snake River Plain.

For more information on flood basalts of the Snake River Plain, see
  Interstate 80 N: Twin Falls — Boise
  U.S. 20: Idaho Falls — Arco
  U.S. 93 A: Shoshone — Arco; Craters of the Moon

Layers of mixed volcanic material and river gravel in one of the Menan Buttes, a few miles north of Idaho Falls. Each layer records a blast of the steam generated when molten magma penetrated water-soaked gravels. See writeup in U.S. 191, Idaho Falls — West Yellowstone.

LEWISTOWN – GREAT FALLS
105 miles

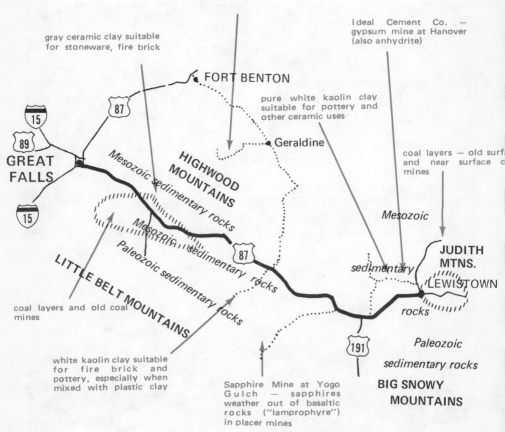

dike rocks, some with
pseudoleucite (reached
from Geraldine)

gray ceramic clay suitable
for stoneware, fire brick

Ideal Cement Co. —
gypsum mine at Hanover
(also anhydrite)

FORT BENTON

pure white kaolin clay
suitable for pottery and
other ceramic uses

GREAT FALLS

Geraldine

coal layers — old surface
and near surface coal
mines

HIGHWOOD
MOUNTAINS

Mesozoic sedimentary rocks

Mesozoic

Mesozoic sedimentary rocks

Paleozoic sedimentary rocks

JUDITH
MTNS.

sedimentary

LEWISTOWN

LITTLE BELT MOUNTAINS

rocks

coal layers and old coal
mines

Paleozoic

white kaolin clay suitable
for fire brick and
pottery, especially when
mixed with plastic clay

sedimentary rocks

Sapphire Mine at Yogo
Gulch — sapphires
weather out of basaltic
rocks ("lamprophyre")
in placer mines

BIG SNOWY
MOUNTAINS

U.S. 87

LEWISTOWN – GREAT FALLS

Lewistown nestles between the Moccasin and Judith Mountains to the north and northeast, respectively and the Big Snowy Mountains to the south.

The Moccasin and Judith Mountains contain a swarm of blister-shaped laccoliths of granite squirted as molten magma between layers of sedimentary rock sometime around 50 million years ago. Most of the laccoliths are quite small, no more than a few miles in diameter.

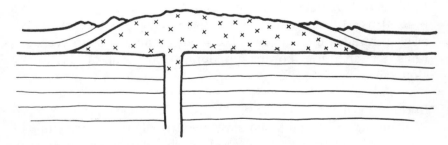

Cross section of a laccolith showing how molten magma injected between layers of sedimentary rock forms a blister-shaped intrusion.

The Big Snowy Mountains are entirely different, being basically a broad arch in the Paleozoic and Mesozoic sedimentary rocks which underlie the high plains. Erosion has peeled off the beds on top of the arch so that the older Paleozoic sedimentary rocks are exposed across the central part of the Big Snowy Mountains, whereas the younger Mesozoic sedimentary rocks form the flanks.

Cross section of eroded arch in sedimentary rocks, showing how older rocks are exposed in the center and younger ones on the flanks.

For much of the distance between Lewistown and Great Falls, the Little Belt Mountains are visible in the distance south of the highway and the Highwood Mountains in the distance to the north. These ranges are quite different.

The Little Belt Mountains are another arch in the rocks underlying the high plains, somewhat similar in many ways to the Big Snowy Mountains but much larger and more complicated. Precambrian igneous and metamorphic basement rocks surrounded by Precambrian sedimentary rocks are exposed in the center of the Little Belt Mountains. Paleozoic and Mesozoic sedimentary rocks form flanks of the range. Some small bodies of molten granite magma intruded into the complex about 60 million or so years ago while the arch was bowing up during formation of the Rocky Mountains.

North of the highway and accessible from Geraldine on County Road 230, are the Highwood Mountains, an extremely interesting group of dark-colored igneous rocks formed roughly 50 million years ago. Some are volcanic rocks but most are dikes and laccoliths intruded as molten magmas into Mesozoic sandstones and cooled there without reaching the surface. The magma squeezed through vertical fractures in the sandstone to make dikes, and bulged between sedimentary layers to make laccoliths shaped like giant cookies several miles across. These are the isolated buttes conspicuous from a distance.

Laccoliths and dikes in the Highwood Mountains are famous among geologists for the unusual rocks they contain. Crystals that formed in the laccoliths as the magma began to cool, floated or sank according to whether they were lighter or heavier than the still-molten liquid. Layers of such crystals accumulated at the top and bottom of the laccolith forming very interesting and unusual rocks.

Molten magma that cooled in the vertical fractures formed dikes which radiate out from centers like spokes in a wheel. Because they are resistant to erosion, the dikes stand above the ground looking like old, tumbledown stone walls crossing the fields. These dikes were the feeder system "plumbing" for a large volcano that formerly rose above the present Highwood Mountains. It has since been almost entirely eroded away leaving only scattered remnants of lava flows as souvenirs of its existence.

Mines in Yogo Gulch, near County Road 239 southwest of Hobson, were for many years one of the world's prime sources of gem-quality sapphires. The stones come from dark-gray dikes which were injected as molten magmas into Paleozoic limestones. Sapphires have been mined both from the dikes and from creek gravels washed down from them. The Yogo Gulch sapphires come in a variety of colors and many are very high-quality stones. Very few are mined now because natural sapphires do not compete very successfully with the inexpensive synthetic ones.

Sapphires are simply a brightly colored and transparent variety of the mineral corundum, a crystalline form of aluminum oxide. Neither sapphires nor corundum are common because most rocks simply do not contain a high enough proportion of aluminum to permit them to form. The sapphires at Yogo Gulch pose an interesting problem because they occur in a kind of igneous rock that does not normally contain such minerals. Probably fragments of clay mudstone, a rock rich in aluminum, were picked up by the hot molten magma while the dikes were being injected and recrystallized to make the sapphires.

All the bedrock exposed along U.S. 89-87 between Lewistown and Great Falls is mudstone and sandstone laid down between 60 and

150 million years ago during the last part of the Mesozoic Era. Most of these rocks escaped being directly involved in the geologic activity that went on during formation of the Rocky Mountains so the sedimentary layers are still lying nearly flat. Several large peat bogs were buried while these sediments were being deposited and have since turned into beds of coal. These were mined rather extensively early in this century but the advent of diesel locomotives and fuel oil and natural gas for home use closed most of the mines by the early 1950's. Now, renewed demand for coal makes it seem likely that the mines will be reopened on an even larger scale, especially because this coal contains very little sulfur so it can be burned with a minimum of atmospheric pollution.

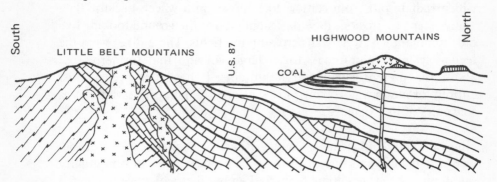

South-north cross section across the line of U.S. 87 about 40 miles east of Great Falls. Volcanoes and laccoliths make up the Highwood Mountains but the Little Belt Mountains are basement rocks and sedimentary rocks intruded by younger granite.

During the last ice age a large ice cap formed in Canada and poured down into the northernmost United States including northern Montana east of the Rocky Mountains. As the ice began to melt, large volumes of water were trapped between the glacier to the north and drainage divides to the south, forming lakes along the edges of the ice cap. One of these, Glacial Lake Great Falls, existed in this part of central Montana. Watch for its shorelines; they usually show up as two perfectly horizontal lines faintly grooved on the sides of hills.

134

Igneous dike standing above surrounding sedimentary rocks like a ruined wall —
Highwood Mountains east of Great Falls.

JACKSON – GRAND TETON NATIONAL PARK – YELLOWSTONE PARK (South Entrance)
60 miles

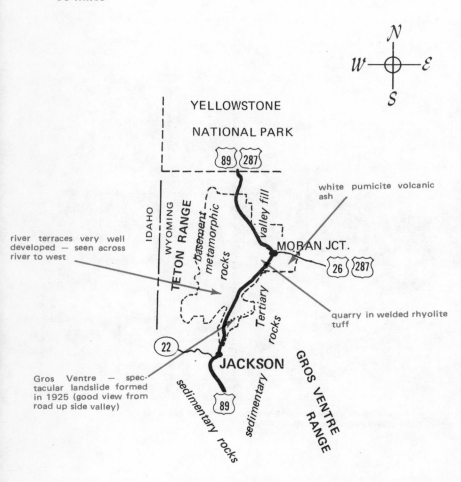

YELLOWSTONE

NATIONAL PARK

89 287

white pumicite volcanic
ash

IDAHO

WYOMING

TETON RANGE

basement
metamorphic
rocks

valley fill

MORAN JCT.

26 287

river terraces very well
developed — seen across
river to west

Tertiary
rocks

quarry in welded rhyolite
tuff

22

JACKSON

GROS VENTRE RANGE

Gros Ventre — spec-
tacular landslide formed
in 1925 (good view from
road up side valley)

sedimentary rocks

sedimentary

89

136

U.S. 89 – 26 – 187

JACKSON – YELLOWSTONE NATIONAL PARK
(GRAND TETON NATIONAL PARK)

Between Jackson and the south entrance to Yellowstone Park, the highway passes through Grand Teton National Park with the magnificent Grand Teton Range dominating the western skyline.

The Grand Tetons are a large block of the earth's crust raised up along faults at the same time the Jackson Hole block was let down during formation of the Rocky Mountains. This movement must have begun about 70-80 million years ago and may well be still continuing. The imposing crest of the range stands about 7000 feet above the floor of Jackson Hole.

Precambrian igneous and metamorphic basement rock consisting mostly of pink and gray streaky-looking gneisses and schists, forms the core of the Grand Tetons. Granite found with it closely resembles the gneiss except that it is not streaky looking. Specimens of these can be seen in the stream gravels along the road.

An interesting geological situation can be seen in Mt. Moran, a large, flat-topped peak due west of Moran Junction. It is made mostly of the Precambrian igneous and metamorphic rocks except for a cap of Paleozoic (Cambrian) sandstone at the top. The sandstone was laid down about 550 million years ago on a flat surface previously eroded on the basement rock. A large, black dike of basalt, visible from the road, runs nearly vertically up the eastern face of Mt. Moran almost to the top where it is cut off by the erosion surface upon which the sandstone was deposited. Since the Cambrian sandstone cuts across the top of the dike, it is clear that it must have been deposited after the dike had been injected. Therefore, the dike must be Precambrian.

Lakes reflecting the eastern face of the Grand Teton Range occupy basins created by large glaciers that formed along the base of the range. Glacial ice pouring down the valleys from the peaks above flowed out onto the floor of Jackson Hole and coalesced to form glaciers along the foot of the range. Large boulders in foreground were dumped by the ice.

Precambrian igneous and metamorphic rocks in the core of the Grand Tetons are overlain by a thick section of Paleozoic limestones and sandstones deposited between about 550 and 200 million years ago. These make up most of the mountain mass and can be recognized from a distance by the fact that they outcrop as long ledges.

The Grand Tetons owe their magnificent craggy profile to carving by very large, closely-spaced mountain glaciers during the last ice age. These came down the east face of the mountains all the way to the valley floor where they spread out and coalesced. During the last ice age, the floor of Jackson Hole Valley adjacent to the Grand Tetons was covered by a continuous sheet of moving ice, called a piedmont glacier, which pushed its way out from the mountains nearly as far as the highway. The piedmont glacier gouged basins in the soft valley floor sediment near the mountains and then dumped its load of debris around their eastern edges to form moraines.

In order to visualize the way the Grand Tetons must have looked during the last ice age we must imagine the higher peaks thrusting up through a sea of ice at their base and clutched in fingers of ice filling the valleys between them.

Most of the ice age glaciers finally melted about 10,000 years ago and now the basins gouged and dammed along the east face of the Grand Tetons are filled with water to form the series of beautiful lakes that reflect the image of the mountains.

A few small glaciers still remain in the Grand Tetons but these are merely shrunken ghosts of the tremendous streams of ice that flowed here during the last ice age. Small glaciers such as we see today are not even remotely capable of carving the kind of landscape their ice age ancestors created.

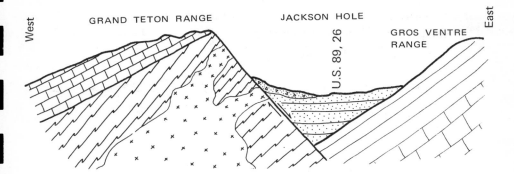

West-east cross section across Jackson Hole. The Grand Teton Range is a block of the earth's crust brought up along a large fault. Glaciers coming down from the Grand Tetons plastered glacial debris over much of the western side of Jackson Hole.

The Grand Tetons so dominate the scene that many people come away from Jackson Hole without having noticed the Gros Ventre Range east of the valley. It is interesting too.

Mt. Leidy, a high peak southeast of Moran Junction, is capped by a gravel conglomerate believed to have been deposited between 60 and 70 million years ago. Gravel lies on top of Cretaceous sandstones which had already been folded and eroded to a flat surface before the gravel was deposited. The Cretaceous rocks were originally deposited as sediments between 60 and 120 million years ago. Clearly, they had been folded, worn down to a flat surface, and then covered with a thick deposit of gravel all before 50 million years ago. Since that time, the whole complex has been uplifted so that we now see it in the top of a high mountain.

About halfway between Jackson and Moran Junction, the Gros Ventre slide can be seen as a red scar on the mountains to the east. This enormous landslide came down the mountain in 1925, dammed the Gros Ventre River, and formed a lake which lasted until 1927 when the slide dam washed out releasing a disastrous flood.

Grand Teton Park is very close to Yellowstone Park where a great deal of volcanic activity has taken place during the last several million years. Between Moran Junction and Yellowstone Park there are numerous exposures along the road of light-colored volcanic rocks similar to those in Yellowstone Park. At its northern end, the Grand Teton Range disappears into the volcanic Pitchstone Plateau of Yellowstone Park.

For information on volcanic rocks in Yellowstone Park, see
Yellowstone National Park (after U.S. 20: Cody — East Entrance)

Massive valley glaciers, closely-spaced, carved the craggy peaks of the Grand Teton Range into a fault block of Precambrian basement rocks overlain by Paleozoic sedimentary rocks.

MAMMOTH HOT SPRINGS – LIVINGSTON
53 miles

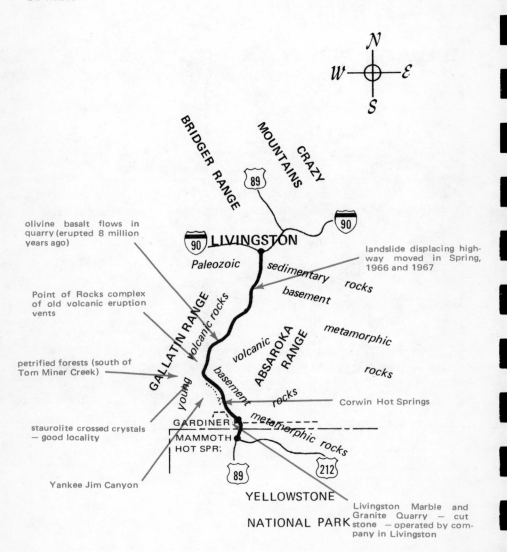

olivine basalt flows in quarry (erupted 8 million years ago)

Point of Rocks complex of old volcanic eruption vents

petrified forests (south of Tom Miner Creek)

staurolite crossed crystals — good locality

Yankee Jim Canyon

landslide displacing highway moved in Spring, 1966 and 1967

Corwin Hot Springs

Livingston Marble and Granite Quarry — cut stone — operated by company in Livingston

BRIDGER RANGE

CRAZY MOUNTAINS

LIVINGSTON

Paleozoic

sedimentary rocks

basement

metamorphic rocks

volcanic rocks

ABSAROKA RANGE

GALLATIN RANGE

volcanic rocks

young

basement rocks

GARDINER

MAMMOTH HOT SPR:

metamorphic rocks

YELLOWSTONE NATIONAL PARK

142

U.S. 89

MAMMOTH HOT SPRINGS – LIVINGSTON

U.S. 89 follows the valley of the Yellowstone River between the Absaroka Range to the east and the Gallatin Range to the west. Both ranges are made largely of volcanic rocks erupted about 50 million years ago on top of a complex older foundation consisting of Precambrian igneous and metamorphic basement rocks overlain by folded Paleozoic and Mesozoic sedimentary rocks. The Yellowstone River has cut down through the volcanic cover into the older rocks providing a good view of the geology along the highway.

Mammoth Hot Springs produces water heavily loaded with dissolved limestone leached from Paleozoic sedimentary rocks below the surface. The dissolved limestone is redeposited around the mouth of the spring to form enormous white travertine terraces. Apparently the spring has issued from different points in the hillside at various times in the past because several old terraces now grown over with plants are scattered within a mile of the ones now active.

The big mountain on the west side of the road at the northern edge of Yellowstone National Park is composed of soft Cretaceous shales overlain by volcanic rocks. The shales don't seem able to bear the weight of the volcanics and the entire northern side of the mountain is slowly coming down in a series of enormous landslides. Look for them south and west of the highway from near Mammoth Hot Springs to a point 2 or 3 miles north of Gardnier.

Five miles northwest of Gardiner a vertical red stripe called the Devil's Slide is conspicuous on the side of the mountain across the river west of the highway. It is an outcrop of Mesozoic shale in a section of the older sedimentary rocks exposed after the river had cut down through the volcanics above. Devil's Slide is in a cliff that contains a sequence of sedimentary rocks spanning the geologic time scale from Devonian (300 million years old) at the north end to

Rimmed travertine pools at Mammoth Hot Springs.

Cretaceous (60 million years old) at the south end. All the beds stand vertically, having been tilted that way as the Rocky Mountains formed.

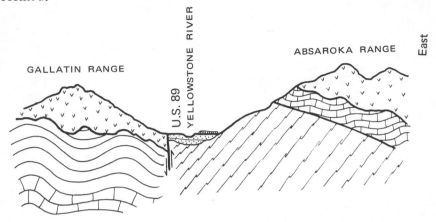

West-east cross section across the line of U.S. 89 about midway between Mammoth Hot Springs and Livingston. Both the Absaroka and Gallatin Ranges are heavily blanketed with volcanic rocks erupted within the last 50 million years.

Several miles north of Corwin Hot Springs the road goes through Yankee Jim Canyon where the river has cut down through the volcanics into hard, metamorphic gneiss belonging to the Precambrian basement. The valley narrows abruptly as it enters the canyon because the hard Precambrian rocks have been faulted up against the much softer sedimentary rocks.

About 8 million years ago, a large basalt lava flow poured down 15 miles of the Yellowstone River Valley between Yankee Jim Canyon and Emigrant. The river has now cut down through this flow but remnants of it can still be recognized as a level surface a hundred or so feet above the road underlain by the coal black basalt which is fractured into vertical columns.

Immediately south of Livingston, the road passes through another narrow canyon. The rocks exposed here are Paleozoic sedimentary formations, mostly limestones, ranging in age from Cambrian (about 550 million years old) to Permian (about 250 million years old).

For information on Mammoth Hot Springs, see
Yellowstone National Park Road: Tower Junction – Mammoth Hot Springs

For information on volcanic rocks in Yellowstone Park, see
Yellowstone National Park (after U.S. 20: Cody – East Entrance)

LIVINGSTON — WHITE SULPHUR SPRINGS — GREAT FALLS
163 miles

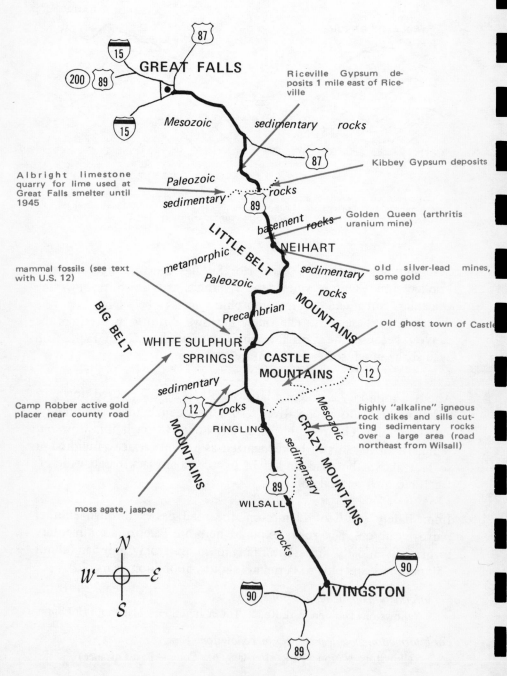

87

15

GREAT FALLS

200 89

15

Riceville Gypsum deposits 1 mile east of Riceville

Mesozoic   *sedimentary   rocks*

87

Kibbey Gypsum deposits

Albright limestone quarry for lime used at Great Falls smelter until 1945

Paleozoic

sedimentary   rocks

89

basement   rocks

Golden Queen (arthritis uranium mine)

NEIHART

metamorphic

LITTLE BELT

old silver-lead mines, some gold

sedimentary

rocks

mammal fossils (see text with U.S. 12)

Paleozoic

Precambrian

MOUNTAINS

old ghost town of Castle

BIG BELT

WHITE SULPHUR SPRINGS

CASTLE MOUNTAINS

12

Camp Robber active gold placer near county road

sedimentary

12

rocks

Mesozoic

CRAZY MOUNTAINS

highly "alkaline" igneous rock dikes and sills cutting sedimentary rocks over a large area (road northeast from Wilsall)

RINGLING

MOUNTAINS

sedimentary

89

moss agate, jasper

WILSALL

rocks

90

N

W ⊕ E

S

90

LIVINGSTON

89

U.S. 89

LIVINGSTON – GREAT FALLS

In the southern part of this route, between Livingston and White Sulphur Springs, U.S. 89 goes right up the middle of the Crazy Mountain Valley, crossing valley-fill sediments laid down between 40 and 3 million years ago during the Tertiary Period when our region was a desert. For much of this distance it follows the Shields River named by Lewis and Clark after one of the men who accompanied them.

Oil geologists are fascinated by the Crazy Mountain Valley because it appears to be a fold formed when Paleozoic and Mesozoic sedimentary rocks were jammed together during formation of the Rocky Mountains. A tremendous thickness of these rocks is crumpled beneath this valley and considerable work is being done in an effort to find deposits of oil trapped within them.

The Crazy Mountains dominate the view to the east. Their deep canyons and sharp peaks make them one of the most picturesquely glaciated ranges in the entire region. The southern part of the Crazy Mountains is composed of volcanic rocks erupted about 50-60 million years ago. The northern part is mostly Mesozoic sedimentary rocks that contain a number of intrusive igneous rocks squirted into them as molten magmas. Some of the igneous rocks are very rare varieties known to occur in only a few places. Unfortunately, these nondescript-looking gray rocks are not attractive to look at – they are the sort of thing that could be loved only by a geologist.

Rising west of U.S. 89 between Livingston and Ringling is the Bridger Range, an uplifted fault-block composed mostly of folded Paleozoic and Mesozoic sedimentary rocks lying on top of a core of Precambrain sedimentary and basement rocks. A very craggy profile was carved into the high peaks of the Bridger Range by glaciers during the last ice age.

Along most of the distance between Ringling and White Sulphur Springs, U.S. 89 follows the valley of the Smith River between the Big Belt Mountains to the west and the Castle Mountains to the north and east. Filling the view north of White Sulphur Springs are the Little Belt Mountains which U.S. 89 crosses.

In the core of the Castle Mountains is an intrusion of granite that pushed its way up through the sedimentary rocks roughly 50 million years ago. Sedimentary rocks pretty well surround the granite and make up most of what is visible from the road. During the last century large silver mines operated in the southern part of the range around the ghost town of Castle, which is accessible from Lennep on Montana 294. Castle had a population of about 5,000 in 1893 when the mines were closed after Congress demonetized silver. Nobody lives there now.

Between White Sulphur Springs and Great Falls, U.S. 89 crosses the Little Belt Mountains, basically a great fold arched upward in the plains east of the main mass of the Rocky Mountains. Mesozoic and Paleozoic sedimentary rocks flank the range while Precambrian sedimentary and basement rocks form the core. Highway 89 crosses the center of the range providing a good view of the wide variety of rocks it contains.

Rocks exposed on the south flank of the range, between White Sulphur Springs and Kings Hill Pass 30 miles to the north, are Paleozoic limestones and sandstones except for a stretch of several miles near the boundary of the Lewis and Clark National Forest where Precambrian mudstones and limestones can be seen.

Neihart, once a busy little mining town is now mostly inactive. Some of the large old mine dumps near the road contain interesting and attractive rock and mineral specimens.

Igneous and metamorphic rocks belonging to the Precambrian basement outcrop in large roadcuts for the 10 miles north of town. Many of these are streaky-looking pink and gray schists and gneisses containing mostly quartz, pink and white feldspar, and black mica or hornblende. North of Neihart there are a number of roadcuts in a beautiful coarse-grained gabbro recognizable as a very dark-colored rock made up of greenish-black augite enclosing large, rectangular crystals of greenish-white plagioclase feldspar. This is an unusually handsome rock which is very attractive when sawed into large slabs and polished.

From a point 10 miles north of Neihart to the area several miles south of the junction with U.S. 87, all the rocks are Paleozoic sedimentary rocks — mostly limestones. Many of the outcrops contain fossils. Mesozoic sedimentary rocks outcrop along the entire route of U.S. 89-87 to Great Falls.

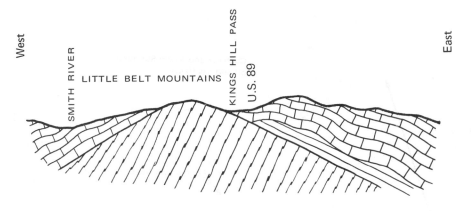

West-east cross section across the line of U.S. 89 where it passes through the Little Belt Mountains. Precambrian basement rocks form the core of the range and are surrounded by Precambrian and Paleozoic sedimentary rocks. Although younger granites are also present in the Little Belt Mountains, none of them occur along the line of this section.

Belt Butte, a few miles north of the intersection of U.S. 87 with U.S. 89, is visible from the highway. Molten magma was squirted between these Mesozoic sedimentary beds to make a layer of igneous rock. Now the whole thing has been carved by erosion so that Belt Butte is left standing as an isolated knob. The layer of igneous rock projects as a ridge like a belt around the middle.

Mesozoic rocks which outcrop along the route of U.S. 89-87 east of Great Falls were laid down along the margins of a shallow sea between 60 and 150 million years ago. Some of these rocks were deposited in swamps along the seashore burying large peat bogs which have now turned into coal. Small coal mines have operated in this area for many years but these are likely to become much larger in the future because much of the coal is very low in sulfur so it can be burned with minimal atmospheric pollution. Large reserves of coal remain to be mined.

GREAT FALLS – BROWNING
126 miles

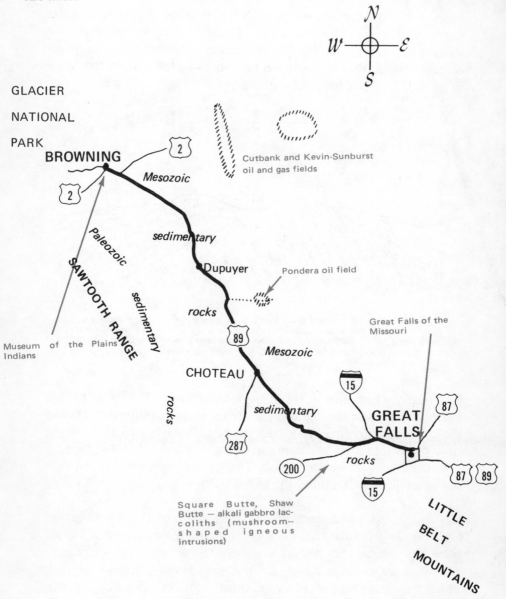

N
W ⊕ E
S

GLACIER

NATIONAL

PARK

BROWNING

GLACIER NATIONAL PARK

2

2

Mesozoic

Cutbank and Kevin-Sunburst
oil and gas fields

Paleozoic

SAWTOOTH RANGE

sedimentary

sedimentary

Dupuyer

Pondera oil field

rocks

89

Museum of the Plains
Indians

rocks

Mesozoic

CHOTEAU

Great Falls of the
Missouri

15

87

sedimentary

287

**GREAT
FALLS**

200

rocks

87   89

15

Square Butte, Shaw
Butte — alkali gabbro laccoliths (mushroom--
shaped igneous
intrusions)

**LITTLE
BELT
MOUNTAINS**

89

150

U.S. 89

GREAT FALLS – BROWNING

Between Great Falls and Choteau, U.S. 89 crosses late Mesozoic (Cretaceous) sandstones and mudstones deposited about 60-80 million years ago, at a time when a shallow sea still flooded the plains of Montana and the northern Rocky Mountains were just beginning to rise to the west. These sedimentary rocks escaped being involved in the crustal movements that formed the Rocky Mountains so their layers are still nearly horizontal.

For about 20 miles west of Great Falls a group of isolated buttes interrupt the skyline in the distance to the south and southwest. These are igneous intrusions called laccoliths; they are discussed at the end of the roadguide to Interstate 15 between Helena and Great Falls.

Between Choteau and Browning, U.S. 89 follows a route across the western edge of the high plains. From every high point on the highway the imposing front of the Sawtooth Range rises like a wall in the west to end the plains that extend nearly unbroken for hundreds of miles to the east. Between Dupuyer and Browning, the high peaks of Glacier Park come into view in the northwest. On a very clear day the Bearpaw Mountains south of Havre can just barely be glimpsed far to the east. This isolated range that pokes up out of the high plains contains some very unusual igneous rocks.

The high plains were formerly much smoother than they now are, and extended eastward from the Rocky Mountain front as an almost unbroken, gently sloping surface. During the last several million years, the streams that flow east from the mountains have cut their valleys down into this old surface. It can still be seen smoothly

151

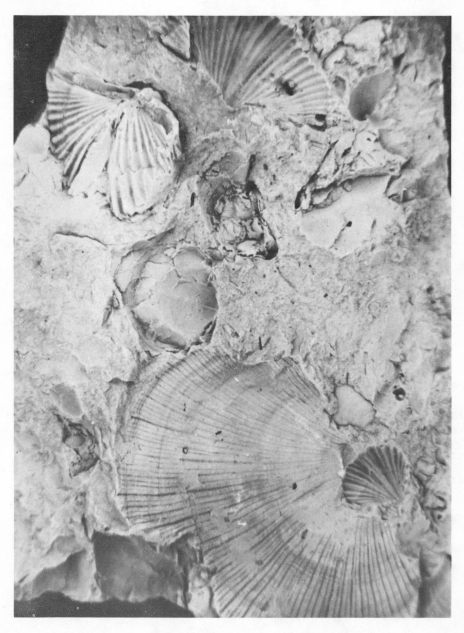

Paleozoic fossils like these brachiopods occur in some of the slices of rock that make up the parallel ridges of the Sawtooth Range west of U.S. 89.

profiled against the sky from many places along the highway. The high plains surface in this area is underlain by thick beds of gravel eroded from the mountains and carried eastward by streams during late Tertiary Time. These are exposed in numerous small roadcuts in places where the road passes high across the old, smooth surface.

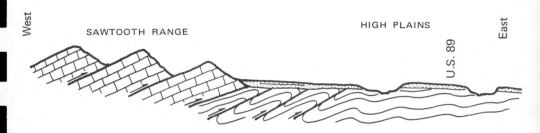

West-east cross section across the line of U.S. 89. Tertiary sediments deposited since movement on the faults, underly the High Plains and lap onto the flanks of the Sawtooth Range.

Bedrock beneath the gravel is Cretaceous marine sedimentary rock deposited about 60 million years ago just before the sea drained away from Montana for the last time. These rocks are exposed in the river valleys where the gravel has been eroded away. Some of the Cretaceous outcrops contain numerous fossils; dinosaur bones have been found in several places along this road.

The valley of Birch Creek north of Dupuyer still clearly shows the effects of the disastrous flood that swept this region in June, 1964 when a heavy snowpack in the mountains was melted by several days of warm rain. Thousands of dead trees along the floodplain high above the creek record the incredible height of the flood waters.

During the last ice age, a great continental glacier covered much of central Canada and poured into northern Montana as far as the area just south of Browning. Another glacier moved east from Glacier Park toward Browning. The countryside around Browning was near the edge of this glacier where large quantities of debris were dropped as it melted. Numerous small ponds formed where large blocks of ice incorporated in the glacial deposits later melted leaving sink holes.

For more information on the Sawtooth Range, see
        U.S. 287: Wolf Creek – Choteau

For information on the rocks in Glacier Park, see the following section (Glacier National Park).

GLACIER NATIONAL PARK

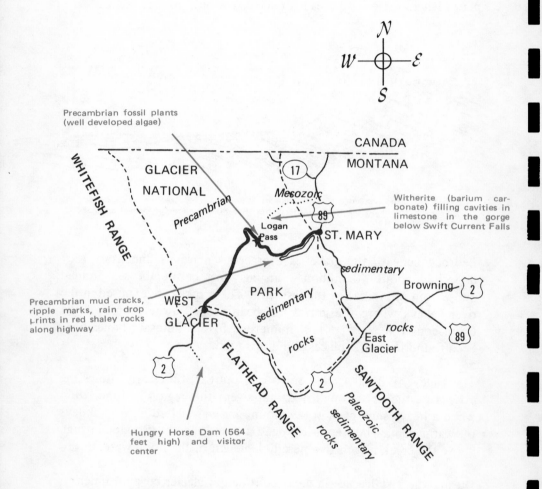

Precambrian fossil plants
(well developed algae)

WHITEFISH RANGE

CANADA
MONTANA

GLACIER
NATIONAL

Precambrian

Mesozoic

17

89

Logan
Pass

ST. MARY

Witherite (barium car-
bonate) filling cavities in
limestone in the gorge
below Swift Current Falls

sedimentary

Browning

2

PARK

WEST
GLACIER

sedimentary

rocks

rocks

89

Precambrian mud cracks,
ripple marks, rain drop
prints in red shaley rocks
along highway

East
Glacier

FLATHEAD RANGE

2

2

SAWTOOTH RANGE

Paleozoic
sedimentary
rocks

Hungry Horse Dam (564
feet high) and visitor
center

GLACIER NATIONAL PARK

Glacier National Park is basically an enormous slab, several thousand feet thick, of Precambrian sedimentary rocks which slid eastward a distance of about 35 miles across the much younger Cretaceous sedimentary rocks that underlie the high plains. The sliding movement seems to have happened about 50 million years ago. Normally geologists expect to find younger rocks on top of older ones; here the situation is reversed so that rocks about a billion years old are on top of rocks less than 100 million years old.

The surface across which the older rocks moved as they slid eastward over the younger ones is called the Lewis Overthrust Fault. It lies nearly flat with a gentle tilt downward to the west. How such large-scale sliding can take place has been a puzzle to geologists for many years, a problem similar to that of getting a large carpet to slide across a floor without being rumpled in the process. It can't be done without greatly reducing the friction in the sliding surface.

Friction in rocks seems to be reduced by the water in them being under high enough pressure to support most of the load. This effectively floats the rocks on top, making it possible for them to glide almost frictionlessly over those beneath. Apparently there must have been water trapped at high pressure in the Cretaceous sedimentary rocks to enable the Precambrian slab to slide eastward over them after having broken loose somewhere to the west. At that time the Lewis Overthrust must have tilted downward to the east instead of to the west as it now does. Otherwise, the Precambrian slab would have had to slide uphill.

The line of outcrop of the Lewis Overthrust runs generally parallel to the eastern and southern margins of Glacier National Park. It can be seen north of U.S. 2 between East Glacier and Marias Pass and west of Montana 49 and U.S. 89 between East Glacier and the Canadian border. It can't be seen on the west side of the park. Cretaceous

View east from the top of Logan Pass, Glacier National Park. Diagonal lines of snow on the top of the peak in the middleground mark two very small faults in the Precambrian sedimentary rock. Sedimentary layers dip gently down to the right.

sandstones and mudstones beneath the Lewis Overthrust outcrop as gently rolling hills covered with aspen shrub while the Precambrian rocks rise above it as bold cliffs. The line of the fault can easily be spotted by watching for this abrupt break in the topography.

Distinguishing one rock formation from another is ordinarily a job for a professional geologist familiar with the area. But in the Precambrian of Glacier National Park anyone can tell the formations apart. Four of them outcrop along the highway.

Directly above the Lewis Overthrust is the Altyn Limestone, the oldest Precambrian formation in the park. White when freshly broken, it weathers to a buff color on old surfaces. It is full of sand grains and pebbles arranged in beds in such a way as to indicate that it was deposited on a beach. Fossil seaweeds exist but are hard to find and not likely to be noticed by someone who doesn't have a lot of time to look for them. They suggest fossil brussel sprouts – of course they are not. Altyne Limestone is in several roadcuts along the north side of St. Mary Lake but the best place to see it is around the parking lot of the Many Glacier Hotel on Swiftcurrent Lake.

The Appekuny Formation, directly above the Altyn Limestone, consists mostly of green mudstones but also contains a few layers of red mudstone and white sandstone. Green Appekuny mudstones contain some ripple marks and mudcracks but these are abundant in only a few places. The Appekuny is the only formation in the park that is mostly green.

The Grinnell Formation, above the Appekuny, consists mostly of red mudstones but also contains a few layers of green mudstone and white sandstone. Mudstones in the Grinnell Formation are full of mudcracks and ripple marks recording wet seasons followed by days of baking sun a billion years ago. Some bed surfaces are dotted with raindrop imprints, telling us of passing showers long ago. Other red formations cap some of the highest peaks in the park but the Grinnell mudstones are the only red formation that outcrops along the road.

A rock wall made of slabs of red and green mudstone from the Grinnell and Appekuny Formations surrounds the parking area at Sunrift Gorge a short distance west of St. Mary Lake. Nearly all the different kinds of sedimentary features in both formations can be seen in this wall. Sunrift Gorge itself is a long straight channel carved

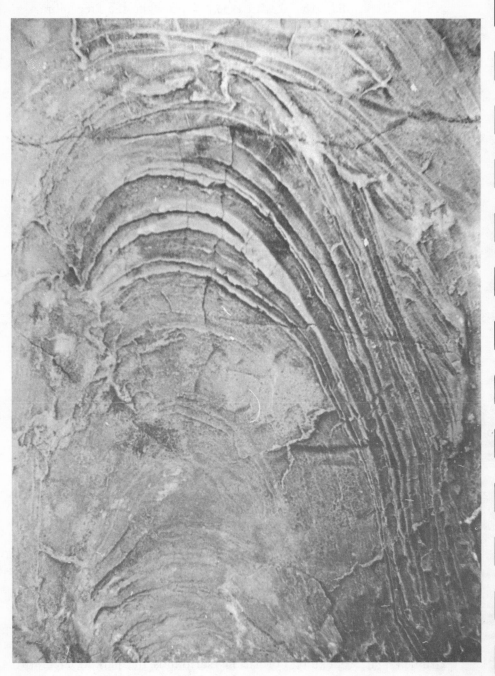

Fossil algae in the Precambrian Siyeh Limestone, Glacier National Park. This picture shows a vertical cross-section of one of the cabbage like structures that apparently developed when the plants grew in a wave-washed environment. Approximately natural size.

where the stream followed a fracture in the Grinnell Formation.

The most conspicuous formation in the park is the Siyeh (pronounced "sigh-ah") Limestone which is on top of the Grinnell Formation and outcrops for many miles along the higher part of the Going-to-the-Sun Highway. Siyeh Limestone is dark gray to black on fresh surfaces and weathers to lighter gray or tan on old surfaces. The dark color is caused by organic material. Many outcrops of the Siyeh are full of fossil seaweeds which come in a variety of forms. Some look like squiggly vertical lines in the rock. These formed when the seaweed grew to the shape of a leaf blade in quiet water and was then buried in lime mud and later crumpled as the mud compacted while becoming limestone. Others suggest fossil brussels sprouts or cabbages packed together in the rock. They appear to have grown where waves were breaking. Fossil seaweeds can be seen in the Siyeh Limestone in many places but one of the best is along the trail between the visitor center on Logan Pass and Hidden Lake. Several prominent ledges near the visitor center are full of them.

Other formations above the Siyeh Limestone can not be seen near the road. Red rocks which form the mountain tops immediately surrounding Logan Pass are in these formations.

A thick layer of molten basalt magma injected between sedimentary beds in the upper part of the Siyeh Limestone forms the black Purcell Sill. Heat from the magma boiled the black organic material out of the adjacent enclosing limestone, bleaching it white both

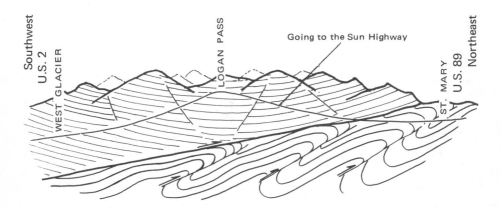

Southwest-northeast cross section across Glacier National Park along the line of the Going to the Sun Highway. The slab of Precambrian sedimentary rocks that slid eastward along the Lewis Overthrust Fault is deformed into a broad fold causing the layers to dip down to the west in the eastern part of the park and to the east in the western part.

159

above and below the sill. So the sill can be recognized from a great distance as a thin black ledge bordered above and below by white bands in many of the high peaks in the park. Analysis of radioactive minerals has shown that the Purcell Sill is 800 million years old. Clearly, the Siyeh Limestone which it intruded must be older.

The Purcell Sill outcrops about at the level of the Going-to-the-Sun Highway at the top of Logan Pass. It can be seen by walking a few hundred feet north from the pass on the trail leading to Granite Park Chalet. Directly above the highway west of the pass, the trail is built right through the bleached zone in the Siyeh Limestone above the sill and then through the sill itself. Start watching the rocks when you get to where handropes have been strung alongside the trail. Fossil seaweeds in the Siyeh show up more beautifully in this bleached zone than in any other easily reached spot. The sill itself is easily recognized as an intensely black rock with fracture surfaces coated by glossy, yellowish-green serpentine minerals.

Although faults are common in the Rocky Mountains, we rarely get a chance to look at them because they are usually covered by soil and vegetation. Glacier Park is an exception. Small faults appear on almost any mountainside, showing how the Precambrian rocks were broken up into blocks which moved up and down short distances.

Diagram showing how small faults offset the layers of Precambrian sedimentary rock in Glacier National Park.

Glacier National Park gets its name from the fact that it is a splendid example of glaciated mountain scenery. Of course the several glaciers which still remain in the park — some of them can be seen from the highway — could never erode such a landscape and are merely shriveled vestiges of the magnificent glaciers once here.

During the last ice age, up until about 10,000 years ago, the area that is now Glacier Park was covered by massive glaciers almost continuous enough to be called an ice cap. To imagine what the park was like when this landscape was carved we must visualize a sea of glistening blue-white ice with a scattering of mountain peaks rising above it like islands.

Heavy snows of the last ice age gathered into glaciers on the mountain slopes, then flowed down the valleys as great slow rivers of ice until they got to a low enough elevation to find a climate warm enough to melt the ice front as fast as it advanced. There the glaciers dropped their load of sediment where the ice melted to form moraines visible today as small ridges of debris looping across the landscape marking the former margins of the ice.

In places the moraine ridges formed natural dams across valleys, helping impound some of the larger lakes around the edges of the park — McDonald Lake, St. Mary Lake, Two Medicine Lake and others. In other places the ice gouged out holes in the bedrock to form rock-rimmed basins that hold the smaller lakes dotting the high country.

Most of the rugged landscape of the park testifies to the work done by glaciers and is typical of mountains everywhere that have been shaped by them. Spoon-shaped cirque basins on the flanks of the high peaks look like some giant gouged them with an ice-cream scoop. They are the places where the glaciers began. The deep valleys with wide, flat floors and steep walls were scraped into that shape by the ice as it flowed through them. Sharp, jagged peaks formed where glaciers gouged a peak from several sides, leaving a gnarled pinnacle as all that remains of what once was a full, rounded mountain.

Today the glaciers are gone and will not return until the next ice age. Streams are doing their own kind of work, slowly removing the marks left by the glaciers and reshaping the landscape into the kind of mountains that streams erode.

For more information on ice age continental galciers, see
>   U.S. 2: Kalispell — Bonners Ferry
>   U.S. 93: Missoula — Kalispell
>   U.S. 93: Kalispell — Eureka

For more information on the Lewis Overthrust Fault, see
>   U.S. 2: Browning — Kalispell
>   U.S. 89: Browning — Chief Mountain

BROWNING – CHIEF MOUNTAIN – CANADIAN BORDER
58 miles

U.S. 89 – Montana 17

BROWNING – CANADIAN BORDER

Between Browning and the Canadian border, U.S. 89 crosses Mesozoic (Cretaceous) sandstones and mudstones deposited as sediments between 60 and 80 million years ago and then intensely folded and displaced by faults roughly 50 million years ago when the front range of the northern Rocky Mountains formed.

During the last ice age glaciers flowing east onto the plains from Marias Pass and Glacier National Park spread out at the base of the mountains where they coalesced to form a large ice field. When this ice melted at the end of the last ice age, about 10,000 years ago, it left behind thick deposits of glacial debris plastered over much of the folded sedimentary rock beneath. These deposits are along much of the part of U.S. 89 that follows the eastern margin of Glacier Park. They make an unevenly hummocky landscape littered with boulders and can be recognized in roadcuts as deposits of clean sand and gravel laid down by glacial streams or of boulders, sand, and clay all mixed together as they were dumped directly from glacial ice.

Glacial deposits along the road east of Glacier Park contain samples of all the different kinds of rock in the park. They are good places to collect a nice set of specimens without committing a federal offense by collecting in the park.

Two Medicine Lake, visible east of the road near Kiowa, and St. Mary Lake, visible east of the road 20 miles north of Kiowa, both occupy basins scoured in the Cretaceous sedimentary rock by large glaciers which came down from the mountains in the park. In both places glaciers, which had been flowing over very hard Precambrian sedimentary rock above the Lewis Overthrust Fault, suddenly found themselves on much softer rock when they crossed the fault and scooped it out to make deep basins. Both lake basins are also dammed at their eastern ends by deposits of glacial debris.

In this view of the eastern front of Glacier National Park, rugged cliffs of Precambrian sedimentary rock rise boldly above low, tree-covered topography eroded in the soft Mesozoic sedimentary rocks beneath. The Lewis Overthrust Fault is marked by the nearly horizontal line of snowpatches near the base of the peak in the center of the picture.

About 5 miles south of St. Mary, U.S. 89 crosses the Hudson Bay Divide between drainages flowing to the Gulf of Mexico and to Hudson's Bay. Excellent exposures of folded sandstones are along the road; some of the roadcuts on the north side of the divide are really spectacular.

All the way from Browning to the Canadian border, the mountains of Glacier Park are visible west of U.S. 89. They rise abruptly from the line of the Lewis Overthrust Fault that separates the hard Precambrian sedimentary rocks above from the much softer Mesozoic sandstones and mudstones below.

At Babb, about 10 miles north of St. Mary, the side road to Many Glacier and Swiftcurrent Lake turns west from U.S. 89. On the way to Swiftcurrent Lake the road passes the northern side of Sherburne Reservoir which floods the site of the first oil field in Montana. Wells drilled here in 1904 produced marginally commercial quantities of oil from the folded Cretaceous sedimentary rocks beneath the Lewis Overthrust Fault at a depth of about 500 feet. This was only a small oil field and has been out of production now for more than 50 years. But there are large oil fields not far away and oil companies continue to prospect for more along the eastern front of Glacier Park and the Sawtooth Range.

The Lewis Overthrust crosses the Swiftcurrent Road a very short distance east of the Many Glacier Hotel which is built on the Precambrian Altyn Limestone immediately above the fault. The best place to look at the Altyn Limestone is in the outcrops around the

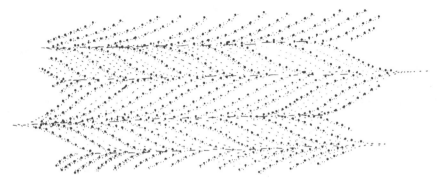

Inclined cross-beds within horizontal layers in a sedimentary rock. Currents of air or water lay down sedimentary beds by depositing successive thin layers of mud or sand. Cross-beds dip down in the direction toward which the current moved.

hotel parking lot. Look for thin layers of pebbles arranged in steeply-tilting "cross beds" cutting across the main layering in the rock. This particular kind of sedimentary structure suggests that the rock was originally deposited as sandy sediment on a beach. No one knows for sure how old the Altyn Limestone may be; certainly at least one billion years must have passed since those pebbles were arranged that way by the surf. Similar cross beds can be found by digging a trench in many modern beaches. So the waves have been washing the pebbles into the same patterns on beaches for at least a billion years.

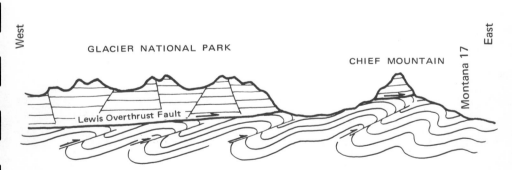

West-east cross section across the line of Montana 17 just south of the Canadian border. Chief Mountain, an erosional remnant, is the easternmost outpost of the Precambrian sedimentary rocks above the Lewis Overthrust Fault.

Highway 17 turns west from U.S. 89 4 miles north of Babb and passes close to the eastern side of Chief Mountain just south of the Canadian border. Chief Mountain is the easternmost outpost of the great slab of Precambrian sedimentary rocks that slid eastward on the Lewis Overthrust. Now it has been completely isolated by erosion so that it stands alone like an island surrounded on all sides by the Cretaceous sedimentary rocks underlying the Lewis Overthrust. Chief Mountain is well known among geologists because it is the best single clue to figuring out the total amount of eastward sliding that took place on the Lewis Overthrust.

For more information on Glacier National Park and the Lewis Overthrust Fault, *see*

Glacier National Park (preceding section)
U.S. 2: Browning — Kalispell

Mountains of the Sawtooth Range and Glacier National Park rise abruptly above the western end of the High Plains near Browning.

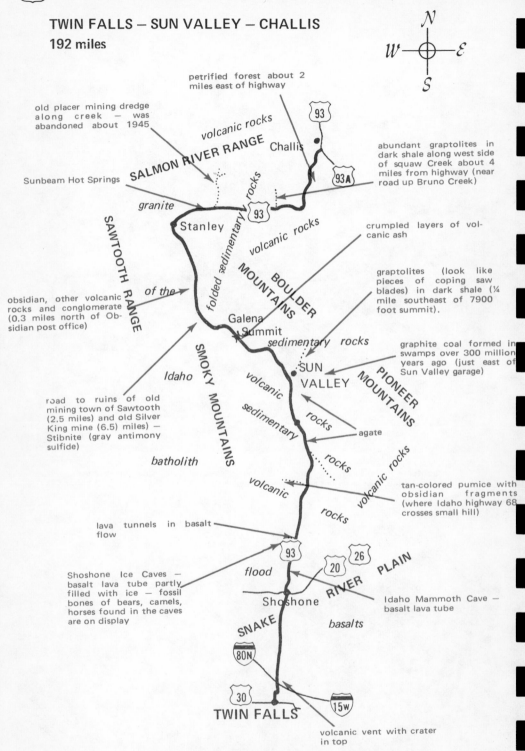

TWIN FALLS — SUN VALLEY — CHALLIS
192 miles

N W E S

petrified forest about 2 miles east of highway

93

old placer mining dredge along creek — was abandoned about 1945

volcanic rocks

SALMON RIVER RANGE

Challis

abundant graptolites in dark shale along west side of squaw Creek about 4 miles from highway (near road up Bruno Creek)

Sunbeam Hot Springs

granite

93A

93

Stanley

volcanic rocks

crumpled layers of volcanic ash

SAWTOOTH RANGE

of the

folded sedimentary rocks

BOULDER MOUNTAINS

graptolites (look like pieces of coping saw blades) in dark shale (¼ mile southeast of 7900 foot summit).

obsidian, other volcanic rocks and conglomerate (0.3 miles north of Obsidian post office)

Galena Summit

sedimentary rocks

graphite coal formed in swamps over 300 million years ago (just east of Sun Valley garage)

Idaho

SUN VALLEY

PIONEER MOUNTAINS

SMOKY MOUNTAINS

volcanic

road to ruins of old mining town of Sawtooth (2.5 miles) and old Silver King mine (6.5 miles) — Stibnite (gray antimony sulfide)

sedimentary

rocks

agate

batholith

rocks

volcanic rocks

volcanic

tan-colored pumice with obsidian fragments (where Idaho highway 68 crosses small hill)

rocks

lava tunnels in basalt flow

93

26

20

RIVER PLAIN

Shoshone Ice Caves — basalt lava tube partly filled with ice — fossil bones of bears, camels, horses found in the caves are on display

flood

Shoshone

Idaho Mammoth Cave — basalt lava tube

SNAKE

basalts

80N

30

15W

TWIN FALLS

volcanic vent with crater in top

U.S. 93

TWIN FALLS – CHALLIS

Between Twin Falls and Challis, U.S. 93 passes through an unusually wide variety of interesting geologic features which are well exposed and easily enjoyed from the road.

Twin Falls is near the southern margin of the Snake River Plain, a high plateau built up of numerous large lava flows erupted during the past several million years. The city takes its name from the waterfalls in the canyon of the Snake River. They can be seen from the bridge south of town, spilling over ledges formed by individual lava flows well exposed in the walls of the canyon. The flows are horizontal but break along vertical shrinkage cracks in the black basalt making some of the ledges look like rows of standing posts.

North of Twin Falls to the area about 15 miles south of Hailey the highway crosses the Snake River Plain which is almost perfectly flat except for a few isolated small knobs marking volcanic vents from which some of the more recent flows were erupted. One of the most easily recognized is Flattop Butte, east of the highway about 8 miles north of Twin Falls. It has a crater in its top.

Several rather fresh lava flows crossed by the highway have intensely black, rather broken-looking surfaces supporting very little vegetation. As time passes, soil will accumulate on these, eventually covering them so plants can grow. Much of the soil on the Snake River Plain is dust blown in by the wind from the deserts to the southwest.

Shoshone Ice Caves are about one-half mile west of the highway, 18 miles north of Shoshone. Tunnels such as these are left in the lava flows when still molten material within runs out from under an already solidified crust leaving the lava flow hollow. Such lava caves frequently contain ice which accumulates there in a very simple way. Cold winter air settles into the cave because it is heavy; warm summer air does not because it is lighter than the air already in the

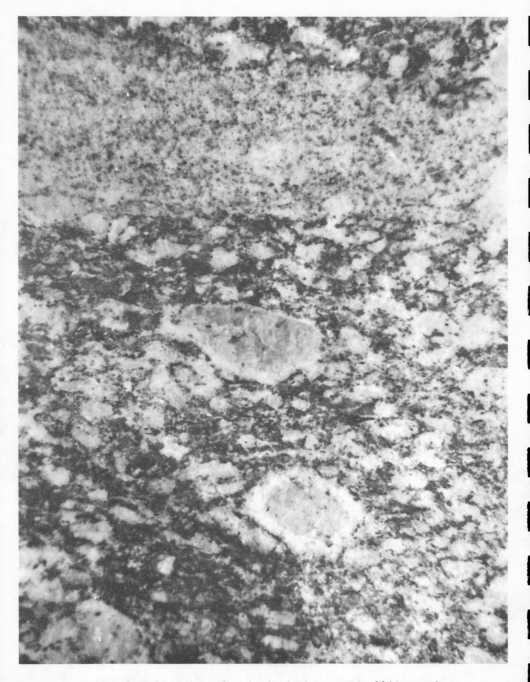

Sawed surface of a specimen of granite showing large crystals of feldspar set in a matrix of smaller crystals of quartz, feldspar and black hornblende. Slightly larger than natural size.

cave. So the cold air stays trapped in the cave all summer and the only new air that gets in is colder than that already inside. Any cave with limited circulation of air is likely to accumulate ice in this way.

The northern edge of the Snake River Plain is easy to recognize because it looks almost like the shore of a lake. An older, mountainous landscape was buried by the floods of lava in much the same way that it might have been submerged beneath the waters of a lake.

Mountains rising on the nothern edge of the Snake River Plain are composed mostly of sedimentary rocks originally deposited beneath the waters of a shallow sea during the latter part of the Paleozoic Era roughly 200 to 300 million years ago. They were intricately folded and broken by faults when the Rocky Mountains were beginning to form about 50 to 80 million years ago. At the same time this was happening, enormous masses of molten granite magma were rising up in the earth's crust in the area to the north to form the Idaho batholith which occupies much of central Idaho. Afterwards the whole region was deeply eroded and carved into mountains by streams before being blanketed under light-colored volcanic ash about 50 million years ago. Now the volcanic rocks are being removed by erosion but they still cover the tops of many mountains and can be seen along the highway for long distances.

U.S. 93 follows the valley of the Big Wood River between Hailey and Galena Summit. Rocks near the road are folded Paleozoic sedimentary rocks, mostly limestones, capped in places by the much younger light-colored volcanics. Higher parts of the Pioneer Range east of the highway are made of granite and metamorphic gneiss and schist.

During the last century and the early years of this one, Ketchum was quite a mining center complete with a smelter. Numerous small mining districts in the mountains nearby produced ores of lead, zinc, silver, and gold from deposits found in the volcanic rocks and along the edges of the granites.

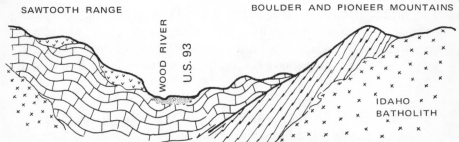

SAWTOOTH RANGE

BOULDER AND PIONEER MOUNTAINS

WOOD RIVER

U.S. 93

IDAHO BATHOLITH

Southwest-northeast cross section across the line of U.S. 93 near Sun Valley. Intensely deformed Paleozoic sedimentary rocks in this area are intruded by the granites of the Idaho batholith and covered in many places by younger volcanic rocks.

Just north of Galena Summit U.S. 93 enters granite of the Idaho batholith which extends north almost to Interstate 90 and northeast into the Bitterroot Range on the Idaho-Montana border. An overlook about a mile north of Galena Summit, provides a wonderful view of the glacially carved peaks of the Sawtooth Range.

Numerous mines have been worked in the Idaho batholith and many of the side roads from U.S. 93 lead to old mining camps and ghost towns. Mineral collecting is frequently quite good on the old mine dumps, partly because the early miners in this remote country had very primitive transportation facilities and could afford to ship only the best handpicked ore, leaving the rest behind. One of the more interesting side roads is the one that turns north from U.S. 93 at Sunbeam, about 14 miles east of Stanley, leading to the ghost towns of Bonanza and Custer in the old Yankee Fork Mining District. This was primarily a silver camp but lead and gold were mined as well. An old gold dredge still sits in the creek near the road.

Approximately 22 miles east of Stanley U.S. 93 crosses the contact between granite of the Idaho batholith to the west and folded Paleozoic rocks to the east. These are similar to the folded Paleozoic sedimentary rocks south of the batholith, are capped by light-colored volcanics, and also contain numerous small ore bodies which have been mined in the past.

Eruptions of light-colored volcanic rocks occasionally buried standing forests of trees about 50 million years ago. Here and there, large quantities of petrified wood are found, including entire logs and large tree stumps still standing as they grew. Good places to see these in their original position are difficult to find near the road, but almost any of the streams near Challis are good places to look for pebbles of petrified wood in the gravels. Trees closely related to the California Sequoias were petrified here, suggesting that the climate 50 million years ago must have been much milder than the one prevailing today.

For more information on flood basalts of the Snake River Plain, see
    Interstate 80 N: Twin Falls — Boise
    U.S. 20: Idaho Falls — Arco
    U.S. 93 A: Shoshone — Arco; Craters of the Moon

For more information on granite of the Idaho batholith, see
    U.S. 95: Boise — New Meadows

SHOSHONE – ARCO
82 miles

N
W ⊕ E
S

LOST RIVER RANGE

WHITE KNOB MOUNTAINS

valley fill

sediments

93A

PIONEER MOUNTAINS

volcanic rocks

Paleozoic sedimentary rocks

Paleozoic sedimentary rocks

ARCO

recent basalt flows with many lava tunnels

20 26

flood

volcanic   rocks

Carey

CRATERS
OF THE MOON

NATIONAL

MONUMENT

PLAIN   basalts

93

flood

93A

lava flows, lava tunnels, cinder cones, perfectly preserved

basalts

SNAKE RIVER RIVER

SHOSHONE

26 20

93

The Great Rift Zone — huge vertical cracks through which much of the basalt lava of the Snake River Plain was erupted

U.S. 93A

SHOSHONE – ARCO

Shoshone is near the middle of the Snake River Plain which stretches away from town in all directions almost as though it were the level surface of a lake. The Snake River Plain is built of basalt lava flows that poured from long fissures during the past several million years and stacked on top of each other to form the plateau. Those that form the present surface were the last to be erupted so are very young geologically. Some are no more than a few thousand years old.

Molten basalt magma is very fluid and runny so it doesn't pile up around the eruption vent to make the volcano but instead spreads out to form extensive lava flows. That is why there are so few volcanoes on the Snake River Plain even though all the rocks are volcanic. Places where the lava welled up out of the ground are sometimes marked by low hills called lava domes. Some can be seen east of U.S. 93 about 3 miles north of Shoshone and again southwest of the highway about 9 miles north of town.

Between Shoshone and Carey, U.S. 93 passes several very rough, black, fresh looking lava flows too young to have acquired enough soil to support vegetation.

Between Carey and Arco, U.S. 93 follows the north edge of the Snake River Plain, skirting the edge of the mountains bounding it to the north. The road crosses several mountain spurs that project out into the flows like peninsulas into a lake.

Mountains north of the Snake River Plain, in this area, are made mostly of limestones laid down in a shallow sea about 220 to 300 million years ago during late Paleozoic Time and then folded when the Rocky Mountains were formed. Light-colored volcanic rocks blanketed these mountains about 50 million years ago; these have since been largely removed by erosion but extensive patches still remain.

Big Southern Butte, a large volcano located southeast of Arco, can be seen from a great distance across the flat Snake River Plain. It is not made of basalt like the lava flows that form the surrounding plain but of light-colored volcanic rocks similar to those on the Yellowstone Plateau.

The northern edge of the Snake River Plain is the part where the most recent eruptions have occurred. One area of very recent activity has been set aside as Craters of the Moon National Monument where an 8-mile loop road takes visitors past a wonderful display of volcanic features, giving a vivid first-hand impression of what happens when a volcano erupts.

For basalts of Craters of the Moon, see
　　　Craters of the Moon National Monument (following section)

For more information on flood basalts of the Snake River Plain, see
　　　Interstate 80 N: Twin Falls — Boise
　　　U.S. 20: Idaho Falls — Arco

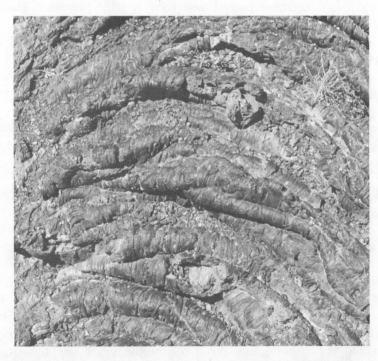

"Pahoehoe" surface of a basalt lava flow on the Snake River Plain. Such ropy surfaces form when a thin crust of solidified basalt is carried along on flowing, molten lava beneath. The tuft of grass gives an indication of scale.

176

CRATERS OF THE MOON

Eruptions created the bleak volcanic landscape of Craters of the Moon National Monument several thousand years ago but the rocks look so perfectly fresh that is easier to imagine their being only a few weeks old.

All the rocks at Craters of the Moon are basalt, but they are very slightly different chemically from the basalt which makes up most of the Snake River Plain and were erupted in a slightly different way. Most of the Snake River Plain basalts welled up out of long fissures in the earth's crust as great floods of lava which poured rapidly over the surface making flows covering dozens or hundreds of square miles. Much smaller eruptions formed Craters of the Moon and part of the lava was coughed out of the vents by escaping steam to make little cinder cone volcanoes. Many geologists believe that these small changes in type of basalt and style of eruption may signal the beginning of the end of volcanic activity in the Snake River Plain. The last eruptions on the older, but otherwise similar, Columbia Plateau resembled those at Craters of the Moon.

Globs of molten magma coughed out of a volcanic vent by escaping steam are usually blown high into the air where they cool and solidify as they fall back around the vent to make a volcanic cinder cone. When such volcanoes erupt at night, they make quite a fireworks display: White-hot globs of magma arc high above the vent, cooling to a glowing red heat as they fall then roll down the sides of the cone. Such pieces of basalt frequently have a streamlined shape and are called volcanic bombs. They are always full of gas bubbles which make them surprisingly light. Cinder cones in the national monument are oval-shaped because the wind was blowing when the eruptions happened.

Occasionally globs of basalt magma are blown more gently from smaller vents and plaster themselves together while still molten, forming a fantastic chimney called a splatter cone. Several of these along the loop road through the national monument are identified by signs.

Some basalt lava flows in the national monument have a very rough and jagged surface formed when a thick solid crust was broken up by continued movement of still molten magma beneath. These are called "aa" flows and they look almost like fields of black rubble. Other flows have a smooth, ropy-looking surface which develops when a thin, quietly flowing stream of lava begins to freeze at the surface, forming a solid skin which then wrinkles as it is carried along by the still flowing lava beneath. These are called "pahoehoe" flows. "Aa" and "pahoehoe" are Hawaiian words used by the natives there to describe the basalt lava flows on their islands. Although they look very different, "aa" and "pahoehoe" flows are actually made of exactly the same kind of rock; the distinctions between them are the result of their having been erupted under slightly different circumstances. Sometimes both kinds of surface can be seen on different parts of the same lava flow.

Lava flows frequently have tunnels in them, formed when molten lava within the flows runs out from under a solid crust leaving the flow hollow inside. Some of these are big enough to enter and walk in but most are much smaller. Inner surfaces of lava tunnels, especially the smaller ones, are often very fancy, being covered with fantastic drippings of basalt. Look at these by getting down near the ground and peeking into the small hollow places under the surface crust of the flow. A flashlight helps.

Pressure ridges form when the surface crust of a lava flow is pushed up as the molten material beneath carries it along while it continues to flow. These look like long, narrow bulges in the flow and they usually have cracks running along their crusts. Pasty molten lava often has squeezed up through the cracks making bulges that suggest black bread dough.

Craters of the Moon National Monument has a name that can be misleading if not properly understood. The round craters seen on the moon through a telescope are not volcanic. They are explosion craters formed when large meteorites hit the moon and exploded on

Spatter cones in Craters of the Moon National Monument formed as globs of molten magma blown out of the vent welded themselves together to build a chimney.

impact. These have nothing to do with the features in the national monument.

But the floors of the largest craters on the moon are filled with large basalt lava flows that do have surface features resembling some of those in Craters of the Moon National Monument, so much so that this area has been used as one of the training grounds for astronauts who study geology before they go to the moon. The black spots that make up the "man in the moon" are large explosion craters floored with black basalt lava flows similar to those in the national monument. Most of the rocks brought back from the moon by returning astronauts have turned out to be basalt very much like that in Craters of the Moon National Monument.

For more information on flood basalts of the Snake River Plain, see
Interstate 80 N: Twin Falls — Boise
U.S. 20: Idaho Falls — Arco

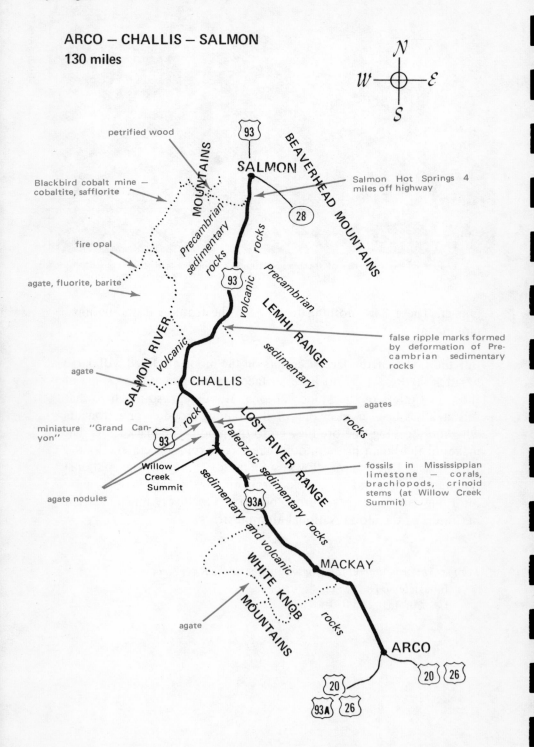

ARCO – CHALLIS – SALMON
130 miles

93 93A

N
W —⊕— E
S

petrified wood

Blackbird cobalt mine —
cobaltite, safflorite

fire opal

agate, fluorite, barite

agate

miniature "Grand Canyon"

agate nodules

SALMON

93

28

Salmon Hot Springs 4
miles off highway

BEAVERHEAD MOUNTAINS

Precambrian sedimentary rocks

93

volcanic rocks

LEMHI RANGE

Precambrian

false ripple marks formed
by deformation of Pre-
cambrian sedimentary
rocks

sedimentary

SALMON RIVER MOUNTAINS

volcanic

CHALLIS

rock

93

agates

LOST RIVER RANGE

rocks

Paleozoic sedimentary rocks

Willow
Creek
Summit

sedimentary and volcanic rocks

93A

fossils in Mississippian
limestone — corals,
brachiopods, crinoid
stems (at Willow Creek
Summit)

MACKAY

WHITE KNOB
MOUNTAINS

rocks

agate

ARCO

20

20 26

93A 26

180

U.S. 93A, 93

ARCO – CHALLIS – SALMON

Between Arco and Mackay the road crosses basalt lava flows on the northern edge of the Snake River Plain. Most of these have acquired enough soil to support some vegetation so the basalt is exposed in only a few places.

From Mackay to Willow Creek Summit the highway follows the valley of the Big Lost River, so named because it completely disappears near Arco where the water soaks into the porous lavas of the Snake River Plain.

East of the highway between Mackay and Willow Creek Summit is the Big Lost River Range which includes the highest peaks in Idaho. They are made almost entirely of Paleozoic sedimentary rocks (mostly limestones) laid down in shallow seas between 500 and 200 million years ago and then slowly folded and broken by faults as the Rocky Mountains were formed during the past 70 million years. In a few places where the trees are thinnest you can see folded beds of limestone from the road.

The Big Lost River Range is highest toward its northern end where its western slope is flanked by some of the most spectacular alluvial fans in the northwest. The road is built along their slopes high above the river which the fans have pushed to the western side of its valley.

West of the highway between Mackay and Willow Creek Summit are mountains similar geologically to the Big Lost River Range even though not nearly as high. In quite a few places, especially near Mackay, it is possible to see folded beds of limestone from the road. Watch for wrinkled layers of rock in low, grass-covered hills.

Very high, jagged peaks can occasionally be glimpsed in the far distance west of the highway; these are in the Sawtooth Range near Sun Valley. They are composed of granites, gneisses and schists formed about 80 million years ago.

About halfway between Willow Creek Summit and Challis, the road winds for a mile through a spectacular small canyon eroded into limestones and dolomites originally deposited in a shallow sea about 375 million years ago (Paleozoic, Devonian Period). These rocks are very black because they are full of organic material. They actually stink when freshly broken. Apparently they were deposited on a stagnant bottom. There aren't very many fossils here but a few nice brachiopods (superficially clam-like shells) can be found with a little patience.

This picturesque little canyon is geologically interesting because the tiny stream that eroded it cut right through a hill of limestone instead of taking a much easier route through softer materials a short distance to the east. Apparently the hill is actually a very old one which was buried under much younger (Tertiary) sands and gravels and then exhumed as these were subsequently eroded away. The stream that cut the canyon began flowing on the younger sediments while the hill was still completely buried and then sawed the gorge down through it as the hill was exhumed.

Between Challis and Salmon, most of the outcrops are light-colored volcanic rocks laid down between 50 and 80 million years ago. These were deposited on top of an older landscape eroded into complexly folded Precambrian sedimentary rocks. Streams have now carved a new landscape in the volcanic rocks, cutting right down through them in places so the older rocks beneath can occasionally be seen along the river. These are much harder to erode than the volcanic rocks so the river passes through the older Precambrian rocks in narrow canyons.

One of the best places to stop and look at the Precambrian rocks is at the little community of Ellis where the Pahsimeroi River joins the Salmon. Immediately north of Ellis steeply dipping beds of black Precambrian slate contain innumerable miniature faults, each offsetting the layers a fraction of an inch, making them look almost as though they contained ripple marks. At the north edge of this roadcut are some mudcracks which have been stretched as the rocks were deformed so that they are now long and narrow instead of blocky in outline.

Volcanic rocks along this road come in many shades of gray, pink, yellow, and red. Occasional cliffs are stained bright green by copper minerals. Most of these rocks have very thick layers and are rather soft. Many of them contain beautiful little crystals of quartz and a few contain large, perfectly cubic crystals of brassy yellow pyrite as much as an inch across.

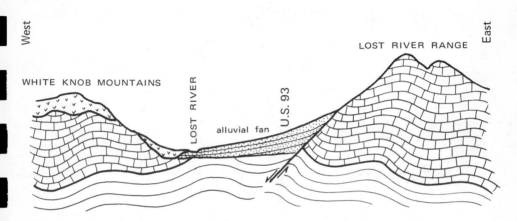

West-east cross section across the line of U.S. 93 south of Willow Creek Summit. Large alluvial fans of water-transported sediment shed from the Lost River Range push the river far to the western side of its valley. Uneroded patches of volcanic rocks still cover parts of the White Knob Mountains.

183

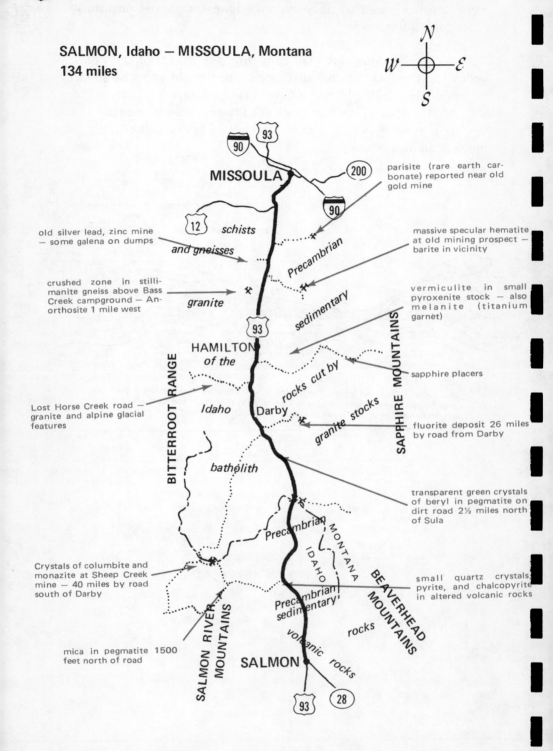

SALMON, Idaho — MISSOULA, Montana
134 miles

parisite (rare earth car-
bonate) reported near old
gold mine

MISSOULA

old silver lead, zinc mine
— some galena on dumps

schists

and gneisses

massive specular hematite
at old mining prospect —
barite in vicinity

Precambrian

crushed zone in stilli-
manite gneiss above Bass
Creek campground — An-
orthosite 1 mile west

granite

sedimentary

vermiculite in small
pyroxenite stock — also
melanite (titanium
garnet)

HAMILTON
of the

sapphire placers

rocks cut by

Idaho   Darby

granite stocks

fluorite deposit 26 miles
by road from Darby

Lost Horse Creek road —
granite and alpine glacial
features

BITTERROOT RANGE

SAPPHIRE MOUNTAINS

batholith

transparent green crystals
of beryl in pegmatite on
dirt road 2½ miles north
of Sula

Precambrian

Crystals of columbite and
monazite at Sheep Creek
mine — 40 miles by road
south of Darby

MONTANA
IDAHO

small quartz crystals,
pyrite, and chalcopyrite
in altered volcanic rocks

SALMON RIVER MOUNTAINS

BEAVERHEAD MOUNTAINS

Precambrian
sedimentary

rocks

mica in pegmatite 1500
feet north of road

volcanic rocks

SALMON

184

U.S. 93

SALMON – MISSOULA

Between Salmon and Darby, Montana the rocks along the road are mostly light-colored volcanics erupted between 20 and 30 million years ago on top of a landscape that had been eroded onto folded Precambrian sedimentary rocks. Modern streams are cutting down through the volcanic rocks, back into the older rocks beneath them, now being exposed by erosion for a second time.

The volcanics can be recognized from a distance as yellow, pink, tan, or gray rocks with very little layering in them. They tend to form rather softly rounded outcrops. Precambrian sedimentary rocks beneath are much harder and contain easily visible sedimentary layers likely to be tilted at almost any angle.

Between Salmon and a few miles north of Lost Trail Pass, much of the volcanic material has been eroded away and the older Precambrian sedimentary rocks are well exposed in many places. Between Lost Trail Pass and south of Darby most of the outcrops are volcanic rocks and the older rocks beneath are seldom seen. Dense forest in the mountains makes rocks of any kind difficult to spot from the road over the pass.

People interested in looking at gneisses, schists, and granite will enjoy taking a side trip down the North Fork of the Salmon River by turning west onto a gravel road at the community of North Fork, 19 miles north of Salmon. Most of the rocks exposed along this road are gneisses and schists; their banded structure gives them the appearance of having a "grain." These are metamorphic rocks formed when granites and Precambrian sedimentary rocks were strongly heated and recrystallized. Some of them still retain ghostly vestiges of their original sedimentary appearance. The Idaho batholith, one of the world's largest bodies of granite, lies a short distance west of this country and considerable quantities of molten granite magma were squirted into the metamorphic rocks while it was forming, mainly between 70 and 90 million years ago. The granite can be recognized as a pink or gray rock, almost structureless and lacking "grain." Both granites and gneisses contain the same minerals — quartz, pink and white feldspar and black mica or hornblende. In some roadcuts near the old gold mining town of Shoup there are rocks which look like granite and gneiss stirred together to give them an appearance suggestive of marble cake. These form when the gneiss gets so hot that it begins to melt into granite magma.

An added, non-geologic attraction to the side trip west from North Fork is provided by several rock shelters along the road once lived in by Indians. These have been partially excavated by archeologists exposing the layers of debris that accumulated as garbage while the shelters were inhabited. Indian paintings done in red ocher adorn the walls.

Members of the Lewis and Clark expedition explored part of the Salmon River Valley along the present route of U.S. 93. Captain Clark is known to have visited Wagonhammer Spring where good exposures of the Precambrian sedimentary rock underlie the volcanics. Lost Trail Pass gets its name from the fact that the Lewis and Clark expedition got lost there and had trouble finding the right pass.

Between Lost Trail Pass and Hamilton there are magnificent views of the Bitterroot Mountains west of the highway. These are made of granites belonging to the Idaho batholith. Valleys in the Bitterroot Range were filled by large glaciers during the last ice age when the wonderful alpine scenery we see today was carved.

Patches of yellowish-white volcanic rocks near the road one mile north of Darby were erupted only about 25 million years ago.

Most of the Bitterroot Range is roadless and impenetrable except on foot or horseback. One of the few good roads into the range is the one up Lost Horse Canyon. It turns west from U.S. 93 at milepost 38 between Darby and Hamilton. As this road approaches the mountains, it winds across large glacial moraines marking the edge of a large glacier that poked its snout several miles out onto the floor of the canyon during the last ice age. Lost Horse Canyon is an outstanding example of how a large glacier improves the splendor of a mountain valley. The bedrock is entirely granite of the Idaho batholith which is crossed by only a few good roads; most of its 14,000-square-mile outcrop area is in primitive country.

On the east side of the Bitterroot Valley is the Sapphire Range, composed of folded Precambrian sedimentary rocks intruded by small masses of granite magma during the time the Rocky Mountains were forming. The range gets its name from the commercial gem sapphire placers on its eastern slope in the West Fork of Rock Creek. They can be reached by taking Montana 38 west from U.S. 93 at the intersection 4 miles south of Hamilton. The placer claims are privately owned but some of the operators welcome visitors who wish to pay a fee ($1.50 per bucket of gravel in 1971) for panning privileges. Like many other Montana Sapphires, the stones from these placers are mostly green and light "cornflower" blue.

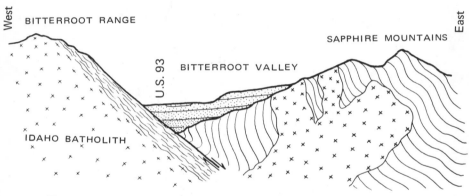

West-east cross section across the Bitterroot Valley near Hamilton. The Bitterroot Valley is a trough formed when the Sapphire and Bitterroot mountain ranges moved along a fault. Uneroded remnants of Tertiary valley-fill form the grassy "foothills" along the base of the Sapphire Mountains.

Between Hamilton and the north end of the Bitterroot Valley near Missoula, the road passes through the lush Bitterroot Valley between the Bitterroot and Sapphire Ranges. All the roadcuts along the highway are in Tertiary valley-fill sediments, and gravels washed out of the canyons of the Bitterroot Range during the last ice age.

Between Lolo and Missoula the road follows the valley of the Bitterroot River past large roadcuts in red and green Precambrian mudstones. A large fault closely parallels this section of the highway and the rocks in the roadcuts are broken and crushed because of movements along the fault.

For more information on granites of the Idaho batholith, see
Idaho 15: Boise – New Meadows

MISSOULA – KALISPELL
121 miles

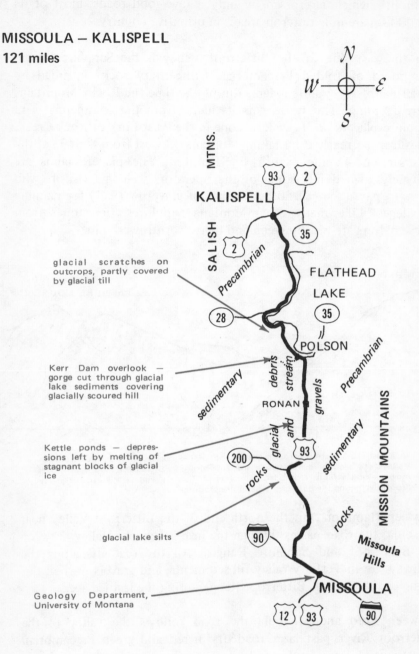

MTNS.

93   2

KALISPELL

SALISH

2   Precambrian

35

FLATHEAD

LAKE

glacial scratches on outcrops, partly covered by glacial till

28   35

Precambrian

POLSON

Kerr Dam overlook – gorge cut through glacial lake sediments covering glacially scoured hill

sedimentary   debris stream   gravels

RONAN

Kettle ponds – depressions left by melting of stagnant blocks of glacial ice

glacial and

93   sedimentary

200

rocks

glacial lake silts

90   rocks

Missoula Hills

MISSION MOUNTAINS

Geology Department, University of Montana

MISSOULA

12   93   90

U.S. 93

MISSOULA – KALISPELL

The Missoula Valley is one of the very few intermountain valleys in the entire Rocky Mountain region that runs east-west instead of north-south. Likewise, the high mountain range immediately north of Missoula, which doesn't seem to have any generally accepted name, is one of the few large ranges in the region that run east-west. Probably this has something to do with the fact that an enormous east-west fault with many miles of displacement runs through the Missoula Valley. Movement on this fault appears to have been horizontal and it seems that the Missoula Valley and hills have been dislocated as the mountains to the north moved westward. This is the same fault that Interstate 90 approximately follows all the way from near Helena to near Spokane.

All the bedrock exposed along the road and in the surrounding mountains between Missoula and Kalispell is Precambrian sedimentary rock, mostly limestones and sandstones. These rocks were originally deposited between 500 million and 1500 million years ago and then intensely folded and deformed during the last 70 million years while the northern Rocky Mountains have been forming.

Arlee is in the Jocko Valley, bounded to the east by the softly rounded Jocko Hills which look very different from the angular, jagged mountains on the south side of the valley and the imposing crags of the Mission Range to the northeast. This difference in appearance has nothing to do with the kind of rock the mountains are made of; all the ranges in the area are composed of very similar Precambrian sedimentary rocks. It is simply because the Jocko Hills, being relatively low, were not glaciated during the last ice age while the higher ranges in the neighborhood were. Had there never been an ice age, all the ranges in the northern Rocky Mountains would today have the same kind of gently rounded shape we see in the Jocko Hills.

Glacially-carved peaks of the southern Mission Range between Missoula and Polson. The big hole scooped in the top of the peak at left is a cirque, one of the typical landforms created by glacial erosion.

Near the end of the last ice age, about 12,000 years ago, the icy waters of Glacial Lake Missoula filled the Jocko and Mission Valleys. Large quantities of pulverized rock flour released from melting glaciers to the north were carried into the lake and slowly settled to the bottom. Now that the lake is gone, these deposits make extensive, level surfaces in the lower part of the Jocko Valley. A large roadcut through them about halfway between Arlee and Ravalli Junction stands as a white bluff on the east side of the highway. The soft lake silts in this roadcut contain layers recording the history of Glacial Lake Missoula. Especially interesting are the varves, thin alternating light and darker bands that can be found by digging into the weathered surface of the exposure. The light bands are silt dumped into the lake as ice melted during the summer and the darker bands are organic remains that settled to the bottom during the long, ice age winters.

Between St. Ignatius and Polson, U.S. 93 runs the length of the Mission Valley, the southernmost end of what geologists call the Rocky Mountain Trench, a fault-block valley that extends continuously for more than 800 miles into northern British Columbia.

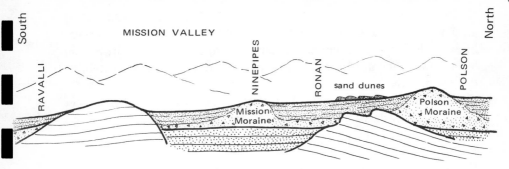

MISSION VALLEY

RAVALLI

NINEPIPES

RONAN

sand dunes

POLSON

Mission Moraine

Polson Moraine

South-north cross section along the Mission Valley (Rocky Mountain Trench) showing glacial deposits on top of valley fill and Precambrian sedimentary rocks. The Mission Moraine is partially buried beneath water-transported outwash derived from the younger Polson Moraine.

Bounding the eastern margin of this valley is the Mission Range, a great slab of Precambrian sedimentary rock, mostly limestone, spectacularly lifted up on a fault that runs along the straight western face of the range. The face of the mountains as seen from the road is very steep, partly because it is the fault surface — now carved by erosion. The craggy alpine topography of the Mission Range shows clearly that there were enormous glaciers in its valleys during the last ice age. A few very small ones that still remain appear as white patches on the high peaks during the late summer.

An enormous glacier filled the Rocky Mountain Trench during the last ice age. Most of the ice formed far to the north in British Columbia and flowed southward almost to St. Ignatius before finally reaching a climate warm enough to melt the ice front as fast as it advanced. Numerous small ponds around Ninepipes National Wildlife Refuge about 8 miles north of St. Ignatius mark places where large blocks of ice buried within the terminal moraine later melted to form sinkholes.

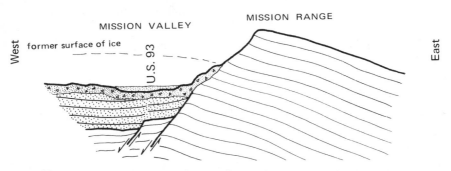

MISSION RANGE

MISSION VALLEY

West

former surface of ice

U.S. 93

East

West-east cross section across the line of U.S. 93 near Ronan. The Mission Range is a great block of Precambrian sedimentary rock lifted up along a fault next to the Mission Valley, the southernmost part of the Rocky Mountain Trench.

191

Melting glaciers leave behind a dismal landscape of sand and watery mud swept by a wind of cold air draining off the remaining ice. Frequently the wind whips the sand up into dunes that drift along for a few years until a growth of plants can get started to stabilize the sand. The little hills covered with shrubby pine trees in the vicinity of Pablo, 7 miles south of Polson, are old sand dunes formed in this way while the big glacier was melting about 10,000 years ago.

Approximately opposite Ronan, 12 miles south of Polson, the Mission Range abruptly changes in appearance. South of Ronan it has the angular and craggy profile typical of mountains that were filled with glaciers during the last ice age. To the north, the Mission Range is rather smooth and gently rounded. The smooth northern part of the Mission Range was completely buried under the ice of the Rocky Mountain Trench glacier. That ice must have been thousands of feet thick!

Polson is on the south shore of Flathead Lake immediately north of the big Polson Moraine which runs as a sizeable ridge completely across the valley from the Mission Range on the east to the outposts of the Salish Range on the west. This moraine marks the southern end of the ice during the last of at least three major glacial advances.

Flathead Lake was originally impounded by the Polson Moraine which functioned as a giant natural earth-fill dam across the valley. Lake water overflowed the top of the moraine to form the southern extension of the Flathead River which promptly began cutting a gorge down through the moraine to drain the lake. It would have succeeded in doing this long ago had the river not happened into a course directly above a buried hill of Precambrian sandstone. As soon as the gorge was cut down through the soft glacial deposits to the level of the buried hill, the river suddenly found itself faced with the task of cutting the rest of the gorge through very hard rock. It has been busily sawing away for 10,000 years now; meanwhile Flathead Lake has survived. Kerr Dam, 7 miles southwest of Polson, is built in the gorge the river has cut through the sandstone hill.

North of Polson, U.S. 93 follows the west shore of Flathead Lake, passing roadcuts in hard Precambrian sedimentary rock and in glacial debris plastered on top of the landscape during the last ice age. In several roadcuts the bouldery glacial debris rests directly on Precambrian rocks. The upper surface of the bedrock roadcuts in these exposures is polished and grooved where the glacier dragged hard rocks embedded in its sole across the bedrock surface. Look in the glacial deposits for rocks with flat surfaces covered with scratches. These were the ones dragged across the bedrock by the glacier. Only glaciers shape rocks in this way.

Chief Cliff stands boldly above the west side of Flathead Lake a short distance north of the community of Elmo. Actually an old river bluff, it stood above a large stream that once flowed here along the edge of the glacier. The stream disappeared when the ice melted about 10,000 years ago but its channel can still be seen by climbing west from the road up to the base of Chief Cliff.

Wildhorse Island, almost directly west of Elmo, is so large that it can easily be mistaken for part of the mainland shore. The rocky hills on Wildhorse Island, like many others in this area, have been sculptured by flowing glacial ice giving them a distinctly streamlined appearance; gently sloping on their northern sides and steep on their southern sides. A herd of wild horses that gave the island its name was removed years ago because they were drastically overgrazing the range. A large herd of Rocky Mountain Sheep roam the island today.

Between the north end of Flathead Lake and Kalispell, U.S. 93 crosses deposits of glacial debris left thickly blanketing the floor of the Flathead Valley when the ice melted at the end of the last ice age. The Flathead Valley, like the Mission Valley to the south, is part of the Rocky Mountain Trench.

For more information on continental ice age glaciers, see
     Glacier National Park (after U.S. 89: Great Falls — Browning)
     U.S. 93: Kalispell — Eureka

For more information on ice age glacial lakes (Glacial Lake Missoula), see
     Interstate 90: Missoula — Lookout Pass
     Montana 28: Plains — Elmo
     Montana 200: Ravalli Junction — Sandpoint
     County 382: Perma — Hot Springs

KALISPELL – EUREKA
67 miles

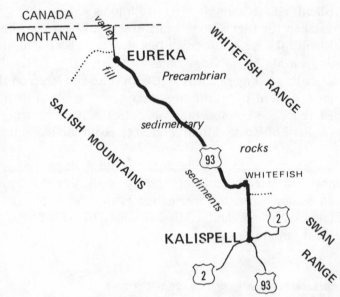

U.S. 93

KALISPELL – EUREKA

From Kalispell to Eureka and on to the Canadian border, U.S. 93 travels through the Flathead Valley which can be followed, under other names, north all the way through British Columbia. Geologists call it the Rocky Mountain Trench.

Ice deeply filled the Flathead Valley during the last ice age, as a massive glacier poured down out of British Columbia as far south as the area south of Flathead Lake. All of the valley floor is deeply covered by debris left behind when the ice melted about 10,000 years ago so the Tertiary valley-fill deposits are now buried.

Numerous lakes along the road owe their origin to the glacier in one way or another. The bigger ones occupy basins gouged out by the ice, then dammed by debris as the ice melted. Must of the small ponds are in places where large blocks of ice were buried in the glacial sediment and then later melted forming sinkholes.

A vivid impression of the depth of the ice that once occupied this valley can be gained by looking north from Whitefish toward Big Mountain, recognizeable by the ski runs and letter "W" on its south face. Big Mountain's lower slopes are thickly forested while the upper ones are rocky and support only scattered forest. The break in topography is at about the lower end of the ski runs. The lower, forested slopes are plastered with glacial debris while the higher, more open, ones are not. Therefore, the former depth of the ice is right at the level where the appearance of the mountain changes. Imagine the entire valley below this level filled with a solid mass of slowly flowing ice!

Between Whitefish and Eureka the valley is heavily forested, as are the mountains, and very little can be seen of the geology. The big mountains east of the highway are the Whitefish Range while the less imposing ones in the distance to the west are known as the Salish Mountains. Like all the mountains in northwestern Montana, these are made entirely of Precambrian sedimentary rocks — sandstones, mudstones, and limestones.

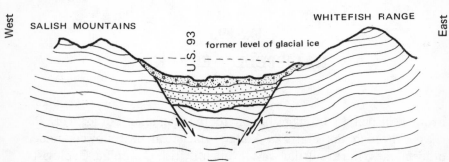

West-east cross section across the line of U.S. 93 between Kalispell and Eureka. The Flathead Valley (Rocky Mountain Trench) is a block of the crust let down along faults. Glacial debris completely covers Tertiary valley-fill sediments in the floor of the valley.

Between Eureka and the Canadian border, U.S. 93 passes through a truly spectacular field of drumlins. These streamlined hills form when a moving glacier plasters mud and boulders onto the ground and then shapes the deposit by flowing over it. Drumlins are always long and narrow with a blunt end facing in the direction from which the ice came and a long, sloping tail dragging out downstream. Since these drumlins have their blunt ends facing north, we can be sure that the ice in this valley flowed from north to south — not a very surprising conclusion. Drumlins usually occur in groups and have sometimes been compared to a herd of giant tadpoles swimming upstream under the ice. Numerous drumlins are found in some of the middle western and northeastern states but these are among the few really good ones in the entire northern Rocky Mountain region.

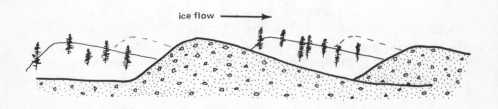

Cross section of drumlins showing how the glacial debris of which they are made is streamlined as it is plastered onto the ground beneath the flowing ice of a large glacier.

Mudcracks (lower left) and ripple marks preserved in the surface of thin slab of Precambrian mudstone preserve memories of mudflats that held pools of water after a rain, then dried in the baking sun more than a billion years ago. Approximately natural size.

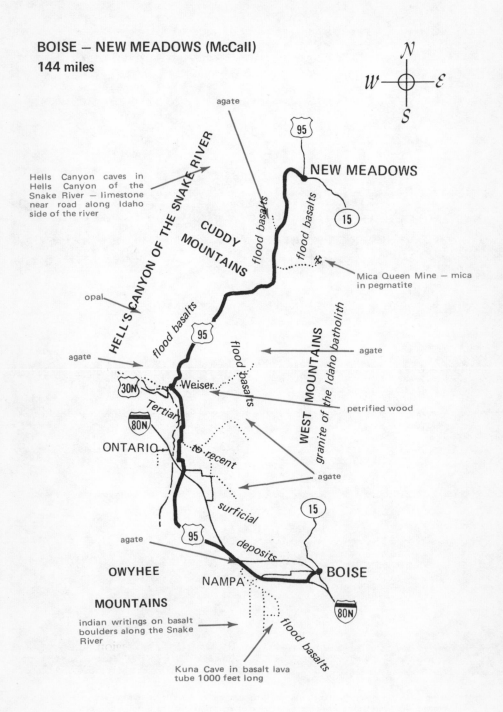

BOISE — NEW MEADOWS (McCall)
144 miles

N
W — E
S

agate

95

NEW MEADOWS

15

Hells Canyon caves in Hells Canyon of the Snake River — limestone near road along Idaho side of the river

flood basalts

flood basalts

CUDDY MOUNTAINS

HELL'S CANYON OF THE SNAKE RIVER

Mica Queen Mine — mica in pegmatite

opal

flood basalts

95

agate

flood basalts

WEST MOUNTAINS

granite of the Idaho batholith

agate

30N

Weiser

petrified wood

Tertiary

80N

ONTARIO

to recent

agate

15

surficial

95

agate

deposits

BOISE

OWYHEE

NAMPA

MOUNTAINS

80N

indian writings on basalt boulders along the Snake River

flood basalts

Kuna Cave in basalt lava tube 1000 feet long

U.S. 95 – Interstate 80N
BOISE – NEW MEADOWS

Boise is at the western tip of the Snake River Plain and near the southeastern margin of the Columbia Plateau. Both are high plateaus built up of layers of flood basalt lava flows erupted from long fissures in the earth's crust. Black basalt lava flows belonging to both plateaus can be seen near Boise.

Interstate 80N between Boise and Ontario passes through the major population center of Idaho. At least part of the rich soils of the area were deposited during periods when this area was a lake because the drainage had been blocked by lava flows.

The mountain range on the distant skyline to the southwest is called the Owyhee Mountains. They are made of granite extensively covered by volcanic rocks and were once the site of large silver mines near the ghost town of Silver City. Rising to the northeast are the West Mountains, made of granites belonging to the enormous Idaho batholith.

The oldest rocks in this region are Paleozoic sedimentary rocks laid down between 225 and 600 million years ago and then folded and intruded by molten granite magma between 60 and 90 million years ago early in the formation of the Rocky Mountains. An incredible quantity of granite magma rose into the crust of this region at that time. It cooled to form the immense Idaho batholith which extends northeastward from Boise all the way across central Idaho into Montana, covering a total area of about 14,000 square miles. The granites in the Owyhee Mountains were intruded about the same time and are probably closely related to those in the Idaho batholith.

After the granites and folded sedimentary rocks had been exposed and carved into mountains by erosion, they were thickly blanketed by light-colored volcanic rocks. These have been largely removed by erosion but still remain in places, capping some of the mountains and filling old valleys.

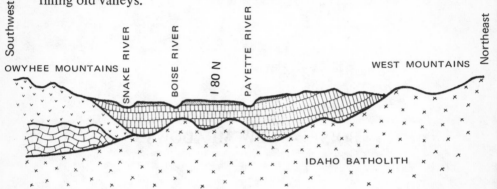

Southwest-northeast cross section across the line of Interstate 80 N showing basalt lava flows burying an older landscape eroded onto granite of the Idaho batholith.

About 40 million years ago eruption of the Columbia River basalt lava floods began from a series of north-south trending fissures running through eastern Oregon and Washington. Flows continued to pile up for about 25 million years until they finally covered much of eastern Washington and Oregon as well as the western edge of Idaho. These Columbia River basalt flows have been deeply carved by stream erosion during the 15 million years that have passed since the eruptions ceased.

About 2 or 3 million years ago another series of very large basalt eruptions began in southern Idaho, building up the Snake River Plain and burying still more of the older landscape. These eruptions have continued into very recent times and there is no reason to suppose that there will not be more in the future.

Between Ontario and New Meadows, U.S. 95 crosses basalt lava flows belonging to the older Columbia River Plateau. The youngest of these are probably a little less than 15 million years old so there has been plenty of time for an erosional landscape to develop. The fissures from which the flows were erupted are crossed by the highway between Weiser and New Meadows. They are now filled with basalt and mostly covered by soil so few can be seen from the road.

Hills west of U.S. 95 about halfway between Weiser and New Meadows are the Cuddy Mountains, an island of older granite rising above a sea of basalt. They were a high group of hills on the older landscape eroded before the basalt eruptions began and the lava flows never piled up deep enough to bury them.

Most freshly erupted lavas are full of holes and many of them bury logs and occasionally standing trees. With passage of time the holes frequently fill with agate and the buried wood becomes petrified. Lava flows on the Columbia Plateau are old enough for these processes to have run their course and eroded enough that the agate and petrified wood is now exposed at the surface. In numerous places on the Columbia Plateau these materials occur in the basalt or the soil covering it and pebbles are frequently found in stream gravels.

For more information on flood basalts of the Snake River Plain, see
    Interstate 80 N: Twin Falls — Boise
    U.S. 20: Idaho Falls — Arco
    U.S. 93 A: Shoshone — Arco; Craters of the Moon

For more information on flood basalts on the Columbia River Plateau, see
    U.S. 12: Kooskia — Lewiston
    U.S. 95: Lewiston — Coeur d'Alene
    U.S. 195: Lewiston — Spokane

NEW MEADOWS (McCall) — LEWISTON
149 miles

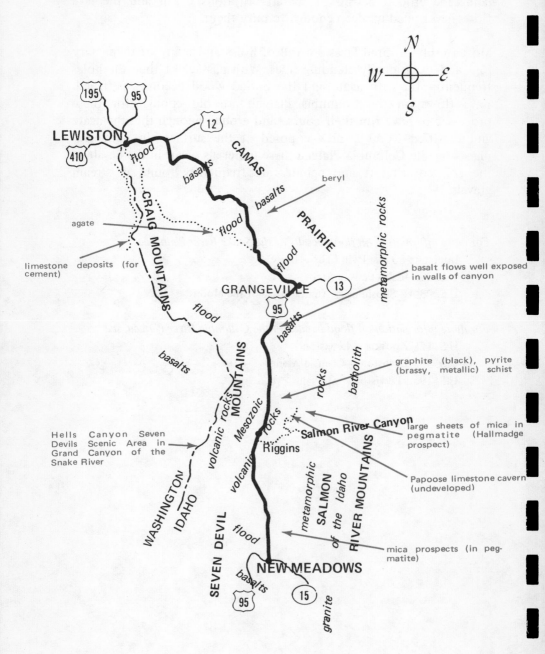

195   95

LEWISTON

410

12

CAMAS

flood

basalts

basalts

beryl

PRAIRIE

agate

flood

metamorphic rocks

limestone deposits (for cement)

CRAIG MOUNTAINS

flood

GRANGEVILLE

13

95

basalt flows well exposed in walls of canyon

flood

basalts

basalts

batholith

rocks

MOUNTAINS

graphite (black), pyrite (brassy, metallic) schist

Hells Canyon Seven Devils Scenic Area in Grand Canyon of the Snake River

volcanic rocks

Mesozoic rocks

Salmon River Canyon

Riggins

large sheets of mica in pegmatite (Hallmadge prospect)

Papoose limestone cavern (undeveloped)

WASHINGTON   IDAHO

volcanic rocks

metamorphic   SALMON   of the Idaho   RIVER MOUNTAINS

flood

mica prospects (in pegmatite)

SEVEN DEVIL

NEW MEADOWS

basalts

95

15

granite

U.S. 95

NEW MEADOWS — LEWISTON

Between New Meadows and Lewiston, U.S. 95 follows a route close to the eastern margin of the Columbia Plateau that was built up layer by layer of large basalt lava flows erupted between 40 and 15 million years ago.

During the 15 million years that have passed since the eruptions ceased, the rivers in this area have cut canyons that bite deeply into the lava flows and in some cases all the way through them into the older rocks beneath. So now the tops of the mountains are capped by lava flows while older rocks are exposed in the deeper canyons. New Meadows is located on one of the high remnants of the eastern margin of the Columbia Plateau.

Between New Meadows and Riggins, the highway follows a canyon the Little Salmon River cut through the black basalt lava flows into the older rocks beneath. In this area, these older rocks are a complicated mixture of sedimentary and volcanic materials originally laid down between 300 and 200 million years ago during late Paleozoic and early Mesozoic Time. They were then tightly folded and intruded by molten granite mgmas between 100 and 70 million years ago while the Rocky Mountains were beginning to form and the granites of the Idaho batholith were rising into the earth's crust a short distance to the east. After they had been folded, these older rocks were carved into mountains by streams and then buried by the basalt lava flows that built up the Columbia Plateau. Now the basalt is being eroded away and the older rocks are once again being exposed and carved into mountains by streams.

For 30 miles north of Riggins, U.S. 95 winds along through the bottom of the deep chasm of the Salmon River past exposures of the older rocks. That basalt lava flows cap the high hills above the canyon has to be taken on faith because they can hardly be seen from the road. West of the river are the Seven Devils Mountains. They form the ridge between the canyon of the Salmon River and the even deeper Hells Canyon of the Snake River about 20 miles to the west.

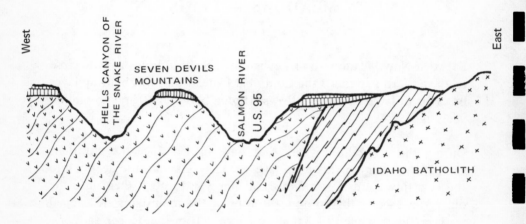

West-east cross section across the line of U.S. 95 between Riggins and Whitebird. The Snake and Salmon Rivers have cut deep canyons down through the basalt lava flows of the Columbia River Plateau, deep into folded Paleozoic volcanic rocks beneath. Remnants of the lava flows cap the higher hills.

The folded Paleozoic sedimentary and volcanic rocks in the walls of the Canyon of the Salmon River come in various shades of gray. They contain a lot of interesting geologic details but these are hard to see from the road. One that might be worth a stop is a graphite-pyrite schist which outcrops around the community of Lucile, 11 miles north of Riggins.

Between 10 and 20 miles south of Grangeville, U.S. 95 ascends the wall of the Salmon River Canyon to the top of the Columbia Plateau by going up White Bird Hill on what must surely be one of the most hair-raising stretches of paved road in the country. It is interesting to reflect, between switchbacks, upon the fact that such a canyon could be eroded in less than 15 million years. It testifies both to the great things done by the slow processes of erosion and to the fact that 15 million years is a very long time indeed.

Grangeville, like New Meadows, is on the Columbia River Plateau. The descent from the high surface at Grangeville to the deep canyon of the Clearwater River at Lewiston is accomplished considerably more gracefully than that to the canyon of the Salmon River at the base of White Bird Hill. U.S. 95 stays on the black basalts of the Columbia Plateau all the way from Grangeville to Lewiston. Over much of the distance they are thinly covered by wind-blown silts.

For more information on flood basalts of the Columbia River Plateau, see
    U.S. 12: Kooskia – Lewiston
    U.S. 95: Lewiston – Coeur d'Alene
    U.S. 195: Lewiston – Spokane

Basalt lava flows break into vertical columns as shrinkage cracks develop in the cooling rock. These may be any size from that of a fencepost to a large log.

LEWISTON – COEUR d'ALENE
112 miles

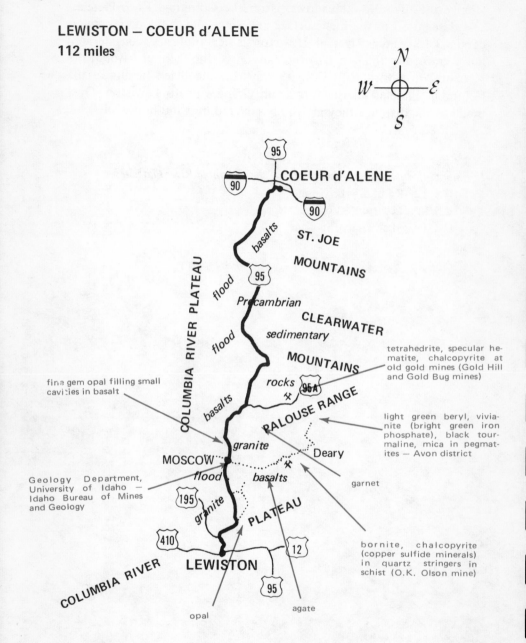

N
W — E
S

95

90 COEUR d'ALENE

90

basalts

ST. JOE

MOUNTAINS

95

flood

Precambrian

CLEARWATER

flood

sedimentary

MOUNTAINS

COLUMBIA RIVER PLATEAU

rocks

tetrahedrite, specular hematite, chalcopyrite at old gold mines (Gold Hill and Gold Bug mines)

fine gem opal filling small cavities in basalt

basalts

95A

PALOUSE RANGE

Deary

light green beryl, vivianite (bright green iron phosphate), black tourmaline, mica in pegmatites — Avon district

granite

MOSCOW

Geology Department, University of Idaho — Idaho Bureau of Mines and Geology

flood

basalts

garnet

195

granite

PLATEAU

410

12

bornite, chalcopyrite (copper sulfide minerals) in quartz stringers in schist (O.K. Olson mine)

LEWISTON

COLUMBIA RIVER

95

opal

agate

U.S. 95

LEWISTON — COEUR D'ALENE

Between Lewiston and Coeur d'Alene, U.S. 95 follows near the eastern edge of the Columbia River Plateau, crossing back and forth between the basalt lava flows and the older rocks they partially cover.

Precambrian mudstones and sandstones originally laid down between 600 and 1500 million years ago are the oldest rocks in this area. These were complexly folded and intruded by large masses of molten granite magma about 60 to 80 million years ago while the Rocky Mountains were beginning to form. A long period of erosion followed during which streams laid the folded sedimentary rocks and granites bare and carved deep valleys into them to make the region mountainous. Then between about 40 and 15 million years ago, a long series of enormous eruptions of molten basalt magma laid down the lava flows to build the Columbia River Plateau and bury much of the older landscape. During the last 15 million years, streams have carved new valleys down into the black basalt lava flows, exposing once again the older rocks beneath them.

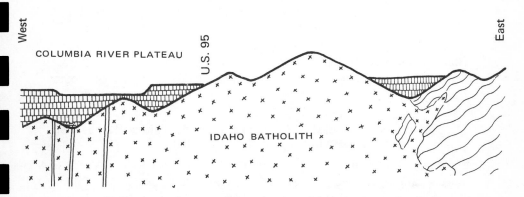

West-east cross section across the line of U.S. 95 north of Moscow. Lava flows of the Columbia River Plateau lap onto an older landscape eroded onto granite intruded into Precambrian sedimentary rocks.

Lewiston is in a deep canyon cut into the basalt lava flows by the Clearwater River. The highway ascends the north wall of this canyon in an impressive series of switchbacks through wonderful exposures of the lava flows then stays on basalt lava flows for most of the distance between Lewiston and Moscow. Relatively little of the basalt is actually exposed on the plateau surface because it is deeply covered in most places by thick soil composed mostly of wind-blown silt. This is excellent agricultural land that supports very productive wheat farms.

The north wall of the canyon of the Clearwater River near Lewiston is peppered with little mounds of soil about the size of an average living room and two or three feet high. These can be seen from town and from the road as it climbs the canyon wall. Similar soil mounds occur in many of the drier parts of the Pacific Northwest. Geologists have been intrigued by these for years and have written quite a literature on them in attempting to explain their origin. Approximately the same number of theories exist as there are geologists who have worked on the problem, so obviously no one is quite sure how they got there. Since nothing happening today seems to be creating these mounds, they must be the relic of some process that went on sometime in the past. Some geologists have suggested that they mark spots where bushes once grew and protected the soil beneath them from erosion while others have suggested that they may be giant ant hills and still others have proposed that they formed during a time when the climate was extremely cold.

Starting from a point several miles south of Moscow and extending all the way to Coeur d'Alene, the road passes through uplands eroded in folded Precambrian sedimentary rocks intruded by small bodies of granite which tend to underlie the higher hills. The larger stream and river valleys are filled with basalt lava flows flooded in from the west. These include the Palouse River near Potlatch, Hangman Creek near Tensed, and the larger valley of the St. Joe River south of Coeur d'Alene.

The mountains visible east of the highway are the Palouse Range near Moscow, the St. Joe Mountains close to Coeur d'Alene, and the Clearwater Mountains between Moscow and Coeur d'Alene. All these ranges are geologically similar, being composed of folded Precambrian sedimentary rocks intruded by large quantities of granite. The granites are the western edge of the Idaho batholith which extends eastward all the way into Montana and covers most of central Idaho. It is one of the larger bodies of granite in the world.

No mountain ranges are visible west of the highway because that area is part of the Columbia River Plateau and is underlain entirely by basalt lava flows.

Coeur d'Alene Lake is a glacial lake with a difference. It is actually south of the farthest extent of the glacier responsible for its formation so does not occupy a glacially scoured basin. The glacier came down from the north through the Purcell Trench as far south as the town of Coeur d'Alene where it dumped large quantities of glacial debris across the valley of the St. Joe River. These glacial deposits formed a natural earth-fill dam after the ice had melted, thereby impounding Coeur d'Alene Lake.

For more information on flood basalts of the Columbia River Plateau, see
    U.S. 12: Kooskia — Lewiston
    U.S. 195: Lewiston — Spokane

For more information on continental ice age glaciers, see
    U.S. 93: Missoula — Kalispell
    U.S. 93: Kalispell — Eureka

COEUR d'ALENE – BONNERS FERRY
84 miles

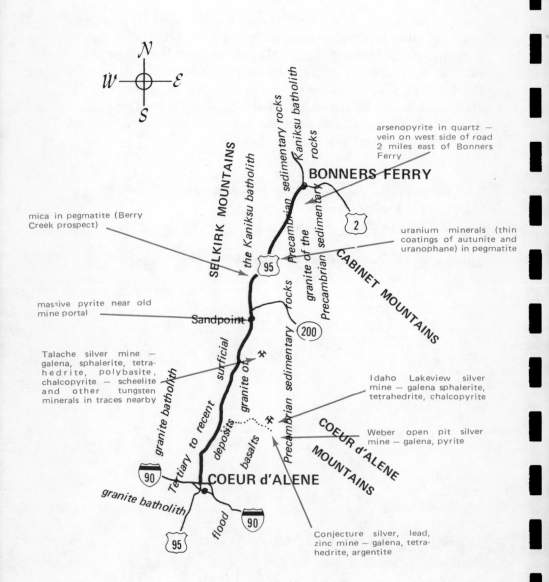

N

W —⊕— E

S

arsenopyrite in quartz — vein on west side of road 2 miles east of Bonners Ferry

BONNERS FERRY

Kaniksu batholith rocks

Precambrian sedimentary rocks

SELKIRK MOUNTAINS

the Kaniksu batholith

mica in pegmatite (Berry Creek prospect)

95

2

uranium minerals (thin coatings of autunite and uranophane) in pegmatite

granite of the Precambrian sedimentary rocks

CABINET MOUNTAINS

massive pyrite near old mine portal

Sandpoint

200

Talache silver mine — galena, sphalerite, tetrahedrite, polybasite, chalcopyrite — scheelite and other tungsten minerals in traces nearby

granite batholith

surficial

granite of

Precambrian sedimentary rocks

Idaho Lakeview silver mine — galena sphalerite, tetrahedrite, chalcopyrite

Tertiary to recent deposits

basalts

Weber open pit silver mine — galena, pyrite

COEUR d'ALENE MOUNTAINS

90

COEUR d'ALENE

granite batholith

flood

90

95

Conjecture silver, lead, zinc mine — galena, tetrahedrite, argentite

U.S. 95

COEUR D'ALENE – BONNERS FERRY

North from Coeur d'Alene, U.S. 95 passes almost 20 miles across the flat surface of Rathdrum Prairie, an extensive lowland that was a lake about 15 or 20 million years ago during the Tertiary Period when the drainage was blocked by lava flows. Rathdrum Prairie held another lake during the last ice age when the drainage was again blocked, this time by glacial ice. The prairie floor is deeply blanketed by glacial debris.

Tertiary Lake Rathdrum, the one dammed by the lava flow, was quite large, extending into the valleys north of Sandpoint and west to the area around Spokane. It also lasted quite a long time, for a lake, and accumulated sediments in its bottom that are now rich collecting grounds for fossil leaves. Most of the good collecting places are west of U.S. 95 in the area around Spokane where the lake beds are not completely buried under later glacial debris.

Rathdrum Prairie is on the eastern margin of the Columbia Plateau, an enormous stack of black, basalt lava flows built up by a long series of eruptions over a period of about 25 million years ending roughly 15 million years ago. The rocks west of Rathdrum Prairie are basalt lava flows; those on the east side are lava flows lapping up against the older rocks that were there long before the flows poured out.

Between the north edge of Rathdrum Prairie and the area just south of Sandpoint, U.S. 95 passes through the Cocolalla Valley between the Cocolalla Hills to the west and the Talache Hills to the east.

Panhandle Idaho contains Precambrian sandstones and mudstones that were intensely folded and broken by faults druing the movements of the earth's crust that affected this area early in the development of the Rocky Mountains between 60 and 90 million years ago. At the same time the Precambrian sedimentary rocks were deformed, they were injected by enormous quantities of molten granite magma that pushed their way upward to form the large Kaniksu batholith as well as many smaller bodies of granite. After the granite was emplaced, the northern panhandle of Idaho was split lengthwise when a long, narrow, north-south valley was let down on faults that run right through the Kaniksu batholith. This valley forms the southern end of the Purcell Trench.

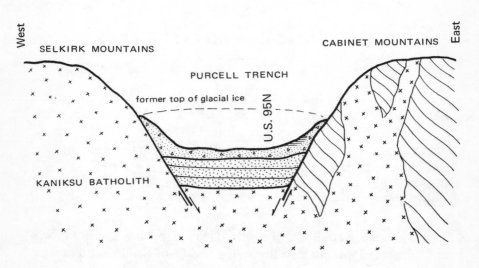

West-east cross section across the line of U.S. 95. The Purcell Trench is let down on faults that run through the Kaniksu batholith between the Selkirk and Cabinet Mountain Ranges. Tertiary valley-fill sediments covered by glacial deposits floor the valley.

The Cocolalla Hills, west of the Cocolalla Valley, are made of granite belonging to the Kaniksu batholith. The Talache Hills, on the east side, are mostly granite but also contain folded Precambrian sedimentary rocks. The Cocolalla Valley itself is a problem because it is obviously too large to have been eroded by the small stream that flows through it today. At one time it must have been the course of a much larger stream. Or it may be a downdropped branch of the Purcell Trench.

Mudcracks (lower left) and ripple marks preserved in the surface of thin slab of Precambrian mudstone preserve memories of mudflats that held pools of water after a rain, then dried in the baking sun more than a billion years ago. Approximately natural size.

BOISE – NEW MEADOWS (McCall)
144 miles

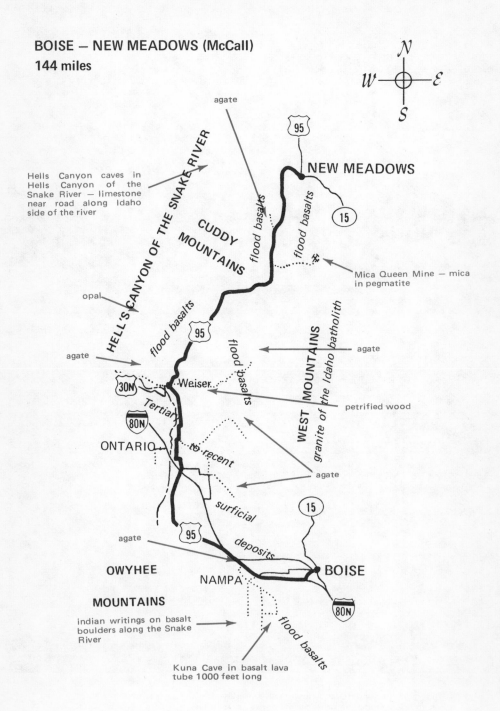

Hells Canyon caves in Hells Canyon of the Snake River – limestone near road along Idaho side of the river

HELL'S CANYON OF THE SNAKE RIVER

CUDDY MOUNTAINS

agate

flood basalts

flood basalts

95

NEW MEADOWS

15

Mica Queen Mine – mica in pegmatite

opal

flood basalts

95

agate

flood basalts

agate

WEST MOUNTAINS
granite of the Idaho batholith

30N

Weiser

petrified wood

Tertiary

80N

ONTARIO

to recent

agate

surficial

15

95

deposits

agate

BOISE

OWYHEE

NAMPA

80N

MOUNTAINS

indian writings on basalt boulders along the Snake River

flood basalts

Kuna Cave in basalt lava tube 1000 feet long

U.S. 95 – Interstate 80N
BOISE – NEW MEADOWS

Boise is at the western tip of the Snake River Plain and near the southeastern margin of the Columbia Plateau. Both are high plateaus built up of layers of flood basalt lava flows erupted from long fissures in the earth's crust. Black basalt lava flows belonging to both plateaus can be seen near Boise.

Interstate 80N between Boise and Ontario passes through the major population center of Idaho. At least part of the rich soils of the area were deposited during periods when this area was a lake because the drainage had been blocked by lava flows.

The mountain range on the distant skyline to the southwest is called the Owyhee Mountains. They are made of granite extensively covered by volcanic rocks and were once the site of large silver mines near the ghost town of Silver City. Rising to the northeast are the West Mountains, made of granites belonging to the enormous Idaho batholith.

The oldest rocks in this region are Paleozoic sedimentary rocks laid down between 225 and 600 million years ago and then folded and intruded by molten granite magma between 60 and 90 million years ago early in the formation of the Rocky Mountains. An incredible quantity of granite magma rose into the crust of this region at that time. It cooled to form the immense Idaho batholith which extends northeastward from Boise all the way across central Idaho into Montana, covering a total area of about 14,000 square miles. The granites in the Owyhee Mountains were intruded about the same time and are probably closely related to those in the Idaho batholith.

After the granites and folded sedimentary rocks had been exposed and carved into mountains by erosion, they were thickly blanketed by light-colored volcanic rocks. These have been largely removed by erosion but still remain in places, capping some of the mountains and filling old valleys.

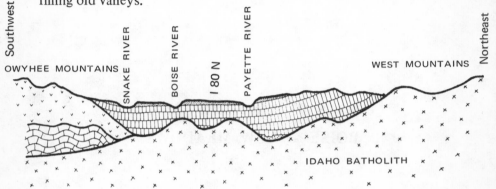

Southwest-northeast cross section across the line of Interstate 80 N showing basalt lava flows burying an older landscape eroded onto granite of the Idaho batholith.

About 40 million years ago eruption of the Columbia River basalt lava floods began from a series of north-south trending fissures running through eastern Oregon and Washington. Flows continued to pile up for about 25 million years until they finally covered much of eastern Washington and Oregon as well as the western edge of Idaho. These Columbia River basalt flows have been deeply carved by stream erosion during the 15 million years that have passed since the eruptions ceased.

About 2 or 3 million years ago another series of very large basalt eruptions began in southern Idaho, building up the Snake River Plain and burying still more of the older landscape. These eruptions have continued into very recent times and there is no reason to suppose that there will not be more in the future.

Between Ontario and New Meadows, U.S. 95 crosses basalt lava flows belonging to the older Columbia River Plateau. The youngest of these are probably a little less than 15 million years old so there has been plenty of time for an erosional landscape to develop. The fissures from which the flows were erupted are crossed by the highway between Weiser and New Meadows. They are now filled with basalt and mostly covered by soil so few can be seen from the road.

200

Hills west of U.S. 95 about halfway between Weiser and New Meadows are the Cuddy Mountains, an island of older granite rising above a sea of basalt. They were a high group of hills on the older landscape eroded before the basalt eruptions began and the lava flows never piled up deep enough to bury them.

Most freshly erupted lavas are full of holes and many of them bury logs and occasionally standing trees. With passage of time the holes frequently fill with agate and the buried wood becomes petrified. Lava flows on the Columbia Plateau are old enough for these processes to have run their course and eroded enough that the agate and petrified wood is now exposed at the surface. In numerous places on the Columbia Plateau these materials occur in the basalt or the soil covering it and pebbles are frequently found in stream gravels.

For more information on flood basalts of the Snake River Plain, see
      Interstate 80 N: Twin Falls – Boise
      U.S. 20: Idaho Falls – Arco
      U.S. 93 A: Shoshone – Arco; Craters of the Moon

For more information on flood basalts on the Columbia River Plateau, see
      U.S. 12: Kooskia – Lewiston
      U.S. 95: Lewiston – Coeur d'Alene
      U.S. 195: Lewiston – Spokane

NEW MEADOWS (McCall) — LEWISTON
149 miles

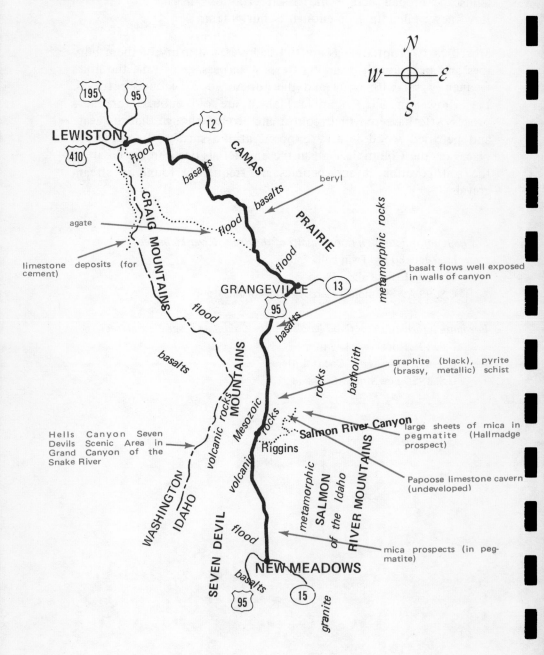

U.S. 95

NEW MEADOWS – LEWISTON

Between New Meadows and Lewiston, U.S. 95 follows a route close to the eastern margin of the Columbia Plateau that was built up layer by layer of large basalt lava flows erupted between 40 and 15 million years ago.

During the 15 million years that have passed since the eruptions ceased, the rivers in this area have cut canyons that bite deeply into the lava flows and in some cases all the way through them into the older rocks beneath. So now the tops of the mountains are capped by lava flows while older rocks are exposed in the deeper canyons. New Meadows is located on one of the high remnants of the eastern margin of the Columbia Plateau.

Between New Meadows and Riggins, the highway follows a canyon the Little Salmon River cut through the black basalt lava flows into the older rocks beneath. In this area, these older rocks are a complicated mixture of sedimentary and volcanic materials originally laid down between 300 and 200 million years ago during late Paleozoic and early Mesozoic Time. They were then tightly folded and intruded by molten granite mgmas between 100 and 70 million years ago while the Rocky Mountains were beginning to form and the granites of the Idaho batholith were rising into the earth's crust a short distance to the east. After they had been folded, these older rocks were carved into mountains by streams and then buried by the basalt lava flows that built up the Columbia Plateau. Now the basalt is being eroded away and the older rocks are once again being exposed and carved into mountains by streams.

For 30 miles north of Riggins, U.S. 95 winds along through the bottom of the deep chasm of the Salmon River past exposures of the older rocks. That basalt lava flows cap the high hills above the canyon has to be taken on faith because they can hardly be seen from the road. West of the river are the Seven Devils Mountains. They form the ridge between the canyon of the Salmon River and the even deeper Hells Canyon of the Snake River about 20 miles to the west.

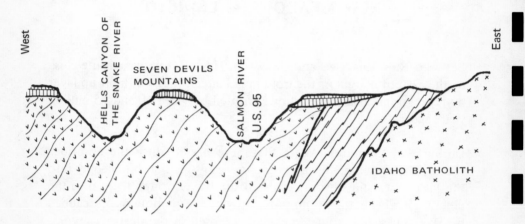

West-east cross section across the line of U.S. 95 between Riggins and Whitebird. The Snake and Salmon Rivers have cut deep canyons down through the basalt lava flows of the Columbia River Plateau, deep into folded Paleozoic volcanic rocks beneath. Remnants of the lava flows cap the higher hills.

The folded Paleozoic sedimentary and volcanic rocks in the walls of the Canyon of the Salmon River come in various shades of gray. They contain a lot of interesting geologic details but these are hard to see from the road. One that might be worth a stop is a graphite-pyrite schist which outcrops around the community of Lucile, 11 miles north of Riggins.

Between 10 and 20 miles south of Grangeville, U.S. 95 ascends the wall of the Salmon River Canyon to the top of the Columbia Plateau by going up White Bird Hill on what must surely be one of the most hair-raising stretches of paved road in the country. It is interesting to reflect, between switchbacks, upon the fact that such a canyon could be eroded in less than 15 million years. It testifies both to the great things done by the slow processes of erosion and to the fact that 15 million years is a very long time indeed.

Grangeville, like New Meadows, is on the Columbia River Plateau. The descent from the high surface at Grangeville to the deep canyon of the Clearwater River at Lewiston is accomplished considerably more gracefully than that to the canyon of the Salmon River at the base of White Bird Hill. U.S. 95 stays on the black basalts of the Columbia Plateau all the way from Grangeville to Lewiston. Over much of the distance they are thinly covered by wind-blown silts.

For more information on flood basalts of the Columbia River Plateau, see
    U.S. 12: Kooskia – Lewiston
    U.S. 95: Lewiston – Coeur d'Alene
    U.S. 195: Lewiston – Spokane

Basalt lava flows break into vertical columns as shrinkage cracks develop in the cooling rock. These may be any size from that of a fencepost to a large log.

LEWISTON – COEUR d'ALENE
112 miles

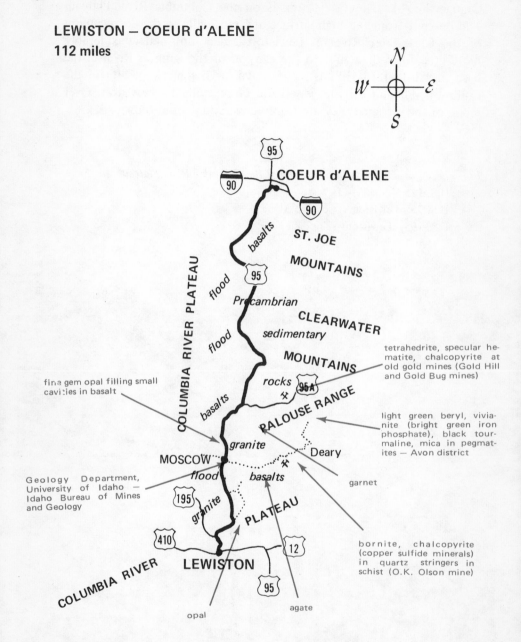

LEWISTON – COEUR d'ALENE map showing U.S. Route 95 with the following labels:

- 95
- 90 — COEUR d'ALENE
- 90
- basalts — ST. JOE MOUNTAINS
- flood — COLUMBIA RIVER PLATEAU
- 95 — Precambrian
- flood — CLEARWATER
- sedimentary — MOUNTAINS
- basalts — rocks — 95A — PALOUSE RANGE
- granite
- MOSCOW — flood — basalts — Deary
- 195 — granite — PLATEAU
- 410 — 12
- LEWISTON
- 95
- COLUMBIA RIVER

Annotations:

- tetrahedrite, specular hematite, chalcopyrite at old gold mines (Gold Hill and Gold Bug mines)
- light green beryl, vivianite (bright green iron phosphate), black tourmaline, mica in pegmatites — Avon district
- fine gem opal filling small cavities in basalt
- garnet
- Geology Department, University of Idaho — Idaho Bureau of Mines and Geology
- bornite, chalcopyrite (copper sulfide minerals) in quartz stringers in schist (O.K. Olson mine)
- opal
- agate

U.S. 95

LEWISTON — COEUR D'ALENE

Between Lewiston and Coeur d'Alene, U.S. 95 follows near the eastern edge of the Columbia River Plateau, crossing back and forth between the basalt lava flows and the older rocks they partially cover.

Precambrian mudstones and sandstones originally laid down between 600 and 1500 million years ago are the oldest rocks in this area. These were complexly folded and intruded by large masses of molten granite magma about 60 to 80 million years ago while the Rocky Mountains were beginning to form. A long period of erosion followed during which streams laid the folded sedimentary rocks and granites bare and carved deep valleys into them to make the region mountainous. Then between about 40 and 15 million years ago, a long series of enormous eruptions of molten basalt magma laid down the lava flows to build the Columbia River Plateau and bury much of the older landscape. During the last 15 million years, streams have carved new valleys down into the black basalt lava flows, exposing once again the older rocks beneath them.

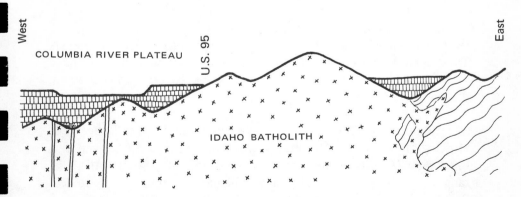

West-east cross section across the line of U.S. 95 north of Moscow. Lava flows of the Columbia River Plateau lap onto an older landscape eroded onto granite intruded into Precambrian sedimentary rocks.

Lewiston is in a deep canyon cut into the basalt lava flows by the Clearwater River. The highway ascends the north wall of this canyon in an impressive series of switchbacks through wonderful exposures of the lava flows then stays on basalt lava flows for most of the distance between Lewiston and Moscow. Relatively little of the basalt is actually exposed on the plateau surface because it is deeply covered in most places by thick soil composed mostly of wind-blown silt. This is excellent agricultural land that supports very productive wheat farms.

The north wall of the canyon of the Clearwater River near Lewiston is peppered with little mounds of soil about the size of an average living room and two or three feet high. These can be seen from town and from the road as it climbs the canyon wall. Similar soil mounds occur in many of the drier parts of the Pacific Northwest. Geologists have been intrigued by these for years and have written quite a literature on them in attempting to explain their origin. Approximately the same number of theories exist as there are geologists who have worked on the problem, so obviously no one is quite sure how they got there. Since nothing happening today seems to be creating these mounds, they must be the relic of some process that went on sometime in the past. Some geologists have suggested that they mark spots where bushes once grew and protected the soil beneath them from erosion while others have suggested that they may be giant ant hills and still others have proposed that they formed during a time when the climate was extremely cold.

Starting from a point several miles south of Moscow and extending all the way to Coeur d'Alene, the road passes through uplands eroded in folded Precambrian sedimentary rocks intruded by small bodies of granite which tend to underlie the higher hills. The larger stream and river valleys are filled with basalt lava flows flooded in from the west. These include the Palouse River near Potlatch, Hangman Creek near Tensed, and the larger valley of the St. Joe River south of Coeur d'Alene.

The mountains visible east of the highway are the Palouse Range near Moscow, the St. Joe Mountains close to Coeur d'Alene, and the Clearwater Mountains between Moscow and Coeur d'Alene. All these ranges are geologically similar, being composed of folded Precambrian sedimentary rocks intruded by large quantities of granite. The granites are the western edge of the Idaho batholith which extends eastward all the way into Montana and covers most of central Idaho. It is one of the larger bodies of granite in the world.

No mountain ranges are visible west of the highway because that area is part of the Columbia River Plateau and is underlain entirely by basalt lava flows.

Coeur d'Alene Lake is a glacial lake with a difference. It is actually south of the farthest extent of the glacier responsible for its formation so does not occupy a glacially scoured basin. The glacier came down from the north through the Purcell Trench as far south as the town of Coeur d'Alene where it dumped large quantities of glacial debris across the valley of the St. Joe River. These glacial deposits formed a natural earth-fill dam after the ice had melted, thereby impounding Coeur d'Alene Lake.

For more information on flood basalts of the Columbia River Plateau, see
    U.S. 12: Kooskia — Lewiston
    U.S. 195: Lewiston — Spokane

For more information on continental ice age glaciers, see
    U.S. 93: Missoula — Kalispell
    U.S. 93: Kalispell — Eureka

COEUR d'ALENE — BONNERS FERRY
84 miles

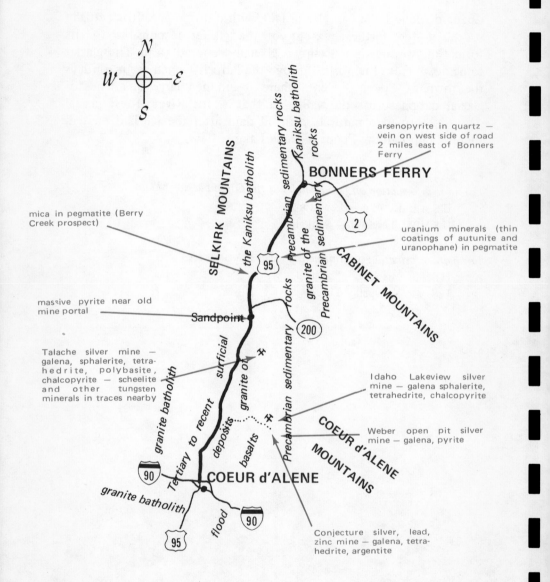

N

W ⊕ E

S

arsenopyrite in quartz —
vein on west side of road
2 miles east of Bonners
Ferry

BONNERS FERRY

Kaniksu batholith

Precambrian sedimentary rocks

Kaniksu batholith rocks

SELKIRK MOUNTAINS

the Kaniksu batholith

mica in pegmatite (Berry
Creek prospect)

95

2

granite of the
Precambrian sedimentary

CABINET MOUNTAINS

uranium minerals (thin
coatings of autunite and
uranophane) in pegmatite

massive pyrite near old
mine portal

Sandpoint

Precambrian sedimentary rocks

200

Talache silver mine —
galena, sphalerite, tetrahedrite, polybasite,
chalcopyrite — scheelite
and other tungsten
minerals in traces nearby

surficial

granite of

granite batholith

Idaho Lakeview silver
mine — galena sphalerite,
tetrahedrite, chalcopyrite

Tertiary to recent

deposits

basalts

Precambrian sedimentary

COEUR d'ALENE
MOUNTAINS

Weber open pit silver
mine — galena, pyrite

90

granite batholith

flood

90

COEUR d'ALENE

95

Conjecture silver, lead,
zinc mine — galena, tetrahedrite, argentite

U.S. 95

COEUR D'ALENE – BONNERS FERRY

North from Coeur d'Alene, U.S. 95 passes almost 20 miles across the flat surface of Rathdrum Prairie, an extensive lowland that was a lake about 15 or 20 million years ago during the Tertiary Period when the drainage was blocked by lava flows. Rathdrum Prairie held another lake during the last ice age when the drainage was again blocked, this time by glacial ice. The prairie floor is deeply blanketed by glacial debris.

Tertiary Lake Rathdrum, the one dammed by the lava flow, was quite large, extending into the valleys north of Sandpoint and west to the area around Spokane. It also lasted quite a long time, for a lake, and accumulated sediments in its bottom that are now rich collecting grounds for fossil leaves. Most of the good collecting places are west of U.S. 95 in the area around Spokane where the lake beds are not completely buried under later glacial debris.

Rathdrum Prairie is on the eastern margin of the Columbia Plateau, an enormous stack of black, basalt lava flows built up by a long series of eruptions over a period of about 25 million years ending roughly 15 million years ago. The rocks west of Rathdrum Prairie are basalt lava flows; those on the east side are lava flows lapping up against the older rocks that were there long before the flows poured out.

211

Between the north edge of Rathdrum Prairie and the area just south of Sandpoint, U.S. 95 passes through the Cocolalla Valley between the Cocolalla Hills to the west and the Talache Hills to the east.

Panhandle Idaho contains Precambrian sandstones and mudstones that were intensely folded and broken by faults druing the movements of the earth's crust that affected this area early in the development of the Rocky Mountains between 60 and 90 million years ago. At the same time the Precambrian sedimentary rocks were deformed, they were injected by enormous quantities of molten granite magma that pushed their way upward to form the large Kaniksu batholith as well as many smaller bodies of granite. After the granite was emplaced, the northern panhandle of Idaho was split lengthwise when a long, narrow, north-south valley was let down on faults that run right through the Kaniksu batholith. This valley forms the southern end of the Purcell Trench.

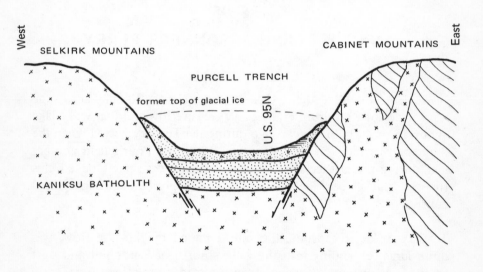

West-east cross section across the line of U.S. 95. The Purcell Trench is let down on faults that run through the Kaniksu batholith between the Selkirk and Cabinet Mountain Ranges. Tertiary valley-fill sediments covered by glacial deposits floor the valley.

The Cocolalla Hills, west of the Cocolalla Valley, are made of granite belonging to the Kaniksu batholith. The Talache Hills, on the east side, are mostly granite but also contain folded Precambrian sedimentary rocks. The Cocolalla Valley itself is a problem because it is obviously too large to have been eroded by the small stream that flows through it today. At one time it must have been the course of a much larger stream. Or it may be a downdropped branch of the Purcell Trench.

From Sandpoint to Bonners Ferry, the highway passes through the southern part of the Purcell Trench which extends far north into British Columbia where it is called the Kootenai Valley. To the west are the granites of the Selkirk Range, and to the east the Cabinet Range is also made of granite where it faces the Purcell Trench. Occasional glacially rounded hills of granite protrude from the valley floor.

During the last ice age, the Purcell Trench held a large glacier that flowed south as far as Coeur d'Alene where it deposited the moraine that impounds Coeur d'Alene Lake. Pend Oreille Lake fills a basin scoured and then dammed by this same glacier.

The Purcell Trench glacier also distinguished itself by damming the drainage of the Clark Fork River near the present site of Pend Oreille Lake, impounding Glacial Lake Missoula. It must have been an enormous glacier because the waters of Glacial Lake Missoula rose to a depth of about 2000 feet at the ice dam before it finally burst, suddenly draining the lake and releasing a great flood that scoured the eastern third of Washington in about the same way that a washtub full of water might scour a child's sandbox. The dry coulees and scabland channels of Washington were eroded by these floodwaters. Apparently the glacier kept advancing and blocking the Clark Fork drainage again and again because there is evidence that Glacial Lake Missoula filled and drained many times.

For more information on Glacial Lake Missoula, see
    Montana 28: Plains – Elmo
    Montana 200: Ravalli Junction – Sandpoint
    County 382: Perma – Hot Springs
    Interstate 90: Missoula – Lookout Pass

For more information on Coeur d'Alene Lake, see
    U.S. 95: Lewiston – Coeur d'Alene

IDAHO FALLS — WEST YELLOWSTONE
109 miles

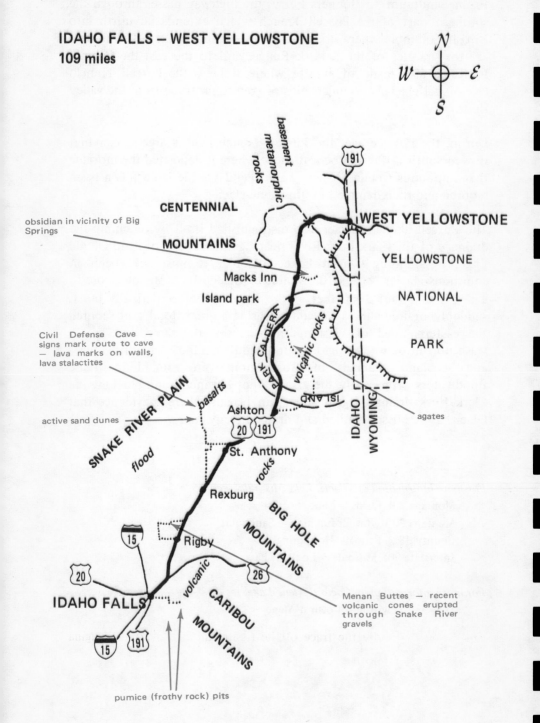

N
W ⊕ E
S

obsidian in vicinity of Big Springs

CENTENNIAL

MOUNTAINS

WEST YELLOWSTONE

YELLOWSTONE

Macks Inn

NATIONAL

Island park

PARK

basement metamorphic rocks

Civil Defense Cave — signs mark route to cave — lava marks on walls, lava stalactites

PARK CALDERA

ISLAND

volcanic rocks

SNAKE RIVER PLAIN

basalts

active sand dunes

Ashton

20 191

agates

IDAHO

WYOMING

flood

St. Anthony

rocks

Rexburg

BIG HOLE

MOUNTAINS

15

Rigby

20

26

IDAHO FALLS

volcanic

CARIBOU

Menan Buttes — recent volcanic cones erupted through Snake River gravels

15 191

MOUNTAINS

pumice (frothy rock) pits

214

U.S. 191 – 20

IDAHO FALLS – WEST YELLOWSTONE

Between Idaho Falls and West Yellowstone the route passes almost entirely over two different kinds of volcanic rocks. In the southern part black, basalt lava flows to the Snake River Plain form a thick pile of lava flows that cover an enormous, crescent-shaped expanse of southern Idaho. The northern part crosses light-colored volcanic rocks similar in many ways to those found on the Yellowstone Plateau.

Menan Buttes, located near the town of Menan about 16 miles north of Idaho Falls, punctuate the skyline north and west of the highway along much of the drive between Idaho Falls and Rexburg. This cluster of five small volcanic cones formed several thousand years ago when molten basalt magma rose along a fissure into the water-soaked gravels underlying the floodplain of the Snake River. Heat from the magma boiled the water causing steam explosions which blew a mixture of river gravels and volcanic rock fragments up out of the floodplain to form the Menan Buttes. The cones are arranged in a nearly straight line about 7 miles long that runs northwest-southeast and is undoubtedly the trace of the fissure along which the magma rose to the surface. It seems likely that all five Menan Buttes formed nearly simultaneously, probably in a matter of a few days. Menan Buttes are among the best known examples of volcanic cones formed by steam explosions and are famous among geologists for their mixture of river gravels and volcanic material.

An interesting closer look at Menan Buttes can be had by turning
west on the secondary road about a mile south of the Snake River
crossing at Lorenzo, 16 miles north of Idaho Falls. About 4 miles
west of the highway the secondary road rises over a small hill, a
remnant of one of the Menan Buttes mostly eroded away by the
Snake River leaving only a crescent-shaped piece of the original cone.
An old gravel pit on the north side of the road, now used as a dump,
provides a wonderful cross-sectional view of the inside of the cone.
Hundreds of layers, each several inches thick, composed of mixed
river gravels and black volcanic rock fragments are exposed in the
walls of the cut. Each layer was deposited as material settled on the
slopes of the cone following a blast of steam from the crater on top.
We can imagine the volcano puffing like a giant steam engine blowing
out a spray of gravel and molten shreds of basalt with every puff.
The high percentage of broken river pebbles testifies to the violence
of the action. See photograph, page 129.

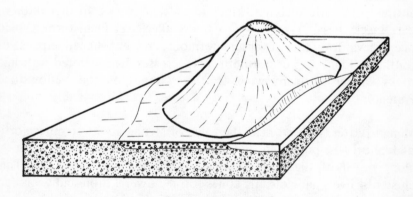

One of the Menan Buttes, a cone of mixed gravel and volcanic material built up
by a series of steam explosions after molten basalt magma rose into the
water-soaked gravels of the Snake River flood plain.

Between Rigby and Ashton are good views of the Grand Tetons,
unmistakably recognizable as a row of pointed peaks rising like a
battlement above the horizon about 40 miles to the east. The lower
mountain front with an even skyline extending north from the Grand
Tetons is the volcanic Yellowstone Plateau. Mountains dimly visible
in the far distance north and west of the highway beyond the Snake
River Plain are composed mostly of Paleozoic sedimentary rocks.

216

Between Rexburg and St. Anthony large tracts of sand dunes appear as low, white patches in the distance west of the highway. These are made of quartz sand which must have been brought down from the mountains by the Snake River and then blown off its floodplain by the wind, because there is no quartz in the black volcanic rocks that underlie this region.

U.S. 20-191 goes right across the Island Park Caldera between Ashton and Island Park. This is a rare treat geologically because the Island Park Caldera is one of the largest in the world as well as being one of the easiest to visualize. Most calderas are very hard to see.

Calderas are large basins that form when the central part of the volcano settles into the space left underground as a large volume of lava is erupted. Normally at least part of the flank of the old volcano is left standing to form a rim around the caldera basin.

Directly north of Ashton is the low south rim of the Island Park Caldera. Some large roadcuts in this rim, between 4 and 6 miles north of Ashton, are well worth a stop. Light-colored volcanic materials were blown from the vent and then settled through the air to form the beds exposed along the road. Some layers contain large fragments of pumice that look almost like pulled taffy and are so full of air bubbles that they will float on water. It is also studded with beautifully formed small crystals of quartz. Several thin beds of volcanic ash are composed entirely of loose, nearly perfectly formed crystals of quartz and feldspar. Look closely for these because they can be mistaken for sand until seen through a magnifier where they make a beautiful sight. On a sunny day the flat faces of the feldspar crystals in these roadcuts reflect spots of light like a thousand tiny mirrors.

Where the road crosses the top of the south rim of the Island Park Caldera, the ridge that forms the rim can be followed with the eye as it curves around to the west and north, tracing the outline of the caldera. The north rim is very low and difficult to see; don't mistake it for the Centennial Range just a short distance farther north which is made of entirely unrelated Paleozoic and Mesozoic sedimentary rocks.

Several dome-shaped hills rise just inside the west rim of the Island Park Caldera. These small, secondary volcanic cones formed when more eruptions took place after the caldera floor had subsided. The best place to watch for them from the road is along the Henry's Fork River where it flows across the flat floor of the caldera south of Island Park.

Only the western half of the Island Park Caldera is visible. The eastern half is buried beneath the volcanic rocks of the Yellowstone Plateau, the flat-topped mountain front east of the floor of the basin.

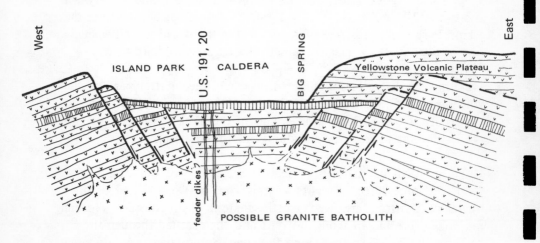

West-east cross section across the Island Park Caldera approximately 20 miles north of Ashton, Idaho. A volcano sank into space created underground by eruption of magma, forming a large basin rimmed by remnants of the original cone. The eastern part of the caldera rim and basin are now buried beneath younger volcanic rocks of the Yellowstone Plateau.

Big Springs is located where the Island Park Caldera disappears beneath the base of the Yellowstone Plateau. Turn east at Macks Inn onto Idaho 84 and drive 5 miles to the springs. The water comes from Yellowstone National Park by soaking down through the volcanic rocks of the Yellowstone Plateau. Many of the rocks in the vicinity of the spring are obsidian (volcanic glass) as beautiful as any to be found in the park and specimens can be collected without committing a federal offense. The trout are protected.

Between Macks Inn and West Yellowstone the highway crosses the edge of the high Yellowstone Plateau which is built up of volcanic rocks. The mountains to the west are the Centennial and Gravelly Ranges; those to the northwest the Madison Range; and those directly north, the Gallatin Range. All these ranges contain complexly folded Paleozoic and Mesozoic sedimentary rocks more or less covered by much younger light-colored volcanic rocks. Both the

Gallatin and Madison Ranges also contain in their cores igneous and metamorphic rocks belonging to the Precambrian basement.

For information on volcanic rocks of Yellowstone Park, see
    Yellowstone National Park (following U.S. 20: Cody — East Entrance)

For more information on flood basalts of the Snake River Plain, see
    Interstate 80 N: Twin Falls — Boise
    U.S. 20: Idaho Falls — Arco
    U.S. 93 A: Shoshone — Arco; Craters of the Moon

Aerial view of sand dunes on the level surface of the Snake River Plain near St. Anthony, Idaho. Direction of wind-transport of sand is from right to left.

WEST YELLOWSTONE – BOZEMAN
91 miles

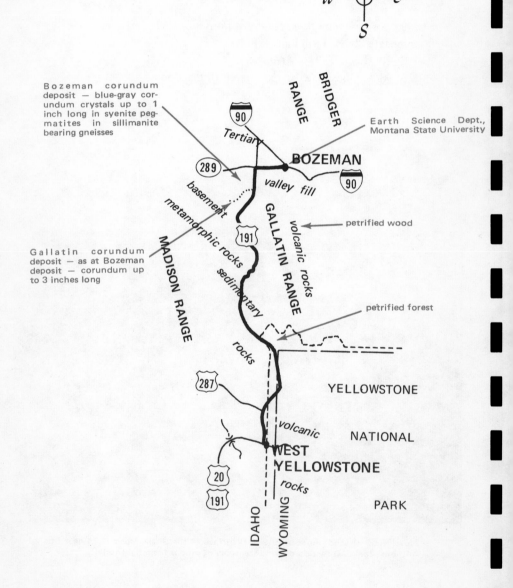

Bozeman corundum deposit — blue-gray corundum crystals up to 1 inch long in syenite pegmatites in sillimanite bearing gneisses

Earth Science Dept., Montana State University

Gallatin corundum deposit — as at Bozeman deposit — corundum up to 3 inches long

petrified wood

petrified forest

BRIDGER RANGE

BOZEMAN

Tertiary

valley fill

basement

metamorphic rocks

MADISON RANGE

GALLATIN RANGE

volcanic rocks

sedimentary

rocks

YELLOWSTONE

volcanic

NATIONAL

WEST YELLOWSTONE

rocks

PARK

IDAHO

WYOMING

U.S. 191

WEST YELLOWSTONE – BOZEMAN

West Yellowstone is on the western edge of the high Yellowstone Plateau formed of light-colored volcanic rocks erupted within the past 2 million years.

About 8 miles north of West Yellowstone, immediately south of the intersection with Hebgen Lake Road (U.S. 287), the highway crosses the Red Canyon Fault Scarp formed during the great Hebgen Lake Earthquake in 1959. The road was displaced during the earthquake, with the side south of the scarp dropping about 15 feet, considerably hampering traffic. It has been repaired now but the fault scarp can still be seen running approximately east-west along the base of the hills west of the highway.

After following the Madison River north of West Yellowstone, U.S 191 crosses into the headwaters of the Gallatin River which it follows all the way to Bozeman. The Gallatin Range to the east and the Madison Range to the west both contain the same two uplifted fault-blocks of Precambrian igneous and metamorphic basement rocks running diagonally in a northwest-southeast direction across the ranges. A mass of folded Paleozoic and Mesozoic sedimentary rocks squashed between the two basement rock blocks also runs diagonally in the same direction through the two ranges.

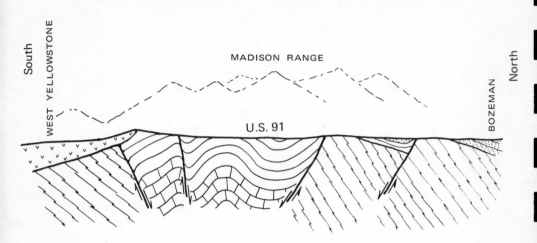

South-north cross section along the line of U.S. 191 between West Yellowstone and Bozeman. Blocks of Precambrian basement rocks and younger sedimentary rocks have been set next to each other by movement along faults.

Capping the Gallatin Range is a thick sequence of dark-colored volcanic rocks erupted on top of the older sedimentary and basement rocks roughly 50 million years ago. These largely cover the older rocks so the Gallatin Range is mostly volcanic. Because the volcanics are similar to those in the Absaroka Range of Wyoming and were erupted at the same time, the Gallatin Range can be thought of as being a northward extension of the Absaroka Range into Montana. Very few volcanic rocks occur in the Madison Range.

The Gallatin Petrified Forest just north of Yellowstone Park is a place where trees were buried in volcanic ash and later petrified through slow replacement of woody tissues by quartz. A number of such petrified forests are known in the Absaroka volcanics. Streams draining from these mountains contain pebbles of petrified wood in their gravels and are excellent places to collect small specimens.

Where the Gallatin River crosses the outcrop area of the Paleozoic and Mesozoic sedimentary rocks, its canyon is relatively wide because these rocks are mostly soft and easily erodible. Where the stream enters the fault-blocks of Precambrian basement rocks, the canyon narrows abruptly because these rocks are very hard and resistant to erosion. The Spanish Peaks Primitive Area in the Madison Range is in one of the basement rock blocks.

Most of the basement rocks are streaky-looking pink, black and gray gneisses. There are also schists, flaky with mica, as well as uniform-looking granite. Areas of basement rock usually contain at least a few unusual rocks and these are no exceptions. Just east of U.S. 101 south of Bozeman are occurrences of the rare mineral corundum. Corundum is the hardest of all minerals, except for diamond, and is used industrially as an abrasive. Clear, nicely colored corundum is the gem-mineral sapphire. None of the specimens near Bozeman are gem-quality but well formed, 6-sided, bluish-gray crystals are common.

For information on Yellowstone Park, see
Yellowstone National Park (after U.S. 20: Cody — East Entrance)

Folded bands of gneiss cut by a small fault. This is typical of the rocks in the Precambrian basement complex.

BIG TIMBER – LEWISTOWN
101 miles

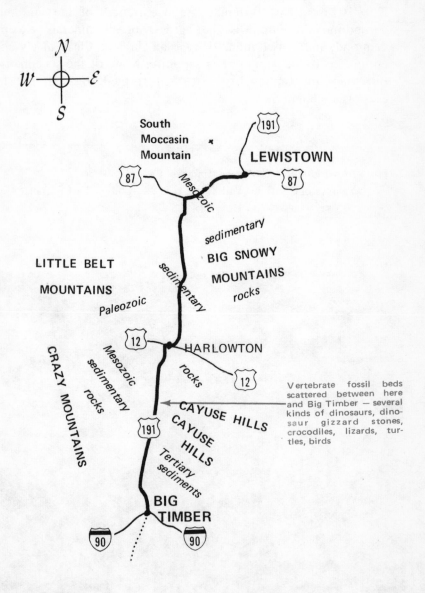

Vertebrate fossil beds scattered between here and Big Timber — several kinds of dinosaurs, dinosaur gizzard stones, crocodiles, lizards, turtles, birds

U.S. 191

BIG TIMBER — LEWISTOWN

Between Big Timber and Harlowton, U.S. 191 crosses beds of sedimentary rocks deposited between roughly 50 and 70 million years ago. Sedimentary layers along the road are still in nearly their original horizontal position showing very little evidence of having been deformed during development of the northern Rocky Mountains. The same is not true of the older sedimentary rocks beneath the surface. They have been buckled into a very deep and complicated downfold that has received a lot of attention from oil companies because some of the rocks may well contain petroleum. But the complicated folding has made it very difficult to find.

West of the highway between Big Timber and Harlowton are the high Crazy Mountains, a volcanic pile erupted at about the same time some of the rocks along the road were being deposited. The Crazy Mountains are high enough to catch a lot of snow in the wintertime and were heavily glaciated during the last ice age. Evidence of this can be seen in their craggy, jagged profile formed when large glaciers carved into the flanks of the peaks from several sides at once. East of the highway are the low Cayuse Hills, made of the same kinds of rock visible along the road. The distant view directly south of Big Timber is filled by the very high, rolling top of the Beartooth Plateau, a block of Precambrian basement rock vertically uplifted along faults during the past 70 million years.

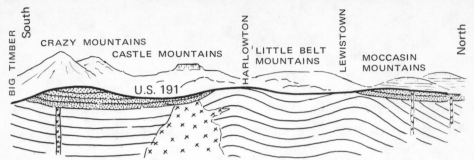

South-north cross section along the line of U.S. 191 between Big Timber and Lewistown. The mountains shown in the background are west of the line of the section which does not indicate their geology. Rocks exposed along the road are mostly Mesozoic sedimentary formations overlain by Tertiary sedimentary deposits.

Sedimentary rocks along the road between Big Timber and Harlowton were deposited on land during the last part of the Cretaceous Period, which ended about 60 million years ago, and the first part of the Tertiary Period that followed. Older Cretaceous rocks outcrop in river valleys beneath the younger Tertiary rocks which generally cap the hills. The rocks consist of layers of mud, sand and gravel washed out of nearby mountains by streams and mixed with volcanic materials either washed in by streams or blown in on the wind.

Numerous vertebrate fossils have been found in a variety of places along the highway between Big Timber and Harlowton. Almost the entire stretch of country from a short distance north of Big Timber to the area about 14 miles south of Harlowton has been richly productive. The American Museum of Natural History has collected extensively in these beds, finding an incredible variety of things ranging from various kinds of dinosaurs, to turtles, small mammals, and even birds. Petrified wood has also been found in a number of places. Fossil bones can be hard to find, even where they are quite abundant, so the only successful collectors are those who keep their eyes open and their noses to the ground.

One of the most interesting kinds of fossils found here are stomach stones — sometimes called "gastroliths." Dinosaurs and some other kinds of animals gobbled stones and carried them in their craws, just as chickens do, using them to grind their food. The mass of stones churning around in the animal's craw acquired a high polish the same way they might if rolled around in a polishing tumbler. Look for isolated, highly polished pebbles all by themselves in beds of mudstone. Don't look for them in beds of gravel where they will have lost their polish by being rolled along with other pebbles.

226

The Cretaceous Period ended when the dinosaurs became extinct so their bones are found only in the Cretaceous rocks exposed in the stream valleys, not in the Tertiary rocks capping the hills. Stomach stones can be found in the Tertiary beds because other kinds of animals besides dinosaurs used them, but they are much more abundant and easier to find in the Cretaceous mudstones.

Between Harlowton and Lewistown, Highway 191 crosses Cretaceous and Tertiary sedimentary rocks with layers still in nearly their original horizontal position. Most of the Tertiary sedimentary rocks are thick beds of coarse gravel washed off the nearby mountains and deposited during the long time when our region had a desert climate and lacked streams to carry the gravel away. This stretch of highway passes through the Judith Basin, named by Captain Clark to honor his fiancée whom he married after the expedition. Judith Basin, later famed for its lush grass, became the site of a great deal of colorful history during the early period of settlement by cattlemen. The great western artist C.M. Russell was a cowboy in this area during his early years in Montana.

East of the Judith Basin are the Big Snowy Mountains, a dome-shaped uplifted arch of the sedimentary rocks underlying the high plains. Paleozoic sedimentary rocks are exposed in the core of the range and Mesozoic sedimentary rocks around the flanks. West of the Judith Basin are the Little Belt Mountains, another large arched uplift of the high plains. Precambrian basement rock exposed in its core is flanked by beds of Paleozoic and Mesozoic sedimentary rock tilted away from the center of the arch. Gem sapphires have been mined for many years in Yogo Gulch on the east flank of the Little Belts.

The Moccasin Mountains are north and the Judith Mountains northeast of Lewistown. Both contain bodies of granite injected as molten magma into Paleozoic sedimentary rocks sometime between 50 and 70 million years ago. Granite magma was squirted between the sedimentary layers where it formed laccoliths shaped like giant blisters several miles across.

For more information on laccoliths, see
      U.S. 87: Lewistown – Great Falls
      Interstate 15: Helena – Great Falls

LEWISTON – SPOKANE
108 miles

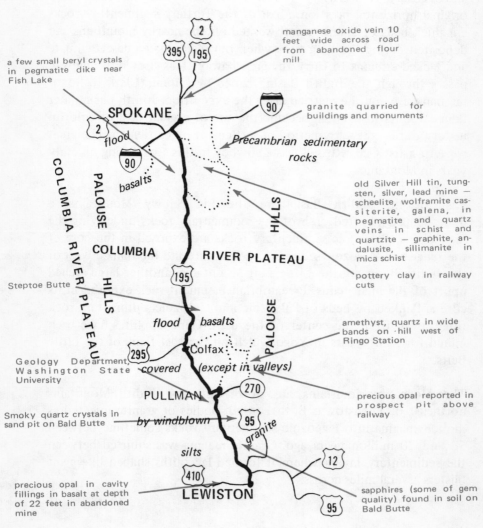

a few small beryl crystals in pegmatite dike near Fish Lake

manganese oxide vein 10 feet wide across road from abandoned flour mill

SPOKANE

granite quarried for buildings and monuments

flood

basalts

Precambrian sedimentary rocks

PALOUSE

COLUMBIA RIVER PLATEAU

HILLS

old Silver Hill tin, tungsten, silver, lead mine — scheelite, wolframite cassiterite, galena, in pegmatite and quartz veins in schist and quartzite — graphite, andalusite, sillimanite in mica schist

COLUMBIA

RIVER PLATEAU

HILLS

Steptoe Butte

pottery clay in railway cuts

flood   basalts

PALOUSE

amethyst, quartz in wide bands on hill west of Ringo Station

Colfax

covered   (except in valleys)

Geology Department, Washington State University

PULLMAN

precious opal reported in prospect pit above railway

Smoky quartz crystals in sand pit on Bald Butte

by windblown

granite

silts

precious opal in cavity fillings in basalt at depth of 22 feet in abandoned mine

LEWISTON

sapphires (some of gem quality) found in soil on Bald Butte

U.S. 195

LEWISTON – SPOKANE

U.S. 195 crosses basalt lava flows of the Columbia River Plateau all the way from Lewiston to Spokane. Great floods of molten basalt magma poured out from north-south trending fissures between 40 and 15 million years ago to cover hundreds of square miles of countryside with lava flows that in many cases are more than 100 feet thick. Long fissures from which many of these flows were erupted are believed to have been approximately along the line of the highway. Of course they are now filled and covered so most cannot easily be seen.

The youngest of these lava flows is about 15 million years old, plenty of time for streams to develop and carve an erosional landscape, making it difficult now to visualize the original flat upper surface of the plateau. A few million years ago this area must have looked about the same way the Snake River Plain in southern Idaho looks today.

Lewiston is in the canyon the Clearwater River has cut deeply into the lava flows. East of Lewiston, where the flows are thinner, the Clearwater River has cut all the way through them into the older rocks beneath. Immediately north of Lewiston the highway ascends the steep northern wall of the canyon in a spectacular series of switchbacks through excellent exposures of the lava flows. Unfortunately, it takes exceptionally strong nerves to appreciate the roadcuts along this breathtaking stretch of road.

229

One of the more interesting geologic features along U.S. 195 is the soil that thickly covers the plateau and supports the wealthy and productive wheat farms in the area. Unlike most soils, this was not developed in place by slow weathering of the bedrock beneath. Instead, it is dust blown in by the wind during times in the past when the climate here was much drier than it is today. Roadcuts in this soil frequently expose thin layers of dust recording the stages in its accumulation.

The small, rolling hills that U.S. 195 crosses in the wheatlands on top of the Columbia Plateau are called the Palouse Hills. They are composed almost entirely of wind-blown dust. Geologists have long been intrigued by the peculiar shape of these little hills that tend to have steep slopes on their northeast faces and gentler slopes on their other sides. Some geologists believe that this is the original shape of the dust dunes that once blew across this country while others maintain that the northeast slopes were steepened by erosion under snowpatches during the last ice age.

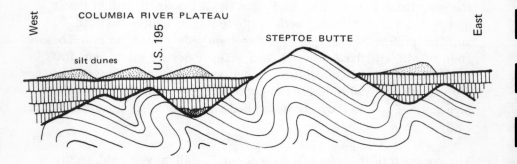

West-east cross section across the line of U.S. 195 between Lewiston and Spokane. Basalt lava flows of the Columbia River Plateau bury an older landscape eroded on folded Precambrian sedimentary rocks. Silt dunes on top of the lava flows make the rolling Palouse Hills.

Black basalt lava flows underlie the wind-blown dust in the Palouse Hills but can be seen in only a few places. Where they do outcrop in stream banks and roadcuts, they show a conspicuous tendency to break into neat vertical columns along shrinkage cracks opened in the basalt as it cooled.

A few miles west of U.S. 195 are the scablands, an extensive tract of dry stream channels cut through the wind-blown dust exposing the basalt beneath. They were eroded in a matter of hours by an incredible flood that scoured across the Columbia Plateau in eastern Washington when the glacier dam impounding Glacial Lake Missoula broke about 12,000 years ago.

For more information on Glacial Lake Missoula, see
    Montana 28: Plains — Elmo
    Montana 200: Ravalli Junction — Sandpoint
    County 382: Perma — Hotsprings

For more information on flood basalts of the Columbia River Plateau, see
    U.S. 95: Lewiston — Coeur d'Alene
    U.S. 12: Kooskia — Lewiston

Rock Creek Canyon, in the Beartooth Plateau, shows the flat bottom and steep valley walls typical of valleys that were occupied by large glaciers during the ice age.

LAUREL – COOKE CITY
(Beartooth Highway)
111 miles

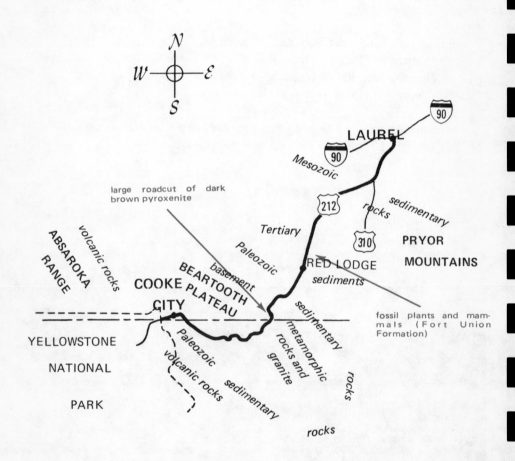

U.S 212

LAUREL – COOKE CITY

(Beartooth Highway)

After leaving Interstate 90 at Laurel, once the home of Calamity Jane, U.S. 212 follows the Clark Fork of the Yellowstone River as far as Rock Creek which it follows all the way to its headwaters in the Beartooth Plateau. The Pryor Mountains, an uplift of Mesozoic and Paleozoic sedimentary rocks, lie in the distance to the southeast. A high rather flat-topped mountain front, the Beartooth Plateau, dominates the skyline to the southwest.

For about 20 miles southwest from Laurel the highway crosses layers of Mesozoic sedimentary rocks still lying in nearly their original horizontal position. Farther southwest, the road passes through Tertiary sands and gravels. These were eroded from the Beartooth Plateau, then deposited as an apron of sediments around its base during the period when our region was a desert.

A few miles north of Red Lodge, the highway passes through gravelly hills of glacial debris laid down during the last ice age. An enormous glacier poured down the canyon of Rock Creek from the Beartooth Plateau and managed to get several miles out onto the plains before it reached an area warm enough to melt the ice as fast as it advanced. These deposits were left where the ice melted.

The Red Lodge to Cooke City segment of the road (Beartooth Highway) crosses right over the top of the high Beartooth Plateau of Wyoming and Montana, winding for miles through barren alpine tundras dotted with small glacial lakes, surely one of the most magnificent drives in North America.

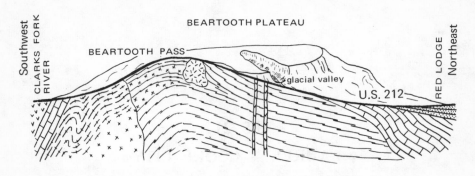

Southwest-northeast cross section and diagram along the line of U.S. 212 as it crosses the Beartooth Plateau, a large block of Precambrian basement rock uplifted along faults during formation of the Rocky Mountains.

The Beartooth Plateau is a big, rectangular block of Precambrian igneous and metamorphic basement rocks raised up along faults during the last 70 million years to form the highest mountain range in our region.

These basement rocks were once covered by Paleozoic sedimentary rocks most of which have been stripped off by erosion since the block was uplifted. Igneous and metamorphic basement rocks are very resistant to erosion so their upper surface, once beneath the sedimentary rocks, remains almost untouched by erosion, giving the Beartooth Plateau a remarkably flat top. Peaks which rise high above this flat surface are uneroded remnants of the Paleozoic sedimentary rocks.

Most of the igneous and metamorphic rocks along the highway are granites and gneisses. These are composed of glassy grains of quartz and pink or white grains of feldspar, along with flakes of black mica and glossy black needles of hornblende. The streaky "grain" or layering of the metamorphic gneisses distinguishes them from the very uniform-looking granites.

Many of the outcrops along the road contain granite and gneiss mixed together looking almost as though they had been stirred with a stick. These rocks formed when the gneiss was heated to the point where it began to melt forming granite magma that moved fluidly, giving the rocks their appearance of having been stirred.

Another of the common rocks on the Beartooth Plateau is amphibolite, composed almost entirely of shiny black needle-shaped crystals of hornblende. Many of the amphibolites have granite magma squirted through them along fractures to form dikes that look like white veins in the black rock. Pyroxenite is a brownish-black rock composed mostly of stubby black crystals of pyroxene. Large outcrops of it are near the eastern margin of the Beartooth Plateau between Beartooth Pass and where the road starts down the edge of Rock Creek Canyon.

Much younger granites were intruded into the Beartooth Plateau when molten magma was squirted through large fractures during the time the block was being uplifted. These are easy to recognize because they contain nicely shaped crystals of pink feldspar about the size of a finger joint, set in a matrix of very fine-grained rock. Crystals of feldspar often weather free of their matrix and can be found loose in the soil around these granites. They make beautifully geometric mineral specimens.

The top of the Beartooth Plateau was almost completely capped by an enormous glacier during the last ice age. Ice moved slowly toward the edges of the plateau – scraping out the lake basins in the top – and then poured glaciers down the stream valleys around the edges. The steep walls and flat bottom of Rock Creek Canyon southwest of Red Lodge are an outstanding example of what glacial erosion can do to a valley.

For Yellowstone Park, see
  Section following U.S. 20: Cody – East Entrance

For more information on Continental ice age glaciers, see
  U.S. 93: Missoula – Kalispell
  U.S. 93: Kalispell – Eureka
  Glacier National Park (after section on U.S. 89: Great Falls – Browning)

For more information on the Beartooth Plateau, see
  Interstate 90: Billings – Big Timber
  Interstate 90: Big Timber – Bozeman

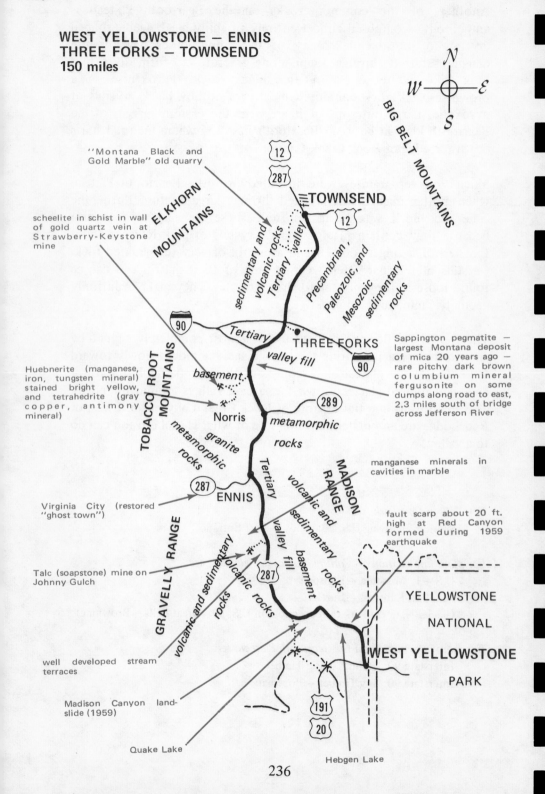

WEST YELLOWSTONE – ENNIS
THREE FORKS – TOWNSEND
150 miles

N
W ✛ E
S

BIG BELT MOUNTAINS

"Montana Black and Gold Marble" old quarry

12
287

TOWNSEND

12

scheelite in schist in wall of gold quartz vein at Strawberry-Keystone mine

ELKHORN MOUNTAINS

sedimentary and volcanic rocks

Tertiary valley fill

Precambrian, Paleozoic, and Mesozoic sedimentary rocks

90

Tertiary

basement

THREE FORKS

90

valley fill

Sappington pegmatite – largest Montana deposit of mica 20 years ago – rare pitchy dark brown columbium mineral fergusonite on some dumps along road to east, 2.3 miles south of bridge across Jefferson River

Huebnerite (manganese, iron, tungsten mineral) stained bright yellow, and tetrahedrite (gray copper, antimony mineral)

TOBACCO ROOT MOUNTAINS

Norris

granite

metamorphic rocks

289

metamorphic rocks

manganese minerals in cavities in marble

Virginia City (restored "ghost town")

287

ENNIS

Tertiary

MADISON RANGE

volcanic and sedimentary rocks

basement

fault scarp about 20 ft. high at Red Canyon formed during 1959 earthquake

Talc (soapstone) mine on Johnny Gulch

GRAVELLY RANGE

volcanic and sedimentary rocks

valley fill

volcanic rocks

287

YELLOWSTONE

NATIONAL

WEST YELLOWSTONE

PARK

well developed stream terraces

Madison Canyon landslide (1959)

191

20

Quake Lake

Hebgen Lake

U.S. 287

WEST YELLOWSTONE — TOWNSEND

West Yellowstone is on the western edge of the high Yellowstone Plateau built up by volcanic eruptions during the past 2 million years.

West of its intersection with U.S. 191, U.S. 287 follows the north shores of Hebgen and Quake Lakes. This stretch of road was involved in the great Hebgen Lake earthquake of August, 1959.

Hebgen Lake is a reservoir impounded by a dam built across the Madison River at the west end of the lake. One effect of the earthquake was to suddenly tilt the floor of this valley down to the north so that the former lake shoreline beside the road is now submerged. Most of this part of the highway had to be rebuilt after the earthquake; much had to be completely relocated onto higher ground. In several places travellers on the present highway can look down at the old road to see it disappear beneath the water. Some of these places are now used for boat launching ramps. Drowned trees still standing in many places along the shore are another indication that the north side of the lake dropped during the earthquake.

At the same time that the north shore of the lake was tilted down and drowned, the south shore was tilted up and drained of water leaving the old beaches high and dry. All this tilting occurred in one sudden jerk during the earthquake.

Another effect of the earthquake was to suddenly lift the Madison Range several feet higher than it had been before. Movement along the fault created a small cliff about 15 feet high, called a fault scarp, which follows the south face of the range approximately parallel to the highway. It is harder to see now than when it was fresh because of new growth of vegetation since the earthquake. Nevertheless, the fault scarp can still be spotted from a number of places along the highway by looking north a short distance up the mountainside.

Part of the fault scarp runs right through the north end of Cabin Creek Campground where a 15-foot high cliff abruptly appeared in the middle of the night where none had been before. Campers awoke to find Cabin Creek flowing over a small waterfall that had not been there when the sun went down. The waterfall has long since been worn away by the stream but the scarp nearby is still there.

Hebgen Dam was badly damaged by the earthquake and seemed about to wash out for several days afterward. Fortunately it held and has since been repaired. A new spillway was built to replace the badly broken old one that can still be seen.

Quake Lake did not exist before the earthquake. It was created when a large rockslide shaken loose from the south wall of the canyon dammed the Madison River by falling into it. The momentum of the rockslide was so great that part of the mass went completely across the canyon and about a third of the way up the slope on the north side before finally coming to rest. A campground is buried here, along with at least 26 people. The landslide scar and slide-mass are still quite freshly preserved so the disaster can easily be visualized.

A Forest Service visitor center on top of the slide mass at Quake Lake displays photographs taken shortly after the earthquake. An earthquake seismograph recorder working in the basement is a most interesting exhibit.

From Quake Lake to Ennis, U.S. 287 follows the Madison River Valley between the Gravelly Range to the west and the Madison Range to the east. The Tobacco Root Range is on the skyline to the northwest along much of this stretch of road. All three of these ranges contain Precambrian igneous and metamorphic basement rocks covered in places by greatly deformed Paleozoic and Mesozoic sedimentary rocks.

Madison Valley is a block of the earth's crust let down during formation of the Rocky Mountains as the mountain range blocks on either side raised up. Like the other such valleys in the region, it is floored by Tertiary valley-fill deposits of mud, sand, and gravel.

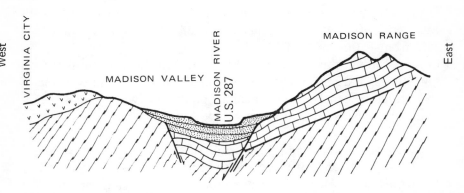

West-east cross section across the line of U.S. 287 about midway up the Madison Valley, a down-dropped fault-block between the high Madison range capped by sedimentary rocks and the lower hills in Precambrian basement rocks to the west. Tertiary valley-fill deposits deeply floor the valley.

At Ennis the Madison River leaves the highway to head east through a narrow gorge it has cut through the north end of the Madison Range. When the river started to flow, this end of the range was completely buried beneath soft Tertiary valley-fill sediments. As these were eroded away, the river was let down onto the top of the once-buried mountains and has sawed its canyon right down through the range.

Most of the route between Ennis and the junction with U.S. 10 goes through gently rolling country between the Tobacco Root Range to the west and the northern end of the Madison Range to the east. For about 5 miles both north and south of Norris, the road crosses igneous and metamorphic rocks belonging to the Precambrian basement. This part of the floor of the Madison Valley is not covered by valley-fill deposits. The Precambrian rocks are mostly streaky-looking gneisses and schists made up of quartz, pink and white feldspar, and black mica or hornblende. They are intruded by numerous dikes of younger granite injected as molten magma into fractures and now visible as white stripes criss-crossing some of the outcrops.

Another area of Precambrian basement rock occurs a few miles farther north, about 5 miles south of the junction with U.S. 10. Here

239

the Precambrian rocks are still overlain by Paleozoic sandstones and limestones whose layers form a series of east-west ridges cut across by the stream which the road follows. Lewis and Clark Caverns, described in the following pages, are a few miles west.

U.S. 10 follows the valley of the Jefferson River to its junction with Interstate 90 a short distance west of Three Forks where the Jefferson forms one of the headwaters of the Missouri. Rocks exposed along this road are Paleozoic and Mesozoic limestones, sandstones, and mudstones, all folded and broken by faults. Some of this structure can be appreciated from the highway by looking for sedimentary beds tilted at various angles.

Between Three Forks and Townsend, U.S. 287 follows the valley of the Missouri River. To the east is the Bridger Range, made of folded Paleozoic and Mesozoic sedimentary rocks lying on top of Precambrian basement rock in the southern part of the range and on top of Precambrian sedimentary rock in the northern part. The tree-covered range to the northwest is the Elkhorn Mountains composed mostly of dark-colored volcanic rocks erupted about 70 – 75 million years ago during the Cretaceous Period.

Townsend is at the south end of Canyon Ferry Reservoir between the Elkhorn Mountains to the west and the Big Belt Mountains to the east. The Big Belts are composed mostly of folded and faulted Precambrian sandstones and mudstones overlain by equally deformed Paleozoic sedimentary rocks. Several small bodies of molten granite magma intruded into these rocks in the central part of the range during the time the Rocky Mountains were forming.

For Yellowstone Park, see
Yellowstone National Park (section following U.S. 20: Cody – East Entrance)

For more information on Precambrian igneous and metamorphic rocks (basement rocks), see
U.S. 212: Laurel – Cooke-City; Beartooth Highway

For information on the Lewis and Clark Caverns, see the following pages.

LEWIS AND CLARK CAVERNS

Lewis and Clark Caverns State Park is on the north side of old U.S. 10 approximately 5 miles west of the junction with U.S. 287. These are truly spectacular caverns, fully the equal of many better known ones in other parts of the country, and the guided tour is well worth the time and money. A little train and cable tramway takes visitors up the side of the mountain to the cave entrance.

Lewis and Clark Caverns are in Paleozoic limestone laid down on the floor of a shallow sea during Mississippian Time about 300 million years ago. Sometime during formation of the Rocky Mountains this thick bed of limestone was folded and badly fractured by movements along a large fault at the base of the mountain near the Jefferson River.

The cave was eroded by rainwater circulating through fractures in the rock. All limestone is soluble in acid and all rainwater is weakly acid so wherever rainwater flows down through fractures in limestone, caves are likely to develop. The solid rock is simply eaten away bit by bit and washed away by the rainwater as it soaks down through the rocks. No one knows for sure when these caves were eroded but it has probably been sometime within the last million years. Geologically speaking, they are very young.

Most visitors to caverns are intrigued by the fascinating shapes of the dripstone formations. These develop after the cave has been eroded when water already saturated with dissolved limestone begins to drip through fractures in the roof. If some of the water evaporates as it enters the cave, the dissolved limestone is precipitated to form the stalactites that hang from the roof like icicles and the stalagmites that rise from the floor like posts. Eventually the two may meet in the middle to form a pillar. Sometimes water trickling into the cave from a crack in the roof deposits dripstone to form continuous curtains that hang from the roof like draperies. For every bit of dripstone deposited in a cavern there must have been an equal amount of limestone dissolved someplace above.

WOLF CREEK – CHOTEAU
67 miles

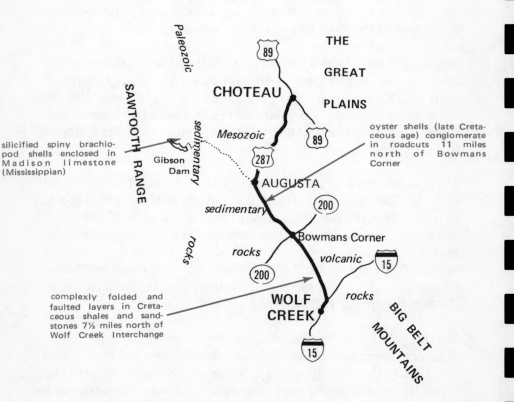

silicified spiny brachio-
pod shells enclosed in
Madison limestone
(Mississippian)

oyster shells (late Cretaceous age) conglomerate
in roadcuts 11 miles
north of Bowmans
Corner

complexly folded and
faulted layers in Creta-
ceous shales and sand-
stones 7½ miles north of
Wolf Creek Interchange

SAWTOOTH RANGE

Paleozoic

Mesozoic

Gibson Dam

sedimentary

rocks

sedimentary

rocks

volcanic

rocks

CHOTEAU

THE

GREAT

PLAINS

AUGUSTA

Bowmans Corner

WOLF CREEK

BIG BELT MOUNTAINS

89

89

287

200

200

15

15

U.S. 287

WOLF CREEK – CHOTEAU

Between Wolf Creek and Bowmans Corner (intersection with Montana 200) the road passes through folded Cretaceous sandstones and mudstones partly covered by dark-colored volcanics.

The sedimentary rocks were laid down near the western shore of a shallow sea between 60 and 80 million years ago, then folded shortly after they were deposited as the Rocky Mountains began to rise to the west.

About 50 million years ago the volcanic rocks were erupted and once completely covered the sedimentary rocks in this area. Most of them have now been eroded away but patches still remain capping many of the higher hills near the road. Their dark color and the fact that many of them contain vertical shrinkage cracks which cause the outcrop to look something like a stockade fence make them distinctive and easy to recognize from a distance.

The folding in this area can be seen from the road. Pick out a prominent ledge of rock and follow it with your eye.

Where the road goes over the crests of the hills between Bowmans Corner and Choteau there are good views of the bold front of the Sawtooth Range to the west. These mountains have a fantastic structure made up predominantly of huge slices of Paleozoic sedimentary rocks that slid eastward over the Cretaceous rocks of the plains and stacked one on top of the other like so many tilted dominoes. This structure is difficult to visualize from the highway but can be seen very nicely by taking a side trip from Augusta into the Sun River Canyon and Gibson Dam.

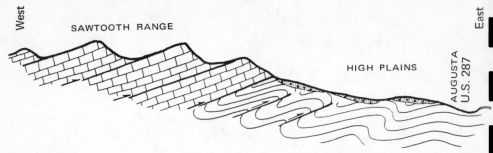

West-east cross section from the Sawtooth Range across the High Plains to U.S. 287 at Augusta. Large slices of Paleozoic sedimentary rock slid eastward and stacked on top of one another to form the ridges of the Sawtooth Range.

The Sun River Canyon Road, about 25 miles long, takes off to the west from the south end of Augusta. It is well graded, gravelled, and easily passable by passenger car except during very wet weather. Take the right turn at Split Rock Junction about 4 miles west of town.

A very large glacier poured out of the mouth of Sun River Canyon during the last ice age and spread out over the plains to make a fan-shaped ice field that extended almost as far east as Augusta. The road to the canyon crosses deposits left by this glacier when it melted about 10,000 years ago. These include a large number of enormous boulders now broken up by water freezing in cracks and splitting the rock.

Along the 4 miles of paved road between the mouth of Sun River Canyon and Gibson Dam, the same massive beds of Madison Limestone (Paleozoic, Mississippian Age) appear over and over again holding up a series of long, north-south ridges separated by valleys. These ridges are the slices of rock which broke up somewhere beneath the surface and slid eastward over the Cretaceous mudstones and sandstones of the plains. Valleys are eroded along the faults. In several places along the road, black Cretaceous mudstone can be seen squeezed almost like toothpaste between the slabs of Paleozoic Limestone.

This same kind of structure is found along the entire length of the Sawtooth Range from Glacier Park south almost to Helena. It extends west far into the Bob Marshall Wilderness Area with the slices of rock becoming progressively older to the west.

244

Explaining the development of the structures in the Sawtooth Range is an interesting problem still hotly debated among geologists. Some claim that these rocks received a strong push from the west while others insist that they simply slid eastward off the uplifted Rocky Mountains under the pull of gravity. The question has considerably more than just academic interest because structures of this type in Alberta have trapped large quantities of oil.

Sun River Canyon is a good place to look at some excellent Mississippian fossils so solidly embedded in large blocks of limestone that they can hardly be collected. A fine place to see them is along the trail leading from the road down to the irrigation diversion dam near the mouth of the canyon. Two kinds of corals are common here: horn corals which look something like cow horns; and colonial corals which resemble large honeycombs in the rock.

Between Augusta and Choteau, Montana 287 crosses complexly folded Cretaceous sandstones and mudstones, poorly exposed for the most part and not easily appreciated from the road. There are no volcanic rocks in this area, perhaps because they have been completely removed by erosion but more likely because they were never laid down here in the first place.

For more information on rocks and faults in the Montana Sawtooth Range, see
    U.S. 89: Great Falls − Browning

BOISE — NEW MEADOWS (McCall)
114 miles

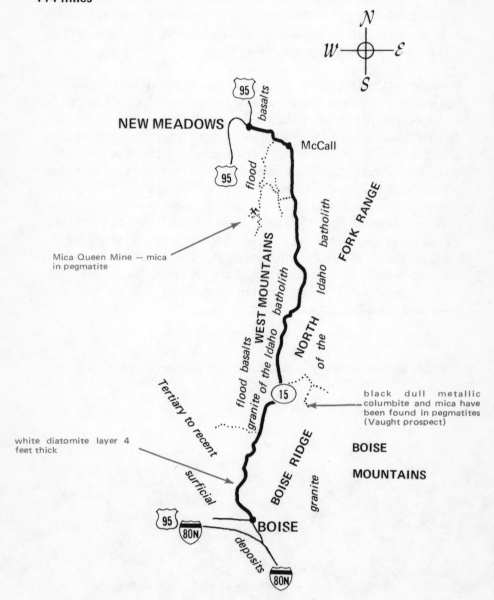

N
W — E
S

95

NEW MEADOWS

basalts

McCall

95

flood

FORK RANGE

Mica Queen Mine — mica
in pegmatite

WEST MOUNTAINS

Idaho batholith

NORTH

of the

flood basalts

granite of the Idaho batholith

15

black dull metallic
columbite and mica have
been found in pegmatites
(Vaught prospect)

Tertiary to recent

white diatomite layer 4
feet thick

BOISE

MOUNTAINS

BOISE RIDGE

granite

surficial

95

80N

BOISE

deposits

80N

Idaho 15

BOISE – NEW MEADOWS

Boise is located at the eastern edge of a large valley with a complicated geologic story, very little of which can easily be seen. Boise Valley accumulated valley-fill sands, gravels and silts during the long interval of the Tertiary Period between about 40 and 3 million years ago when a desert climate prevailed. The story is complicated by the fact that the Boise Valley is located on the eastern edge of the Columbia Plateau and was flooded by some large basalt lava flows during the time between 40 and 15 million years ago when that volcanic area was active. Further complications are added by the fact that the Boise Valley is also located at the western edge of the Snake River Plain and was again flooded by large basalt lava flows when that volcanic area was active during the most recent several million years. So this is an area where valley-fill sediments are interlayered with basalt lava flows associated with both the Columbia Plateau and the Snake River Plain.

Rising in the distance southwest of Boise on the far side of the Snake River Plain is the Owyhee Range composed of granite and various kinds of volcanic rocks. Tradition has it that the name is a corruption of the word "Hawaii" – apparently someone spelled it the way he thought it sounded.

North of Boise and east of Idaho 15 is the Boise Ridge. It is composed of granites belonging to the Idaho batholith which intruded into this area between 70 and 90 million years ago during the Cretaceous Period. From the north edge of the Boise Valley to McCall, the highway follows the valley the North Fork of the Payette River has eroded into these granites. Although the Idaho batholith is one of the largest bodies of granite in the world, it is one of the hardest ones to see. Most of its enormous outcrop area of more than 14,000 square miles is in the nearly roadless and almost inaccessible wilderness of central Idaho. Idaho 15 is one of the very few good roads that cross a large enough part of this batholith to give a traveller some impression of the immensity of this vast body of monotonous granite that extends northeastward about 200 miles into the Bitterroot Mountains along the Montana-Idaho border without being crossed by another paved road in all that distance. Of course, there are other rocks besides granite in that vast country, but the granite overwhelmingly dominates.

Most of the granite contains crystal grains large enough for the individual minerals to be identified without using a magnifier. Most abundant by far is feldspar which comes in pink and white grains that tend to be blocky in outline and frequently show flat faces. Quartz is much less abundant and appears as irregular clear to grayish, glassy-looking grains. Most specimens are peppered with black minerals which may be either flat flakes of mica or needles of hornblende.

Even though the granite is monotonous, not all of it is exactly the same. Proportions of the minerals vary from place to place and so does the grain size of the rock. In some areas the feldspar crystals are very large — as much as two inches across.

Extremely coarse-grained granite with crystals of all minerals several inches across is called pegmatite and can sometimes be seen filling fractures to form dikes. Pegmatites are always interesting to mineral collectors because they frequently contain unusual minerals that usually occur in large, well formed crystals. Aplite is a very fine-grained variety of granite which has a sugary look and also occurs in dikes. Pegmatites and aplites often occur together in the same dike. Watch for them in roadcuts.

Between McCall and New Meadows the highway leaves the granite, crossing onto the much younger coal-black basalt lava flows of the

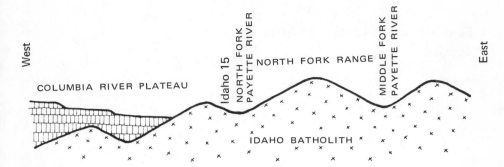

West-east cross section across the line of Idaho 15 north of Boise. Basalt lava flows of the Columbia River Plateau lap over an older landscape eroded onto granites of the Idaho batholith.

Columbia Plateau. These were erupted over the granite after it had already been exposed and carved into mountains by erosion. Since the flows in this area are at the top of the Columbia Plateau, they must be among the younger ones erupted sometime around 15 to 20 million years ago.

For more information on flood basalts of the Columbia River Plateau and the Snake River Plain, see
> U.S. 95: Lewiston – Coeur d'Alene
> U.S. 195: Lewiston – Spokane
> Interstate 80 N: Twin Falls – Boise
> U.S. 20: Idaho Falls – Arco
> U.S. 93 A: Shoshone – Arco; Craters of the Moon

For more information on granite of the Idaho batholith, see
> U.S. 12: Missoula – Kooskia

ELMO (Flathead Lake) – PLAINS
46 miles

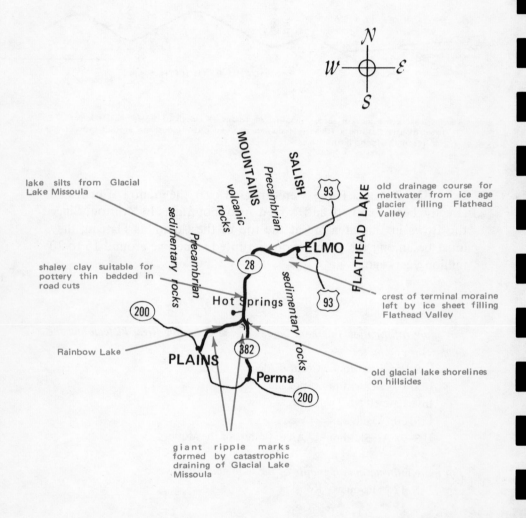

N
W — *E*
S

lake silts from Glacial
Lake Missoula

shaley clay suitable for
pottery thin bedded in
road cuts

Rainbow Lake

old drainage course for
meltwater from ice age
glacier filling Flathead
Valley

crest of terminal moraine
left by ice sheet filling
Flathead Valley

old glacial lake shorelines
on hillsides

SALISH

MOUNTAINS

*Precambrian
volcanic
rocks*

*Precambrian
sedimentary
rocks*

FLATHEAD LAKE

*sedimentary
rocks*

ELMO

Hot Springs

PLAINS

Perma

giant ripple marks
formed by catastrophic
draining of Glacial Lake
Missoula

93
28
93
200
382
200

Montana 28

PLAINS — ELMO

For people interested in glacial geology the highway between Plains and Elmo offers one of the most fascinating drives in the region.

Most of the roadcuts along this highway expose monotonously interlayered thin beds of Precambrian mudstone and sandstone probably laid down in a shallow sea well over 1 billion years ago. These rocks have been folded and slightly recrystallized by heat so that now they are more accurately described as slate and quartzite than mudstone and sandstone.

The glacial geology is complex and unusual. During the last ice age a large glacier blocked the drainage of the Clark Fork River in northern Idaho to a depth of 2000 feet, backing up the water to form Glacial Lake Missoula. This enormous lake with many large arms filled many of the valleys in western Montana. The ice dam broke and the lake drained suddenly, releasing a catastrophic flood that scoured the floors of several valleys in western Montana and then poured across eastern Washington where it carved out the channelled scablands. All this happened about 12,000 years ago, probably within a few days.

Most of the distance between Plains and Elmo is in the very large Little Bitterroot Valley which held an enormous quantity of water when Glacial Lake Missoula existed. When the lake drained, a large part of this water poured over the divide between Rainbow Lake and Hot Springs and then southward toward Plains. The rush of water scoured out the bedrock basins now occupied by Rainbow Lake and the swampy areas north of it. Angular debris scoured from these basins was swept several miles down the valley to the south and then deposited to form an enormous debris delta.

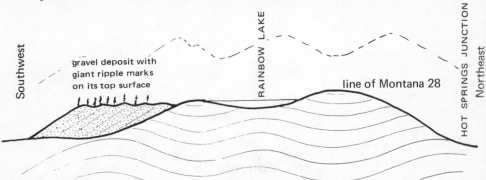

Southwest-northeast cross section along the line of Montana 28 between Plains and Hot Springs Junction. Water draining southwestward during sudden emptying of Glacial Lake Missoula scoured the basin of Rainbow Lake into hard Precambrian bedrock. It dumped the debris into the valley below as a large deposit of gravel with giant ripple marks on its surface.

The most impressive view of this is to be had while driving north from Plains. The road starts up the valley of a small creek which appears perfectly normal for several miles and then abruptly ends at a steep wall of angular debris which the highway ascends in a long grade. This is the front slope of the debris delta. At the top of the grade the road goes for several miles across a nearly level but slightly undulating surface before it finally comes to Rainbow Lake. This surface is the top of the debris delta and the undulations are giant ripple marks similar to those made by water carrying sand in a creek bed except that these are 15 or 20 feet high and made of coarse gravel instead of sand. They are covered by a scrubby growth of trees which grow poorly because water drains rapidly down through the coarse gravel, making the soil very dry.

Rainbow Lake is lovely and peaceful now. It is hard to imagine the angry rush of water that scoured it out of hard bedrock in a few hours when Glacial Lake Missoula drained. But any other origin is even more difficult to imagine. That big pile of angular gravel down the valley with ripple marks on it had to come from somewhere and something had to move it.

The Little Bitterroot Valley north of Hot Springs is very dry and somewhat barren. It hardly seems possible that it could once have held one of the arms of an enormous icy lake. But the evidence is clear and can be seen from the road. Most of the floor of the valley is covered by deposits of light gray glacial silt which contain thin, alternating light and dark layers (varves) recording the ice age summers and winters of the years when the lake was here. And the valley walls are faintly scored by at least two dozen perfectly horizontal shorelines recording different water depths. An early geologist compared these to musical staves drawn on the sides of the mountains. Shorelines are easier to see on the east side of the valley because the prevailing winds drove the waves against that side of the lake.

For 13 miles west of Elmo the road goes through a valley called the Big Draw. Once the course of the Flathead River, it was blocked by debris deposited by the large Flathead Valley glacier to the east. Meltwater swept glacial gravels released from the ice westward down the valley filling it to a depth of more than 200 feet.

Numerous stream beds are still plainly visible on the gravel surface in the Big Draw. These are channels of streams which have not carried water since the ice melted about 12,000 years ago and will not again until the next ice age brings a new glacier into the Flathead Valley to spill meltwater over the top of the moraine and down the Big Draw. Nevertheless, the highway department has carefully installed culverts where the road crosses the channels, presumably in preparation for the next ice age.

Highway 28 crosses the top of the glacial moraine 5 miles west of Elmo. There is a wonderful view of Flathead Lake from this place, made more impressive by the thought that the whole valley up to the level of the moraine was once filled with flowing glacial ice.

For more information on Glacial Lake Missoula and the giant flood which drained it, see
     County 382: Perma — Hot Springs
     Montana 200: Ravalli Junction — Sandpoint
     Interstate 90: Missoula — Lookout Pass

POLSON – BIG FORK – CRESTON
(East side of Flathead Lake)
42 miles

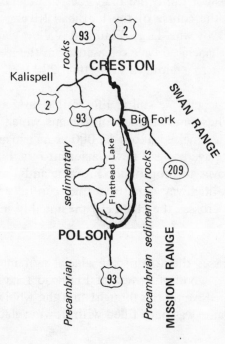

Montana 35

POLSON – BIGFORK – CRESTON

The road between Polson and Creston winds along through apple and cherry orchards on the east shore of Flathead Lake. The northern end of the Mission Range is east of the lake; the low hills west of it are the Salish Mountains. Both are composed of Precambrian sedimentary rock.

Flathead Lake occupies a basin scooped in the Flathead Valley by the big glacier that flowed down this valley from Canada during the last ice age. The lake is more than 300 feet deep; the deepest parts are along the east side just a short distance offshore.

Thick deposits of debris plastered by the glaciers on the slopes of the Mission Range near the south end of Flathead Lake form moraines. Several roadcuts a short distance north of Polson show them to be a light-colored jumble of angular boulders and clay. Many of the finest orchards in this area are growing on rich soil developed on these glacial deposits.

Bedrock outcrops along this section of highway are all Precambrian limestones tilted upward along a fault to form the Mission Range. The road follows the line of this fault rather closely for most of the distance between Polson and Bigfork, past many roadcuts of fractured rocks crushed by movement of the fault.

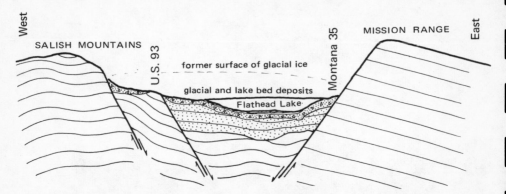

West-east cross section across the line of U.S. 93 showing how the Flathead Valley (Rocky Mountain Trench) is let down on faults between the Salish and Mission Ranges. Tertiary valley-fill sediments covered by glacial debris floor the valley.

The area around the southern part of Flathead Lake has frequent small earthquakes — none of them damaging — that have been closely studied by geologists using seismographs. They are caused by movements along a fault which cuts across the lake in a northwest-southeast direction, intersecting the east shore at a point several miles north of Polson.

For more information on continental ice age glaciers, see
    U.S. 93: Missoula — Kalispell
    U.S. 93: Kalispell — Eureka

The lower Flathead and Mission Valleys are bounded to the east by the Mission Range, a great slab of Precambrian sedimentary rock raised and tilted eastward by movement on a fault. In this view, taken a short distance south of Polson, a small pond formed where a block of ice was once incorporated in glacial deposits forms the foreground.

GREAT FALLS – MISSOULA
177 miles

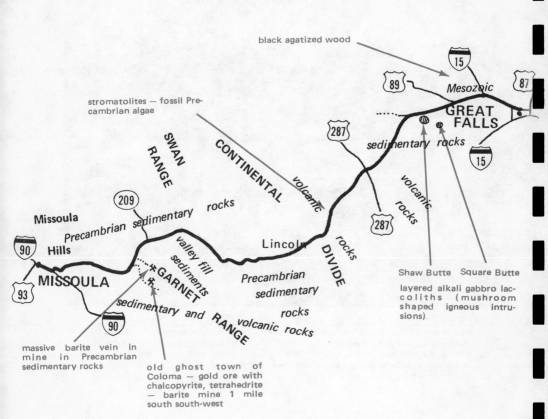

black agatized wood

stromatolites – fossil Precambrian algae

Mesozoic

SWAN RANGE

CONTINENTAL

GREAT FALLS

sedimentary rocks

volcanic

rocks

209

Missoula

Precambrian sedimentary rocks

Hills

90

MISSOULA

93

valley fill

sediments

GARNET

Lincoln

DIVIDE

volcanic

rocks

Shaw Butte   Square Butte

Precambrian
sedimentary

rocks

sedimentary and RANGE

volcanic rocks

layered alkali gabbro laccoliths (mushroom
shaped igneous intru-
sions).

massive barite vein in
mine in Precambrian
sedimentary rocks

old ghost town of
Coloma — gold ore with
chalcopyrite, tetrahedrite
— barite mine 1 mile
south south-west

Montana 200

GREAT FALLS – MISSOULA

From Great Falls to Simms, Montana 200 follows the Sun River past occasional outcrops of brown sandstone laid down about 70 to 80 million years ago during the Cretaceous Period when this area was near the shore of a large shallow sea that stretched away hundreds of miles to the east and south. The Rocky Mountains were just beginning to rise to the west. These sedimentary rocks east of the main mass of the Rockies escaped being much involved in mountain building so their layers are still nearly horizontal.

Several isolated high buttes interrupt the skyline south of the road between Great Falls and Simms. These are large igneous intrusions, called laccoliths, which formed when molten magma was injected between beds of sandstone to form blister-shaped bodies enclosed in the sedimentary rocks. These spectacular laccoliths are well worth a closer look, easily had by taking the secondary road from Simms south to Cascade. This short side trip is briefly described in the roadguide dealing with Interstate 15 between Helena and Great Falls.

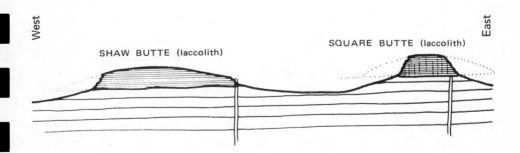

West-east cross section through two large laccoliths between Interstate 15 and Montana 200 west of Great Falls. Eroded parts of the laccoliths, great blister-shaped intrusions of igneous rock, are restored by dotted lines.

At Simms the highway leaves the Sun River to head southwestward toward Rogers Pass over the continental divide. The rocks between Simms and the pass are mostly Cretaceous sandstones, mudstones, and volcanics which become tightly folded close to the mountains.

From Rogers Pass to Missoula the bedrock is almost entirely folded Precambrian sedimentary rocks, mostly red and green mudstones. These contain numerous small bodies of granite intruded as molten magmas sometime between 30 and 80 million years ago. A number of the granites have metallic ore bodies associated with them so the region has seen many small mining ventures over the years. During the late 1960's, the Anaconda Company found a large ore body of copper near the old Mike Horse Mine located south of Montana 200 a few miles west of Rogers Pass. This may someday become the site of a large open-pit mine similar to the Berkeley Pit in Butte.

Highway 200 follows the canyon of the Big Blackfoot River from its headwaters at Rogers Pass to its mouth just east of Missoula where it joins the Clark Fork. A large valley glacier flowed down the upper part of this canyon during the last ice age and left several morainal deposits of glacial debris which the highway crosses in the vicinity of Lincoln. Recognizable as small ridges crossing the valley floor, they partially dam the drainage to create marshy areas on their eastern (upstream) sides. Roadcuts through the moraines expose a mixture of boulders, sand, and clay all jumbled together.

More glacial deposits are around Clearwater Junction where Montana 200 meets County 209. These hummocky low hills of debris were left by an enormous glacier that came down the Swan Valley all the way from its northern end. This was a branch of the still larger glacier that filled the Mission Valley on the other side of the Mission Range.

Where the highway crosses the Blackfoot River about 6 miles southwest of Clearwater Junction, the valley floor is strewn with enormous boulders of Precambrian mudstone much too large to be moved by the present stream. Apparently the river was at one time dammed by glacial deposits to form a lake a short distance upstream from this point. The dam burst, as such dams often do, and the lake washed out sometime during the last few thousand years releasing a flood that carried these boulders several miles down the valley.

Four miles east of Bonner an interesting outcrop of Precambrian sandstone is made easy to spot by a little roadside rest with a spring and some restrooms on the south side of the road beside an enormous boulder. The sandstone is white with purple cross-beds of a type which indicates that the sand was originally deposited by streams that flowed here more than 600 million years ago. Blocks of this material are easily collected from the talus slope behind the spring. Sawed and polished, they make very striking bookends.

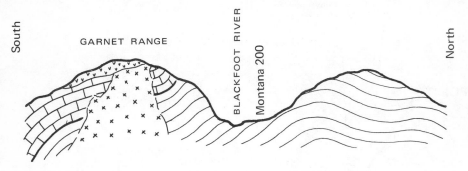

South-north cross section across the line of Montana 200 near Lincoln. Volcanic rocks cap the Garnet Range which also contains intrusive granites. Rather gently-folded Precambrian sedimentary rocks north of the Blackfoot River probably contain some faults even though these are not shown in the section.

South of Highway 200 between Lincoln and Bonner is the Garnet Range where the folded Precambrian sedimentary rocks have been intruded by granites and capped in places by volcanic rocks approximately 25 million years old. There was a lot of gold mining in the Garnet Range during the early days and several interesting ghost towns still remain. One of these, Coloma, can be reached by turning south from the highway at the Greenough Store about 7 miles southwest of Clearwater Junction.

For more information on ice age glaciers, see
    U.S. 93: Missoula – Kalispell
    U.S. 93: Kalispell – Eureka
    Glacier National Park (after U.S. 89: Great Falls – Browning)

For more information on the laccolith Buttes west of Great Falls, see
    Interstate 15: Helena – Great Falls

RAVALLI JCT. — THOMPSON FALLS
SANDPOINT
139 miles

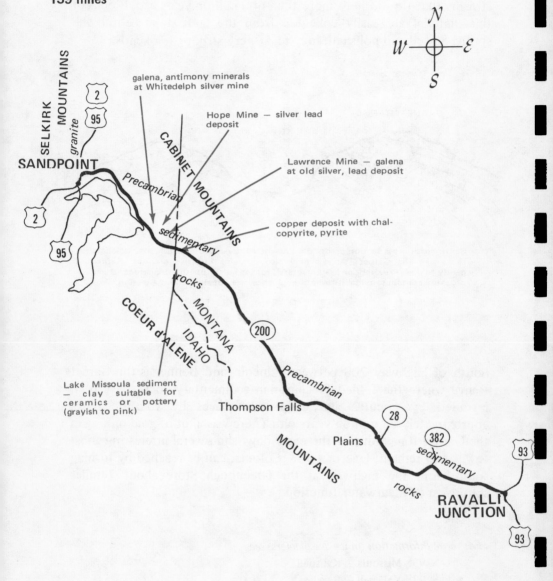

Montana-Idaho 200

RAVALLI JUNCTION (U.S. 93) — SANDPOINT

For most of the distance between Ravalli Junction and Sandpoint, Highway 200 follows the Flathead River along the route taken by the great rush of water released about 12,000 years ago when a glacial ice dam near Sandpoint broke and Glacial Lake Missoula suddenly drained. Water flowed northwestward down this valley during those hours at a rate estimated to have been between 8 and 10 cubic miles per hour! The flood washed much of the soil off the valley walls providing better bedrock exposures than are normally seen in this wet and heavily forested part of our region.

The narrow stretch of valley west of Perma constricted the floodwaters and shows the most spectacular scouring. Nearly all the soil was stripped from the valley walls and floor, leaving craggy outcrops of bedrock. Many of the tributary gulches are dammed about halfway up the valley wall by sand and gravel swirled into them by eddies as the water rushed past.

Before the dam burst, the entire route of Highway 200 was flooded by Glacial Lake Missoula, so lake sediments undoubtedly accumulated all along what is now the river floodplain. Most of these soft silts were swept out with the lake water but a few patches somehow survived and can be seen along the road. They are easy to recognize as very pale, pinkish-gray silts which make rather soft-looking outcrops. Lake silt is very weak and will slide if given the slightest excuse; Highway 200 is built on this material in the vicinity of Dixon (about 7 miles west of Ravalli Junction) and has had to be rebuilt after slides.

Bedrock exposed along the highway between Ravalli Junction and Pend Oreille Lake is almost entirely Precambrian sandstone and mudstone laid down between 600 and 1500 million years ago, then tightly folded with formation of the Rocky Mountains during the last 70 million years. Several large sills of coarse-grained, black basalt (diabase) were squirted as a molten magma between the sedimentary layers about 800 million years ago. One of these is exposed in large black roadcuts on both sides of the highway about 1 mile east of Perma. Small intrusions of granite, intruded as molten magmas while the Rocky Mountains were forming, are not easily visible from the road.

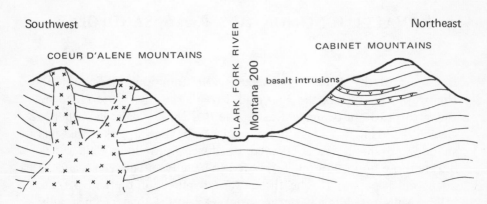

Southwest-northeast cross section across the line of Montana 200 from the Coeur d'Alene to the Cabinet Mountain Ranges. Mountains in this area are made of gently-folded Precambrian sedimentary rock intruded by small masses of granite.

Strangely, the mountains south of the highway between Ravalli Junction and Plains don't seem to have any generally accepted name. Some maps show them as the Ninemile Divide but they are more often referred to as "Them mountains out by Ninemile Creek." No high mountains rise immediately north of this stretch of road, but occasionally the Craggy pinnacles of the Mission Range appear in the distance to the northeast. They are made of Precambrian limestone.

The mountains south of the highway between Plains and Pend Oreille Lake are most often called the Coeur d'Alene Range although some maps refer to them as the Northern Bitterroots. North of this stretch of road is the Cabinet Range. All these mountains are composed mostly of the same kind of Precambrian mudstones and sandstones that outcrop along the highway.

Pend Oreille Lake is in the Purcell Trench, a long, narrow block of the earth's crust let down along faults during formation of the northern Rocky Mountains. The trench extends far north into British Columbia where it filled with ice during the last ice age to form a glacier that flowed as far south as Coeur d'Alene Lake. This was the same glacier that flowed across the Clark Fork River, forming the ice dam that impounded Glacial Lake Missoula. It was very large — the ice thickness north of Pend Oreille Lake has been estimated to have been about 5,000 feet — and it made a good enough dam to back the river up to a depth of about 2,000 feet. But the dam was no better than that and finally burst, releasing the lake water to go rushing down the valley toward Spokane and then on across eastern Washington where it eroded the channelled scablands.

The Selkirk Mountains, west of the Purcell Trench, and the western end of the Cabinet Range, east of the Purcell Trench, are both made by granite intruded into this area as a molten magma between 60 and 90 million years ago to form the Kaniksu batholith. Granite of the Kaniksu batholith outcrops along highway 200 in roadcuts about 12 miles east of Sandpoint. The Purcell Trench fault block was let down after the granite magma had cooled and passes right through the batholith.

For more information on Glacial Lake Missoula and the giant flood which drained it, see
    Montana 28: Plains — Elmo
    County 382: Perma — Hot Springs
    Interstate 90: Missoula — Lookout Pass

ENNIS — VIRGINIA CITY — WHITEHALL
69 miles

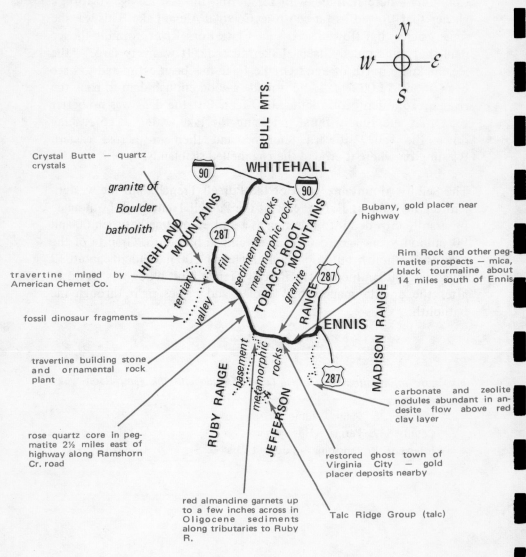

Crystal Butte — quartz crystals

granite of Boulder batholith

BULL MTS.

90 WHITEHALL 90

HIGHLAND MOUNTAINS

287

fill

sedimentary rocks

metamorphic rocks

TOBACCO ROOT MOUNTAINS

granite

RANGE

287

Bubany, gold placer near highway

Rim Rock and other pegmatite prospects — mica, black tourmaline about 14 miles south of Ennis

ENNIS

MADISON RANGE

travertine mined by American Chemet Co.

tertiary valley

fossil dinosaur fragments

travertine building stone and ornamental rock plant

RUBY RANGE

basement metamorphic rocks

JEFFERSON

287

carbonate and zeolite nodules abundant in andesite flow above red clay layer

rose quartz core in pegmatite 2½ miles east of highway along Ramshorn Cr. road

restored ghost town of Virginia City — gold placer deposits nearby

red almandine garnets up to a few inches across in Oligocene sediments along tributaries to Ruby R.

Talc Ridge Group (talc)

Montana 287
ENNIS — WHITEHALL
via
VIRGINIA CITY

Montana 287 from Ennis to Whitehall by way of the Virginia City area takes the traveller through one of the most notorious gold mining camps of the old west.

Ennis is in the Madison Valley, a large, down-dropped fault block floored by valley-fill sediments deposited during the Tertiary Period between 40 and 3 million years ago when our region had a desert climate.

The mountains dominating the skyline east of Ennis are the Madison Range composed largely of igneous and metamorphic rocks belonging to the Precambrian basement. These are overlain by sedimentary rocks deposited during the Paleozoic and Mesozoic Eras and then folded as the Madison Range block was uplifted during formation of the Rocky Mountains. A number of the highest peaks in the Madisons are capped by thick beds of coarse gravel called the Sphinx Conglomerate that are somewhat mysterious in that no one is quite sure how old they are or how they got there — an interesting unsolved geologic problem.

Northwest of Ennis is the Tobacco Root Range, composed mostly of Precambrian igneous and metamorphic basement rocks flanked by much deformed layers of Paleozoic and Mesozoic limestones, sandstones, and mudstones. A very large mass of molten granite magma rose into the center of the Tobacco Root Range during Cretaceous Time, about 70 million years ago, while the mountains in this area were first rising.

Far in the distance southwest of Ennis are the Gravelly and Snowcrest Ranges where Precambrian igneous and metamorphic basement rocks are still largely covered by folded and faulted Paleozoic and Mesozoic sedimentary rocks not yet stripped away by erosion. The Gravelly Range gets its name from the fact that, like the Madison Range, it is partially capped by gravels.

West of Ennis, Highway 287 climbs a long grade up a sloping surface underlain in its lower part by valley-fill deposits laid down during the Tertiary· Period. Higher up the valley-fill sediments disappear and the surface is underlain by igneous and metamorphic rocks belonging to the Precambrian basement. Several roadcuts along this stretch of highway contain granite pegmatites containing very large crystals of quartz, pink and white feldspar, and mica. These are attractive mineral specimens.

At the top of the hill west of Ennis a scenic pullout features a large sign identifying the major peaks of the Madison Range. The stone foundation of the sign is made of boulders of the gravel conglomerate that caps many of those peaks. For most of the distance between this point and Virginia City the road crosses volcanic rocks laid down on top of the Precambrian basement about 40 million years ago.

Alder Gulch, between Virginia City (once the capital of Montana) and Nevada City, a short distance to the west, was the scene of feverish placer mining for gold beginning in the summer of 1863 and for several years thereafter. Mining still continues in the district but at a very low rate. Gravel deposits in the creek have been worked and reworked, first by hand methods and later by dredges, so that now virtually nothing remains of the attractive stream that flowed here a century ago. The original sources of the creek gold were lode deposits in the Precambrian igneous and metamorphic basement rocks which were also mined. Particles of gold are much heavier than any other kind of material found in streams so they lag behind and are concentrated deep in the gravels while lighter rocks are carried away.

Montana 287 follows the Ruby River Valley most of the distance between Nevada City and Twin Bridges. The Ruby Range southwest of the highway is composed mostly of Precambrian igneous and metamorphic basement rocks except for a small patch of folded sedimentary rocks at its northern tip.

For a few miles south of Twin Bridges, the high peaks of the Pioneer Range are on the skyline far to the west. These are composed of Paleozoic and Mesozoic sedimentary rocks complexly folded and intruded by large bodies of granite magma as they were uplifted into mountains.

Between Twin Bridges and Whitehall, Montana 287 follows the Jefferson Valley bounded by the Tobacco Root Range to the east and the Highland Mountains to the west. The isolated small group of mountains south of the Highland Range is McCarty's Mountain, a large body of granite intruded about 70 million years ago into Paleozoic sedimentary rocks which form the flanks of the mass. In their southern part the Highland Mountains are Precambrian igneous and metamorphic basement rock, overlain by much folded Paleozoic limestone, and intruded by granites of Cretaceous age (roughly 70 million years old). The northern part of the Highland Range is much simpler, being composed almost entirely of 70-million-year-old granite belonging to the Boulder batholith which extends continuously northward all the way to the vicinity of Helena.

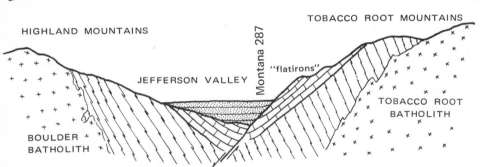

Northwest-southeast cross section across the line of Montana 287. The Jefferson Valley is let down on a fault between the Highland Mountains and the Tobacco Root Mountains. Both ranges contain large masses of granite intruded during formation of the Rocky Mountains.

Prominent "flatirons" — vertical slabs of sedimentary rock — stand along the west face of the Tobacco Root Mountains toward the north end of the range near Whitehall. These are Paleozoic limestone deposited in a shallow sea about 300 million years ago. Lewis and Clark climbed them on their way west to get a view of the country ahead while searching for a route through the Rocky Mountains.

For more information on Precambrian basement metamorphic rocks, see
U.S. 212: Laurel — Cooke City (Beartooth Highway)

CLEARWATER JCT. — BIG FORK
85 miles

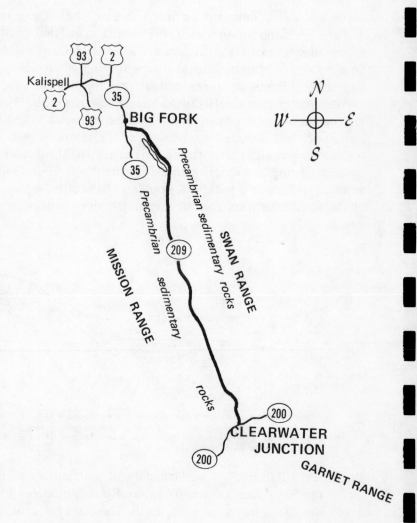

County 209

CLEARWATER JUNCTION (MONTANA 299) – BIGFORK

(Swan Valley Highway)

The "Swan Valley Highway" runs the length of the Swan Valley between the Mission Range to the west and the Swan Range to the east. Good views of the mountains are infrequent because of heavy forest cover but where visible their spectacular craggy profile shows that they were heavily glaciated during the last ice age.

Geologically, the Mission and Swan Ranges are much alike. Both are great, eastward-tilted fault-blocks of Precambrian limestone full of fossil seaweeds. It is difficult to get in to see these because both ranges are almost entirely roadless but similar fossils outcrop along the road in Glacier Park and other places.

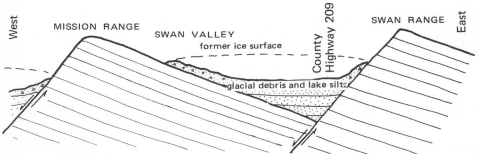

West-east cross section across the line of County 209 in the Swan Valley. The Mission and Swan Ranges are eastward-tilted blocks of Precambrian sedimentary rock brought up along faults. Glacial deposits bury Tertiary valley-fill sediments in the floor of the valley.

During the last glacial period the Swan Valley was entirely filled with glacial ice. A branch of the large glacier that filled the Flathead Valley to the west came over the top of the low northern end of the Mission Range and flowed down the Swan Valley as far south as Clearwater Junction. The floor of the valley is completely covered by glacial debris left when the ice melted at the end of the last ice age about 10,000 years ago. A chain of lakes along the highway occupies basins scooped out by the moving ice then dammed by debris dumped when the ice melted.

Just west of Bigfork the Swan River does an interesting thing by taking a shortcut to Flathead Lake through a narrow gorge it has cut in the low, northern end of the Mission Range. Had it detoured just a couple of miles to the north, the river could have gotten around the end of the range without cutting any gorge at all. The stream appears to have been deflected into this course when glacial ice blocked the valley to the north. By the time the ice melted, the gorge had already been cut so the stream continued to flow through it instead of taking the easier route around the northern end of the range.

For more information on continental ice age glaciers, see
> U.S. 93: Missoula – Kalispell
> U.S. 93: Kalispell – Eureka
> Glacier National Park (after U.S. 89: Great Falls – Browning)

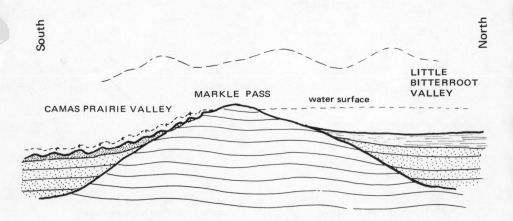

South-north cross section along the line of County 382 where it goes over Markle Pass between the Little Bitterroot Valley and Camas Prairie. Giant ripple marks were left in Camas Prairie by water pouring southward through the pass during sudden drainage of Glacial Lake Missoula.

County 382

PERMA – HOT SPRINGS

(See map, Montana 28)

This short stretch of road passes through flood deposits as spectacular as any to be seen anywhere in the world. The flood happened when Glacial Lake Missoula suddenly drained after the ice dam impounding it broke late in the last ice age, perhaps 12,000 years ago.

Hot Springs is in the southern end of the Little Bitterroot Valley which held one of the major arms of Glacial Lake Missoula. When the ice dam broke, the enormous quantity of water in the valley poured over the tops of several passes as though it were spilling out of an overflowing bathtub. A major part of the overflow spilled southward through Markle Pass down into Camas Prairie creating giant ripple marks.

A neat, round pond north of the highway is right in the top of Markle Pass exactly on the drainage divide – a most unlikely place for a pond. Apparently there was a whirlpool here powerful enough to pluck a sizeable hole in the hard, sandstone bedrock.

For 5 miles south of Markle Pass the floor of Camas Prairie is covered by giant ripple marks left by the flood. The largest ones on the slope just below the pass are 30 feet high. Except for their size, these ripple marks are similar to those that form in sand on the bottom of a fast-moving stream.

The experience of driving through a roadcut in a ripple mark is well worth the trouble of driving to the north end of Camas Prairie.

For more information on Glacial Lake Missoula, see
Montana 28: Plains – Elmo
Montana 200: Ravalli Junction – Sandpoint
County 382: Perma – Hot Springs
Interstate 90: Missoula – Lookout Pass
U.S. 95: Coeur d'Alene – Bonners Ferry

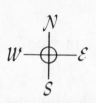

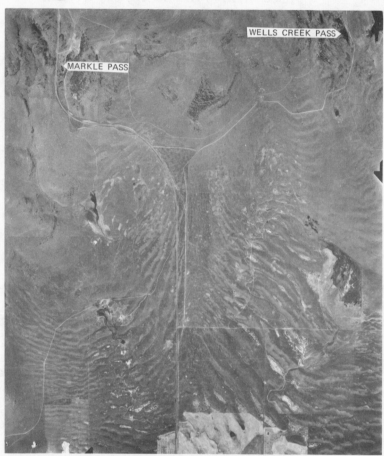

The giant ripple marks in Camas Prairie photographed from an airplane flying at an elevation of approximately 14,000 feet above the ground. Water flowing southward through Markle Pass and Wells Creek Pass created two patterns of giant ripple marks that meet along a line just east of County Road 382. Lakes were scoured in the tops of the passes by great whirlpool eddies.

GLOSSARY OF TECHNICAL TERMS

Amphibolite
A black, grainy metamorphic rock composed mostly of amphibole (hornblende).

Aplite
A variety of granite that can be recognized by the fact that it is finer-grained than most granite and has a sugary appearance. Almost always found in dikes.

Basalt
A very common black igneous rock, most often volcanic but also found as intrusions such as dikes and sills.

Batholith
A very large body of granite. Most batholiths outcrop over areas of hundreds of square miles and some of them cover thousands of square miles.

Caldera
A large basin formed when the ground sinks, as a large quantity of molten magma beneath is erupted through a volcano. Most calderas are several miles across.

Cirque
A large, amphitheater-shaped basin carved into the side of a mountain by a glacier. Looks almost as though a mile-sized bite had been taken out of the mountain with a giant ice-cream scoop.

Complexly folded
A term used to describe rocks that have been deformed into very complicated folds – sometimes referred to as "striped toothpaste geology." A carpet crumpled up from one end gives a similar effect.

Conglomerate
A sedimentary rock originally deposited as gravel. The pebbles make conglomerate easy to recognize.

Drumlin
A streamlined hill formed when a moving glacier plasters rock debris onto the ground surface beneath its bed. Most drumlins are a half mile or more long and anywhere from 50 to 250 feet high.

Dike
A thin sheet of intrusive igneous rock formed when a fracture in the earth's crust is squirted full of molten magma.

275

Fault

A fracture in the earth's crust, the two sides of which have moved past each other.

Fault block

A segment of the earth's crust that has moved up or down along faults.

Fault scarp

A cliff formed where a fault breaks the ground surface. Many of the straight mountain fronts in the northern Rockies are fault scarps.

Feldspar

The most abundant mineral in most igneous and metamorphic rocks. Comes in several varieties but usually occurs as either pink or white translucent crystals with a blocky outline.

Floodplain

The part of river valley subject to flooding during times of high water.

Granite

A very common pink or gray intrusive igneous rock having individual mineral grains large enough to be seen easily without a magnifier. The minerals are quartz, which looks glassy, feldspar, which may be either pink or white, and a nearly black mineral which is usually either mica or hornblende.

Gneiss
(Pronounced "nice")

A common metamorphic rock that typically has a streaky appearance usually with distinct light- and dark-colored bands. Gneiss may contain mica but if there is enough of it to make the rock flaky it is called schist.

Hornblende

A mineral, the commonest variety of amphibole, that occurs in many igneous and metamorphic rocks. Can be recognized by the fact that it occurs in long, narrow crystals that have a glossy black color.

Igneous rock

Any rock that forms by cooling of a molten magma. If the magma was erupted at the surface through a volcano the resulting igneous rock is volcanic. If it cooled within the earth, it is intrusive.

Intrusion

A body of igneous rock that was squirted into older rock as a molten magma.

Intrusive rock A body of igneous rock that cooled while enclosed in other rocks instead of being erupted to the surface through a volcano. Most intrusive igneous rocks cooled very slowly so they contain mineral grains large enough to see. This makes them easy to recognize.

Laccolith A cookie or gumdrop-shaped igneous intrusion formed when a blister of molten magma is squirted between layers of igneous rock. Most laccoliths are a mile or more in diameter.

Lava Any molten magma poured out onto the earth's surface through a volcano.

Limestone A kind of sedimentary rock composed mostly of the mineral calcite. The original sediment was a limey mud. Limestones are generally white or gray but they may also be tan, brown, or even black. Most limestones were originally deposited in shallow sea water and usually fossils can be found with a careful search.

Lode deposit A deposit of valuable minerals in bedrock as distinct from placer deposits which are in river gravels.

Magma Any molten rock. Magmas erupted from volcanoes are called lava and cool to form volcanic rocks. Magmas that are not erupted but cool within the earth's crust, form intrusive igneous rocks.

Metamorphic rock Any rock that has been recrystallized at a red heat deep within the earth's crust. Most metamorphic rocks contain mineral crystals large enough to see and have a streaky or grainy appearance.

Mesozoic The interval of time between the beginning of the Triassic Period about 225 million years ago and the end of the Cretaceous Period about 70 million years ago. (See Geologic Time Scale.)

Mica A common mineral in igneous and metamorphic rocks that can be recognized by the fact that it splits easily into thin, flat flakes. Comes in many colors but brownish black and clear yellowish white are the only common ones.

Moraine A deposit of rock debris laid down by ice at the margin of a glacier. Can usually be recognized as low, hummocky ridges running across the landscape. Moraines are made of mud, sand, gravel, and boulders all mixed indiscriminately together and not separated into distinct layers.

Mudstone A sedimentary rock that was originally deposited as mud. Even though most of the mudstones in the northern Rockies are now very hard rock, most of them look exactly like what they are — mud hardened into rock. They come in most colors: gray, yellowish to brownish, green, red, or black.

Outcrop Any exposure of bedrock at the surface of the ground. Rocks that have been moved from their original position by any process of erosion are not outcrops.

Overthrust fault A fault that is nearly horizontal so the rock above it has moved over the top of the rock below.

Paleozoic The interval of time between the beginning of the Cambrian Period about 600 million years ago and the end of the Permian Period about 225 million years ago. (See Geologic Time Scale.)

Pegmatite A very coarse-grained variety of granite having crystals at least an inch or more across and rarely up to several feet across. Almost always occurs in dikes. Many pegmatites contain unusual minerals and most of them are good places to collect attractive mineral specimens.

Placer A deposit of valuable minerals in stream gravel. Heavy minerals, such as gold, sapphires, or diamonds frequently form placer deposits because they sink to the bottom of the stream gravels.

Precambrian The interval of time between the ages of the oldest known rocks — more than 3 billion years — and the beginning of the Cambrian Period about 600 million years ago. (See Geologic Time Scale)

Pumice A light-colored volcanic rock so full of air bubbles that it looks somewhat like a sponge. Many specimens of pumice are light enough to float on water.

Pyroxene　　A mineral frequently found in dark-colored igneous or metamorphic rocks. May be many colors but the commonest kind of pyroxene occurs in short, stubby crystals with a dark brown or dull black color.

Pyroxenite　　A dark brown or black rock composed mostly of the mineral pyroxene.

Quartz　　A common mineral. Occurs in most kinds of rocks (except in a few black igneous or metamorphic rocks and in limestone) usually as glassy-looking grains. There are innumerable varieties of quartz that include such diverse things as sand grains, agate, petrified wood, amethyst, rock crystal and so on. At least one entire book has been written on the varieties of quartz. They all have exactly the same chemical composition – silicon dioxide.

Recrystallized　　A term used to describe a rock in which the original mineral grains have grown to form new, larger grains.

Sandstone　　A sedimentary rock originally deposited as sand. Close examination of most sandstones shows that the original sand grains are still visible even though cemented tightly together.

Sedimentary rock　　Any rock formed of loose sediment such as sand, mud, or gravel deposited on the earth's surface.

Schist　　A common metamorphic rock that typically has a streaky or grainy appearance and contains enough mica to be flaky. Very similar to gneiss – the distinction between schist and gneiss is not very important.

Siliceous sinter　　A rock formed by deposition of dissolved quartz from hot water. Usually forms a white crust around geysers and some hot springs. Also called "geyserite."

Sill　　A body of rock formed by injection of molten magma between layers of sedimentary rock. Most sills are thin and flat, shaped like the layers of sedimentary rock in which they occur.

Tertiary　　The interval of time between the end of the Cretaceous Period about 70 million years ago and the beginning of the ice ages about 3 million years ago.

Travertine A rock formed by deposition of dissolved calcite (limestone) from water. Commonly found around hot springs. Stalactites and stalagmites in caves are also made of travertine.

Valley fill Sedimentary material such as mud, sand, or gravel deposited in a valley.

Varves Layers of sediment deposited according to the seasons of the year. It is possible by counting the layers in a varved deposit to determine the number of years during which the sediments were laid down.

Weathering The term applied to the processes that cause solid rock to decay into soil.